More Advance Praise for *Climb*

"Michelle Gadsden-Williams, a senior executive and leader in diversity and inclusion, is set to electrify readers with her corporate journey. In her first book, *Climb*, she shares her passion, her drive, and her tools and tactics for success. The fact is, over the course of her career, she has learned to overcome some of the most serious professional and personal obstacles. In 2018, we are particularly in need of Gadsden-Williams's optimistic and inspirational voice."
    —**Sylvia Ann Hewlett, founder and CEO, Center for Talent Innovation**

"Gadsden-Williams has used her personal story of resiliency to provide invaluable insight into how to build a fulfilling life, not just a career. . . . Think of her as your personal mentor, not advising you on what you should do, but rather guiding you to help you discover your personal voice and path."
    —**Linda A. Hill, Wallace Brett Donham Professor of Business Administration and faculty chair of the Leadership Initiative at Harvard Business School; author of *Being the Boss***

"Leaders use strategies to reach their goals, and in this book, Gadsden-Williams demonstrates how *you* also must do the same: set goals for your personal well-being, and incorporate those goals into corporate culture so that you can take your career to the next level."
    —**AJ Johnson, actress and healthy-living coach**

"In a world of self-proclaimed giants and rhetorical ideologues, understated pragmatism is what helps people like you and me transform our lives. *Climb* is practical, it's transparent, and it's genius. Michelle Gadsden-Williams brings a career rooted in dynamic performance and impact to present the best road map from here to excellence I've ever read. It will challenge and inspire while simultaneously providing step-by-step directions to personal and professional metamorphosis. Whether you're trekking the mountains of the global marketplace or ascending the peaks of personal development, *Climb* will help you get there. Pick it up today!"
    —**Jeff Johnson, managing principal, JIJ Communications**

"This might be 2018, but things still aren't coming up rosy for black women in corporate America. Michelle Gadsden-Williams has played at the highest levels in the corporate world, and in *Climb*, she offers valuable insight that is crucial to the development of the next generation of black female business leaders."
    —**Roland S. Martin, senior analyst, *Tom Joyner Morning Show***

"What Michelle Gadsden-Williams has boldly done is share her experiences, not only in the workplace but of her life in general. This is highly valuable to all women, women of color in particular, and men who want to advance in the world of managing and harnessing diverse human capital. This book is a selfless look at the struggles, good and bad, that Gadsden-Williams has faced . . . Most importantly, it tells women of color to always be aware of their strength and to work toward empowering others."   **—Savannah Maziya, group CEO, Bunengi**

"Michelle Gadsden-Williams combines firsthand accounts, historical data, scientific research, and down-to-earth how-to advice to help women in the workplace. This is an informative book for all, but especially women of color who feel they cannot break through the concrete ceiling to achieve success. *Climb* is a bold, inspiring manifesto for professional career women on what it takes to climb to corporate heights in America."   **—Soledad O'Brien, journalist**

"Michelle Gadsden-Williams gives us the gift of her wisdom and candor. Too often our struggles are hidden from the outside world so we are led to believe we are the only ones. Gadsden-Williams weaves together her deep industry expertise with her personal story to give actionable success tips to navigate the workplace on your own terms. Bravo, Michelle!"

—Lisa Skeete Tatum, founder and CEO, Landit

CLIMB

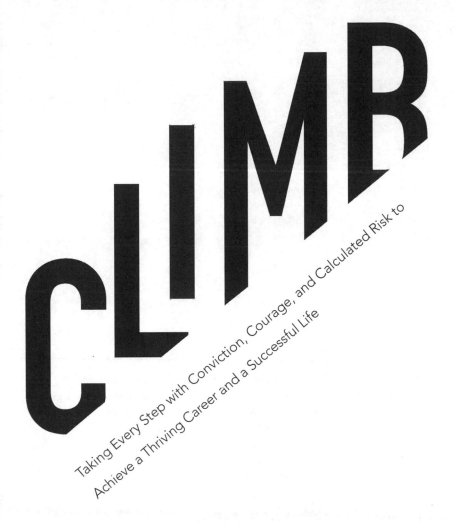

Taking Every Step with Conviction, Courage, and Calculated Risk to Achieve a Thriving Career and a Successful Life

Michelle Gadsden-Williams

with

Carolyn M. Brown

OPEN
LENS

Published by Open Lens/Akashic Books
©2018 Michelle Gadsden-Williams

ISBN: 978-1-61775-624-5
Library of Congress Control Number: 2017956850

First printing

Open Lens
c/o Akashic Books
Brooklyn, New York, USA
Ballydehob, Co. Cork, Ireland
Twitter: @AkashicBooks
Facebook: AkashicBooks
E-mail: info@akashicbooks.com
Website: www.akashicbooks.com

ALSO AVAILABLE FROM OPEN LENS

Pressure Makes Diamonds:
Becoming the Woman I Pretended to Be
by Valerie Graves

Getting It Right
by Karen E. Osborne

And Then I Danced:
Traveling the Road to LGBT Equality
by Mark Segal

The Roving Treee
by Elsie Agustave

Makeda
by Randall Robinson

For my grandmothers:
Elizabeth Polite Gadsden,
Rosalie Grant, and Essie C. Williams

Climb: *to rise, to ascend, to go upward with gradual or continuous progress*

Almost crumbling to the ground, she stopped. Looking at how far she had traveled, and all it had taken to get there, she recognized her strength. The strength she had inside of her, the strength she had gained along the way—her inner power. And so, she stood up, standing tall, she faced forward and continued on.

—Terri St. Cloud

TABLE OF CONTENTS

INTRODUCTION

I was sitting in the United Airlines lounge at Newark International Airport waiting to board a flight to Miami, on my way to an annual women's conference that I looked forward to attending every year. While waiting to board the plane, I slowly sipped on a cup of hot tea and responded to a few e-mails that I received on my iPhone. As I was typing, a young woman with wavy blond hair, a big smile, and glasses approached me from behind, tapped me on the shoulder, and said, "Are you Michelle Gadsden-Williams?"

Although she startled me, I calmly replied, "Yes, I am."

She then told me, "I saw you walk into the lounge a few moments ago, I just want to tell you how much your work at Novartis meant to me—how much it inspired me and so many others."

This woman was a pharmaceutical sales representative working out of Novartis' Pennsylvania location. She had witnessed several of my presentations during previous sales meetings. "Thank you for being a role model for women," she continued that day, showering me with accolades. "We were so sorry to see you leave a few years ago, but we've watched your career continue to blossom. You have an incredible story." She went on, describing me as courageous, and acknowledging my vast experience as the leader of diversity at a few multinational organizations. "You should consider sharing your story like Sheryl Sandberg, Carla Harris, and others. I'm sure that you have a lot of experiences to share. Anyway . . . I just wanted to say thank you."

With glassy eyes I asked her, "What is your name?"

"Debbie," she answered.

We then chatted for thirty more minutes before I had to depart to my gate. It was a brief yet powerful interaction. It was serendipitous, given that I had dreamed of writing a book about my career and experiences. But I had my reservations. Would readers find my story compelling or interesting? Debbie's comments that day certainly led me to believe that I had something meaningful to share.

Debbie had not realized during our conversation that not only had I departed Novartis, but I was no longer laboring in corporate America. A few months prior to my encounter with Debbie, I had just resigned from my position as managing director and global head of diversity at Credit Suisse to pursue entrepreneurial ventures. As a matter of fact, my last day in that role had been just a few days before our interaction at the airport in February 2015. I had a C-Suite position at a major organization that most professionals dream of—global, influential, impactful, and above all, it was the position that I had worked incredibly hard for during my twenty-five-plus years in corporate America. And here it was—I had just "tapped the mat" like a wrestler and quit my job to become a full-time entrepreneur along with my husband of twenty-one years, David Jamal Williams. *Who does that?* I do, apparently.

But my decision was indeed rational and well-thought-out. I knew exactly what I was doing by resigning and what the implications would be. David and I had talked about the pros and cons of my decision, and even covered the worst thing that could happen. I had led a lifetime of taking calculated risks, which all resulted in wonderfully positive outcomes. Why would this life-altering decision be any different? I also sought the counsel of my father, a retired executive, who

17

coached me to think logically about the decision and to remove emotion from the equation. I also had an invaluable ecosystem of family, friends, colleagues, and others who were personally invested in my success. Given all those factors, I had everything that I needed to branch out on my own. At the end of the day, should my entrepreneurial venture not work out, I knew I could always reinvigorate a corporate career by keeping my relationships alive and nurtured . . . which was exactly what I did!

I dove right into cofounding a business, Ceiling Breakers LLC, alongside my husband David, with the caveat that if a corporate opportunity should present itself, I would certainly consider it. You must keep your options open and be prepared for rare opportunities that may reveal themselves, some in the oddest of ways.

The primary goal of Ceiling Breakers is to help women and people of color reach their full potential as well as to assist corporations with enhancing their diversity and inclusion strategies. Based in New York City, it is a multifaceted company focused on three streams of business: diversity consulting, media-driven women's empowerment initiatives, and diverse entertainment investments. Ceiling Breakers is the outgrowth of an online community that gives women a place to share their struggles and successes in breaking down barriers. Contributors from all ethnicities and varying career backgrounds are tasked with providing a wealth of knowledge to inform and inspire.

Ceiling Breakers' platform was meant to provide every woman with a digital playbook to break through barriers to achieve a thriving career and a successful life. You could say that it served as a stepping stone for my writing a book. Besides the fact that executive coaching was one of many services that my company provided, I really wanted to get to know some next-generation leaders. So, in the fall of 2016, I accepted an invitation to participate in a professional leadership development program that was sponsored by the nonprofit The Partnership, Inc., New England's premier organization dedicated to enhancing the competitiveness of the region by attracting, developing, retaining, and convening multicultural professionals. One of the many things that they do is design leadership programs to prepare professionals for all career trajectories—entry level to C-Suite—from a wide range of industries and sectors. At this point, I knew I wanted to write a book, hence I thought this program would be a great way for me to gain exposure to a group of multicultural professionals and to get a better sense of what they were thinking of in terms of next steps.

I was invited by The Partnership's president and CEO, Carol Fulp, to attend an immersion-week seminar with an incoming class of next-generation executives (NGEs) in Cambridge. Prior to The Partnership, Carol was senior vice president of corporate responsibility and brand management at John Hancock Financial. Carol and I served together on the Harvard Women's Leadership Board at the Kennedy School of Government. The participants were high-potential individuals from diverse fields and backgrounds. These were professionals who were ready to take that next step in their career. In essence, the program prepares multicultural talent to act and think like a senior executive. The format consists of a four-day immersion experience, a five-month leadership incubator with executive coaching and peer support, a capstone retreat, and access to a national, cross-industry network of peers and opinion leaders. At the end of the program, the participants graduate. Essentially, it's almost like a mini-MBA in this short period of time.

I served as an executive coach to a cohort of seven professionals who were hosted at the Endicott House at MIT, the private research university in Cambridge. Over the course of four days, in addition to individualized coaching sessions, we talked as a group about our experiences in the workplace, as well as topics like innovation, polar recessions (facilitated by top notch bankers), and what it's like being the only person of color in the room.

All the executive coaches had to facilitate what was referred to as the Lifeline exercise, designed to expose one's personal and professional journey and development. Everyone must chart the course of his or her life from birth to present day, highlighting the most significant events that have occurred in their lives and shaped who he or she is as a human being and as a professional. When done correctly, it can be emotionally taxing, because you are supposed to walk everyone in the group through your life's journey. The payoff is that you gain insight on how you make decisions, how you show up in the workplace, and how you react to major life events.

I, too, participated in the Lifeline exercise. It was important for me to go through this with my cohort to demonstrate how I got to where I am in my career. Meaning, I had to sit and think about all the things that were significant to me and drove me as a professional. I thought about everything that I'd been through and all that I'd endured. I recalled every opportunity that presented itself to me. I examined some of the low points and high points in my life, but more importantly, how those occurrences or dealings influenced how I led and engaged with others to succeed in the workplace.

Everyone in that room was a person of color who aspired to do more and to be more. I helped them step out of their comfort zone. For instance, there was a Chinese man in our group. Like many of the other professionals who were in IT, he was accustomed to working hard and keeping his head down. It's a situation where you sit in front of a computer all day, you code, and then you go home. So, you don't feel the need to interact with people. As one can imagine, this exercise was very uncomfortable for him. In the culture of his upbringing, you don't talk about your family and you don't talk about personal events in your life. I told him to use this exercise to step out of his comfort zone and to start extending himself to others, even in a casual way. I explained how this was a safe space—kind of like the slogan: *What happens in Vegas stays in Vegas.*

It can be a challenge to get people of color to realize that they must be courageous and open themselves up a little bit more to individuals who can make the difference in how they are perceived in terms of leadership. If somebody asks you on Monday morning, "What did you do over the weekend?" and you look at them like, *That's none of your business*, or whatever the case might be, it's because you're not used to someone peppering you with such questions. Culturally, for some people, it's almost viewed as an invasion of their privacy. This is why it's important to take the time to understand the politics, unwritten rules, and norms within that corporate environment. We must let people get to know us on a different level, but also use that opportunity to educate people for whom this is not common practice. These interactions are what I see as teachable moments.

The next-gen professionals in that room were incredibly smart and bright. We discussed what tools they needed in their own personal or professional toolkit to get that next promotion. One woman's challenge was around being disorganized, due to the large volume of work that she had on her plate. She didn't have a lot of support, so she was all over the place. She felt like she was flying by the seat of her pants half the time. I told her: "Why don't you think about getting a chief of staff or someone who works for you? A high-potential individual who can be your number two, your deputy." She needed to do a better job at delegating responsibilities, such as having someone help prepare for meetings and distribute materials. "If you are a leader, then you must perform and behave like one," I explained.

Another member of the cohort was an introvert—a severe one. She didn't speak up or advocate for herself enough and she wanted to do a better job at getting noticed and volunteering for stretch assignments. Her perspective had been: *If I keep my head down and just do a good job, somebody will pay attention and I'll get promoted.*

But I said to her: "It's great that you're good at what you do, but it requires more than just keeping your head down, because sometimes people don't pay attention. If you're not present and you're not exuding the attributes of a true leader, you could get passed over since they don't know what you want to do or they think you're happy with where you are. You've got to step out of your comfort zone, so let's do some exercises that will get you out of your safe space."

One of those tasks that I asked her to do was to initiate a call that we would host as a team; this way she would take the lead on the call. She would engage everyone and make sure all parties spoke; everyone had an opportunity to provide feedback and peer coaching.

Another participant was a young Latina who was a chief of staff in the political arena. Given the fact that she was one of the few people of color in her office, she constantly felt as if she was a token. It was this sense of: "Oh well, if it's Hispanic issues, let's go to her, she should know what to do. Issues that pertain to African Americans, go to her because she is a minority, so she should know."

But her feeling was: *Why do I have to be that person? Why can't they just do the research like everybody else? Why do I have to be the go-to for all things minority?*

Everyone has their own unique issues and challenges. It's really getting them to think differently about the scenario or about how they react. Meaning, not falling into the, *Why me?* And more about, *Why not you?* I explained to her that she should use this as an opportunity to educate people or to display her talents. Consequently, the next time her congressional colleagues interface with someone who looks like her, it won't be foreign to them. So, utilize your difference—being the only woman or the only person of color in the room—to your advantage. Sometimes these tough lessons, these life experiences, are happening for a reason—to teach you and others something.

Leadership development programs like the one I led are beneficial to any professional who is willing to take advantage of the entire experience. The Partnership provides instruction and coaching with these world-renowned academics. Course leaders aren't just spouting theory but they are giving professionals pragmatic examples of how to be more innovative and how to be a better leader. For me, and for the members of that cohort, the coaching doesn't end after the program concludes. I left the door open, saying, "Look, a few months of coaching for thirty to forty-five minutes is not a lot of time. If you want to extend the coaching opportunity, I'm open to it as long as the partnership organization is supportive of it."

Participating in the leadership program reinforced my decision to write a book about my career path and to target diverse professionals. I know that the next chapter in my life has everything to do with helping the next generation of leaders to aspire higher. In many ways, that Lifeline exercise solidified and validated where I currently stand as a professional, why I enjoy doing what I do now, and, most importantly, how I feel about what I've accomplished over the last twenty-five-plus years.

I have come to learn that first and foremost, not only should you strive to be successful in your career, but you should also think of ways where you can add value to your organization. Most of us get caught up in this myopic view of: *I need to get to the top and there is a linear way to do that.* Sometimes we need to think broader about the roles that we play. One of the things I have always said to my mentees, especially the young women, is that in any organization that I have entered, my ultimate goal is to leave the organization in better condition than when I got there. That is what success is to me. You must think broader about the role that you play and the impact that you have.

I always tell professionals that you must work hard at building your internal brand. Your peers and colleagues need to know who you are no matter where they sit in the organization and no matter where *you* sit in the organization. I have sat in that room when decisions are made about top talent. Oftentimes, it's mostly white guys who are there; they're usually the critical mass. There may also be white women in the room in some instances, and one or two people of color, if any at all. It's no fault of theirs if they just don't know who you are or what you do or how you add value to the organization.

The harsh reality is that there are broad-stroke assessments and assumptions about certain people in the workplace. Over the years, I have witnessed different adjectives being used for people in accordance to gender, race, religion, sexual orientation, and nationality. For example, sometimes men and women are described differently in terms of their leadership style. "Oh, he's aggressive, he's assertive, he's a leader. But she's too aggressive, she's too assertive, she has sharp elbows."

It's about more than overcoming biases in the workplace, especially for women of color. One thing that we as women of color cannot afford to do is take a backseat in terms of managing our careers. We cannot wait for that tap on the shoulder to say, "You're promoted," or, "I'd like you to take on this stretch assignment." As corporate professionals, women must do a better job of positioning themselves, branding themselves, and talking in very prescriptive terms with their direct managers and HR about their aspirations and what they want to do next. You can't be shy about talking those things up, because that is the only way it's going to happen with respect to advancing within your organization and in your career.

I've seen people derailed over one small comment. Now, they aren't given a chance. They won't have a shot in hell because someone said, "Oh, she doesn't speak up in a meeting." Well, the reason why she doesn't speak up might be a demonstration of respect for the higher authority figure in the room or a cultural nuance. But she needs and deserves to receive feedback and positive reinforcement, so that is an area that she can work on. We need to challenge some of the unconscious biases that happen in these conversations about advancing high-potential talent.

To be candid, it has always been my intention to write a book about my climb up the corporate ladder. I have had a wonderful corporate career. I would like to continue to help future female leaders to realize their God-given potential and ambitions. Over the years, I have been approached by many women asking for sage advice or counsel on how they, too, can design a career plan and strategy, reinvent themselves after a career setback, have better work/life balance, position themselves for the next big job, plan an elegant exit strategy if they want to pursue entrepreneurship or reenter the workplace after a short hiatus.

As I finished writing this book, I was presented with an executive position as managing director of Inclusion & Diversity North America at Accenture, a leading global professional services company with more than 400,000 people servicing clients across forty industries in 120 countries, providing innovative solutions in strategy, consulting, digital technology, and operations. I accepted the job offer. Off-ramps and on-ramps are part of the career journey. I view my entrepreneurial ride as another extremely positive experience. I've learned a lot about myself in the process and will now have a fresh perspective and a different lens about business models and so forth as I transition back into corporate America. I've accomplished quite a bit since I left two years ago and I'm grateful to have had an opportunity to take a step back, catch my breath, and reenter the corporate arena with a new sense of energy and vigor.

As a woman of color and corporate executive who has worked for several Fortune 500 companies, traveled around the world, lived and worked in Switzerland for close to ten years, been honored and recognized by some of the world's most prestigious organizations and publications (*Ebony, Essence, Black Enterprise, Fortune, Forbes,* and the *Wall Street Journal,* to name a few), and sat on seven nonprofit boards— all while managing a chronic illness—I believe that I have something new to say about tackling the most pressing issues and barriers facing professionals, specifically women, in today's workplace.

The title of this book, *Climb*, speaks volumes about my career trajectory and professional journey. I am passionate about helping women of color climb in corporate America— to ascend the rungs from wherever they are standing in their career and within whatever organization they are employed. My goal is not to focus squarely on academic theories and statistics like other self-help books. This book will focus on addressing and dissecting obstacles, offering pragmatic solutions and key steps to ensure that you are fully equipped to tackle today's most pressing workplace issues and to advance into positions of leadership. I want to offer tools to help you build your own professional playbook. *Climb* is about staying to true to yourself as you take every step, and follow more than one path until you reach your goal and achieve your highest aspiration—whatever it may be.

1

THE BEGINNING OF MY ASCENT

*It's a heavy burden to look up at the mountain
and want to start the climb.*
—Abby Wambach

I have been a fighter since the day of my birth on May 21,
1969. At the time, I weighed four pounds eleven ounces
and my older—by three minutes—identical sibling, Monique, weighed five pounds four ounces. Due to my small
size, I had to stay in the NICU for an additional week until
I reached five pounds; only then was I discharged from the
hospital to go home with my family.

Growing up as a twin is a unique experience. There is a
lot of complexity, whether you are identical or fraternal. It is
a common thought that twins are two people who look alike,
dress alike, and like to play pranks by switching roles—think
the Walt Disney film *The Parent Trap*, be it the 1961 original
version with Hayley Mills or the 1998 remake starring Lindsay
Lohan. One actress did double duty playing her own sibling in
those films. But it was real-life identical twin sisters Tia and
Tamera Mowry who won our hearts playing long-lost twins in
the ABC nineties sitcom *Sister, Sister*.

While Monique and I have a close, special bond, I didn't
realize I was a twin until people pointed it out at school. It was
when I was around age five, just attending kindergarten. In
our youth, most people could not tell us apart, except for our

parents, grandparents, a few aunts, and maybe some cousins. The physical appearance was quite striking. Monique and I were truly identical. Growing up people would say, "Hi, twin," instead of calling us by our names. That didn't sit well with me. There was one instance when I snapped back: "You know, I'm not twin. It's *part* of my identity. It is not my full identity. My name is Michelle and her name is Monique. Let's be clear about that."

Oftentimes, our family and neighbors would refer to Monique and me as a pair—not as two separate individuals with different goals, dreams, and aspirations. Despite identical appearances, studies show that twins prefer their own identities, especially as they grow older. So, I was no different in this respect. I always wrestled with trying to find my own sense of self and unique identity outside of my twin.

I am aggressive, creative, inquisitive, and talkative. I am an extrovert by nature. I draw my energy from people. I make friends easily and have no problem with expressing my opinions to anyone who is willing to listen. My mother often told me that mouth of mine would one day get me into trouble. As a child, I demanded a lot of attention. Anytime I would come home from school or simply walk into the house, I would slam the door. It was my way of announcing, *I'm here!*

Now, Monique on the other hand was the smarter of the two of us; she was more cerebral and analytical. She certainly has more advanced degrees than I do. Monique holds a BS in organizational pyschology, a MEd in counselor education, an ED in educational leadership, and a JD from the Birmingham School of Law. Need I say more? We have a younger sister by eleven years, Alicia, who has a BS in business administration and an MS in interdisciplinary studies.

Under-achievers is certainly not a term used to describe

either of my sisters, who very much wanted to experience being part of a more racially diverse student body. That was one
of the reasons why they chose to attend a historically black
college and university (HBCU). I chose to attend Kean College, a liberal arts institution located in Union, New Jersey,
where I graduated with a BS in marketing and a BA in communications. I also hold an MS in organizational dynamics
from the University of Pennsylvania.

We were raised by Southern parents with Southern values
in a middle-class African American household in North Edison,
New Jersey. Our parents, Anna Lee and Herbert Gadsden Jr.,
were both born and reared in Beaufort, South Carolina, and
migrated north in the 1960s. They were part of the exodus of
African Americans from below the Mason-Dixon Line in the
face of the injustices of Jim Crow laws. The rise of an African
American middle class throughout the 1960s was the result of
economic growth, public policy, higher education, and Southern flight.

Our neighborhood and school were not very diverse at all.
I graduated from high school with fewer than ten other black
students (including Monique) out of a class of over six hundred students. Diversity was not one of North Edison's strong
suits at that time. Today, however, Edison is primarily middle
class with more than seventy-five ethnic communities represented. Indeed, in 2009, Edison was ranked as one of "America's 10 Best Places to Grow Up" by *US News & World Report*.[1]

Albeit, the black middle class does not come to mind
when most people think of black life in America. "Over the
years, wildly popular and celebrated pop culture television se-

---

1 Luke Mullins, "America's 10 Best Places to Grow Up," *U.S. News & World Report*,
August 19, 2009, https://money.usnews.com/money/personal-finance/real-estate/arti-
cles/2009/08/19/americas-10-best-places-to-grow-up.

ries such as *The Cosby Show, The Fresh Prince of Bel-Air,* and the more current *Black-ish* and *Empire,* have planted images of black economic success and postracial progress in American society," according to *Pacific Standard* magazine.[2] But my real-life childhood experience was in a black middle-class family.

My parents believed in what I would define as unrelenting straight talk. Every morning as we prepared to go to school, my father would ask Monique and I the same questions: "So, girls, what do you want to do? Who do you want to be?" These were very sophisticated questions to ask kindergartners, but that's my dad! That whole analytical thinking and thought process, that's how he's wired. After the first day of school, he would ask, "Where did you sit?" He wanted to make sure that we sat in the front of the class. He was very adamant that we were present at all times and allowed our voices to be heard. He taught us the importance of articulating and expressing our thoughts at a very early age.

He made it a point to ask us very specific questions like: "What are your strengths? What aren't you good at? What are your weaknesses? How can you turn that around?" We didn't know it at the time but he was nurturing our gifts and talents. He was shaping our futures in a way that was meaningful for us, as well as our mom and himself, in terms of how they parented. That daily verbal exercise prepared me to think critically about what I wanted to be when I grew up. I would talk to people and say, "Okay, so this is what I'm going to do. This is how I'm going to do it. This is when I'm going to do it." By the time I was ten years old, I could recite my own personal "elevator pitch" about "Who Am I?"

---

2 Charles D. Ellison, "Are We Talking Enough About the Black Middle Class?" *Pacific Standard,* April 13, 2015, https://psmag.com/news/are-we-talking-enough-about-the-black-middle-class.

Like most middle-class families, our parents tried to develop our skills through close supervision and organized activities. There weren't too many things they didn't expose us to.
My sisters and I were involved in countless extracurricular activities. We took lessons in dance, piano, and voice. We were
into gymnastics and cheerleading. In a three-year period, I
played the violin, clarinet, and flute.

Monique and I loved track and field the most. We participated in the sport from middle school all the way through high
school. It provided us with a forum to demonstrate our true
talents as athletes. We were disciplined and fast on our feet.
We were sprinters. Monique ran the 100- and 200-meter dash. I
ran the 400-meter dash. We were true competitors who loved
the sport and we garnered a lot of local and even national
attention. We were local "celebrities" and we knew it!

But it's not about being popular, it's all about being re-
silient. As an athlete, you must learn how to deal with disappointment and then get back out there and do it again. In
track, you can go from hero to zero in a matter of seconds.
Meaning, you can be first at the top of the race but come in
last place by the end of the race. You come to understand
there's a strategy to everything that you do. You must design
the strategy that's going to work best for you to get the win.
That may mean starting out of the blocks as fast as you can, or
hanging back and then sprinting toward the finish line.

The same applies to a career: There are wins. There are
losses. There is a point in time where you must reinvent yourself in some cases or recalibrate after a loss; such as you would
if you were unsuccessful in getting a raise or promotion, or
an assignment didn't go as planned. We all have a tendency
at times to derive our self-worth from our performance. If we
succeed, then we're worthy people. If we fail, we're losers. I

learned how to separate myself from my performance, and so should you.

John Maxwell's 2007 book on the subject, *Failing Forward: Turning Mistakes into Stepping Stones for Success*, describes failures as life experiences that didn't turn out the way you intended. His advice is simple. Don't obsess over the situation and don't use absolute language like, "I'm never going to succeed," or, "I'm always going to fall short of my goal." Don't dwell in self-pity by ruminating on, *Why me?* Instead focus on, *What can I learn?* Even when we fail at a goal, we aren't failing as a person. That's what it means to learn to fail forward.

I learned not only how to bounce back from defeat, I know for sure that running track helped cultivate my leadership capabilities. I learned how to work with a team. I knew how to be an individual with the understanding that I'm also part of a squad. It's not just "I," it's "We." Working as a group and knowing the role that you play is important to the success of the team.

I am grateful that my parents also taught me stick-to-itiveness. A daddy's girl, I observed how my father navigated the tough terrains of corporate America as a black man working in the sixties, seventies, and up until his retirement in 2003. He was the benefactor of affirmative action but not any kind of "perceived" preferential treatment. Dad was deserving of his managerial ranking in corporate America because of his aptitude and his attitude.

As fate would have it, his initial intent was never to enter corporate America. He spent years working in a manufacturing plant, then in 1968 at age twenty-eight, he decided to go back to school. He became a computer programmer at TRW Inc., a Fortune 500 company specializing in industrial products. He devoted thirty-five years to the same company, advancing from the manufacturing floor to an office position in senior management. He went from programming computers to production planning. Later, he was put in charge of the IT department. Out of 150 employees in total at the company, my father had sixty of those staffers working under him at some point. He recalls being one of two managers who were awarded $50,000 worth of stock at a reduced price in TRW. He had designed some computer systems that were financially beneficial to his employer.

After graduating high school and throughout our college years, Monique and I spent four summers and Christmas breaks working with our father. We were placed in the customer service, production, purchasing, and accounting departments at TRW. We both developed a good business sense and understanding of the inner workings of a corporate environment. After hearing my father talk about his struggles and seeing his pain from barriers set before him because of discrimination, I had to think long and hard about whether I wanted to pursue a career working for a major corporation. But our father showed Monique and me how to rise above it all. In the end, we both entered corporate America; though I stayed on while Monique left to pursue a career in academia.

Unlike our father, who stayed put at the same company, my own corporate career journey spans twenty-seven years. I have worked at six major companies—Phillips–Van Heusen, Wakefern Food, Merck & Co., Novartis, Credit Suisse, and now Accenture—across four different industries: apparel, consumer goods, pharmaceuticals, financial and professional services. I also lived as an expat in Europe for eight years.

Dad retired at age sixty-three, while I was age forty-six when I made the life-altering decision to bid farewell to my corporate gig as managing director and global head of diversity and inclusion at a top financial services firm to start my own venture in 2015. It was a bold move. Yet I understood that it was okay to take off-ramps at some point on your road to success, because you can always find on-ramps again to the corporate highway. Things may not work out the way you planned or a new opportunity can reveal itself at any point in time and you have to be ready! That's why it is critical to keep your mentors and sponsors close and your ecosystem of former colleagues even closer. You never know when you're going to need them to attest to your performance and leadership.

Adjusting Your Corporate Footprint

Just as I did when I was a little girl, it is important for you to create a personalized elevator pitch describing your career aspirations. Recite it aloud and often. It is totally fine if your pitch changes over the course of your career. Granted, I didn't dream of being in HR as a little girl. But I was very clear that I wanted to become one of the top people in whatever career I chose. I started my career in marketing. That was my major in college and it was always of interest to me. I enjoyed fashion, so I decided to go to the Fashion Institute of Technology (FIT), which is part of the State University of New York. I had a part-time job when I was in high school working at a department store called Bamberger's, now known as Macy's.

They didn't have housing available for local freshmen at the time, so I had to commute from New Jersey to New York City every day, and I didn't care for that trek too much. Not to mention that I was mugged, twice. After being rescued by a Guardian Angel near the Madison Square Garden arena, I thought, *Okay, we've got to do something different. This is just not going to work.*

After one year, I decided to transfer from FIT to a liberal

arts college in New Jersey that accepted students in the second semester. Kean College was once known as New Jersey State Teachers College and was renamed in 1997. I learned a lot about myself there. One thing I discovered was that the curriculum was not very difficult for me—I was acing every class. That was due in large part to my desire to learn, and a passion for the subject. I went from being an average high school student to a top-of-my-class college student. I did what every college student typically does: I spent a lot time on campus, made a lot of friends, and went to a lot of parties.

When I graduated from Kean, I started working full-time at Bamberger's as part of their Management Training Program. At that time, there were no jobs available for recent college grads like myself. The job market was horrible, and I knew eventually I wanted to move out of my parents' house and buy my own car. I said to myself, *I'll just work here full-time, and then leave and get a real job at some later date.*

The reason I was admitted into Bamberger's Management Training Program was because when I worked part-time at the store, I sold fragrances and became one of their highest-producing sales reps on the night shift. Their thinking was: *Wow! If she can sell the hell out of fragrances, she would probably be great at selling merchandise, and besides that, she's going to school.*

Again, this goes back to my competitive nature, the need to get the win, always wanting to be on top. I made it a point to be the best salesperson. In part, it was the art of persuasion. I think, if anything, many times I would oversell the product. I'd say, "Oh, this eye cream, it's $100, but it does this, that, and the other thing." So I would almost embellish the attributes of the product just to get the sale.

A lot of students who had interests in becoming buyers or

working in the fashion industry also went through that Man-agement Training Program, which lasted eighteen months. It was very competitive. There were twenty-five of us in there at the same time. The endgame, depending upon how well you did in this program, was that you would be promoted to assis-tant manager of a department, where you would learn how to manage teams of people and merchandise. Bamberger's pro-gram was my training ground in terms of managing people, budgets, time sheets, vendors, and inventory. I was assigned to a department where I later became the department manager.

In general, programs designed around training, develop-ment, or leadership building are vitally important because they not only help to strengthen workplace skills but often lead to opportunities for career advancement. When an op-portunity presented itself to me to work at the Phillips–Van Heusen Corporation, thanks in part to a friend of mine who was employed there in HR, I applied for and was accepted into a product development position. Phillips–Van Heusen, commonly referred to as PVH Corp., is an American cloth-ing company, which owns brands like IZOD. These days PVH Corp. is best known as the parent company behind wildly suc-cessful apparel lines including Calvin Klein, Tommy Hilfiger, and Speedo. I spent six years there, working with different factories around the world, managing orders, and making sure the goods made it to the stores. It was still fashion and retail to an extent, but it was more on the corporate side. There was no interaction with customers every day and I did not have to work weekends and holidays . . . YES!

I liked what I did, though I didn't love it. It was import-ant for me to align my career goals and interests according to what I envisioned myself doing for the duration of my career. I would impart that same advice to anyone early in their career.

The job or work that you do should always support your end-game, which in my case was to be at the highest level of senior management within my field at an organization.

When I decided to leave Phillips–Van Heusen I was a senior production manager, where I had been responsible for the production and distribution of private label sweaters and active wear for the intercompany retail divisions that billed $24 billion annually. In 1995, I went to work for another consumer goods company, Wakefern Food Corporation, which is regarded as the largest member-owned wholesale distribution cooperative in the US. Today it supplies groceries and other merchandise to more than three hundred supermarkets under the ShopRite, the Fresh Grocer, and PriceRite banners. I entered Wakefern as part of a leaders-in-training program and upon graduating was placed in a full-time role. Even though it was entry level, I was identified as high-potential talent and had a great deal of exposure to the CEO and his direct reports. I was promoted very quickly in that company, from an HR administrator to a staffing and diversity administrator in 1997.

During my tenure at the retail level there were a significant number of people of color employed at the grocery stores, but on the corporate side, not so much. There were very few people of color in leadership roles—I can recall three managers out of twenty or so. I remember there was one African American male who sat on the executive committee and reported directly to the CEO. There were smatterings of African Americans at Wakefern. Put it this way: there were so few of us that we all knew each other by first name and each person's job function.

Sometimes an opportunity may not present itself, but that shouldn't stop you, because you can carve your own career path. I essentially created an instrumental role for my-self where I worked very closely with the leaders within the company. One of my assignments was to go out and bench-mark other companies in different industries to see how they managed diversity. Some would either be corporate clients of Wakefern or people we had done business with. I put together a presentation about what good diversity practices looked like or could look like. I went to Texaco and PepsiCo. I met with their heads of diversity and I talked to different people within their organizations. I called all around, read a lot of articles about the gurus of diversity and how they were making in-roads. It took me a couple of months, but I collated all this information and then presented it to Ernie Bell, who was my mentor and the VP of HR at the time. I said to him: "I think we should do this."

He replied, "I do too. If we do this, do you want to lead it?"

I said, "Absolutely." So, in essence, I created a job for myself.

Despite this noteworthy accomplishment, the work was still not challenging enough, at least in my mind. I decided to depart Wakefern after laboring there for four years. The move was prompted by Ernie. He came to Wakefern from General Electric, a mammoth company (ranked No. 11 on the 2016 Fortune 500 list with $140.3 billion in revenues). He was in his mid to late forties. One day he told me: "Michelle, you know, you're incredibly talented. But there's just not a lot of opportunity here at this company. I would suggest you go to a bigger company that has more opportunity for someone like you, who has aspirations to do bigger and better things in HR." This is a prime example of how and why you should share your career goals and interests with your manager or an HR rep. Allocate timelines to accomplish your goals and track your progress.

The glass ceiling was certainly there at Wakefern and I was not patient enough to wait for a crack to open. I wanted to learn. I wanted to grow. I wanted to consider other opportunities, other avenues that could get me closer to my goal. I applied for a job at the American pharmaceuticals giant Merck & Co. (ranked No. 72 on the 2016 Fortune 500 list with $39.4 billion in revenues). I got a job working in their strategic staffing function. Yet I left that company after another four years, once again not wanting to bump my head against a ceiling.

Women of Color Must Break a Concrete Ceiling

Did I perceive a powerful position as the means to achieving my professional goals? You bet. I was confident that I would reach C-level status and I would succeed in that role.

I created a vision board for myself that detailed my career goals and I planned strategically on how to achieve them. As black women, why shouldn't we aspire to climb to the top? There is an understanding, however, that the challenges ahead of us often do not lie with our aspirations or abilities, but the organization itself.

Black women are nearly three times more likely than white women to aspire to a position of power with a prestigious title.[3] Yet, white women are twice as likely as black women to attain one, according to the Center for Talent Innovation's (CTI) 2015 report, "Black Women: Ready to Lead," which explores black women's pursuit of powerful jobs within US corporations and uncovers eye-opening numbers around ambition, vision, and barriers. Despite their wanting a top job and honing the qualifications to earn it, 44 percent of black women

---

3 Sylvia Ann Hewlett and Tai Wingfield, "Black Women: Ready to Lead," Center for Talent Innovation, 2015, http://www.talentinnovation.org/publication.cfm?publication=1460.

are more likely to feel stalled in their careers, as compared to 30 percent of white women.[4]

Moreover, those black women who've battled their way into the upper-middle realms of corporate America languish there despite their formidable credentials—49 percent of the black women compared to the 40 percent of white women surveyed for the CTI report hold graduate degrees. "Black women who are ready to lead—whose qualifications, track record, drive, and commitment make them ideal candidates for executive roles—stick firmly to the marzipan layer, in sight of the C-Suite, but seemingly not in the sights of those who occupy it," say the report's authors, Sylvia Ann Hewlett, CTI's founder and CEO, and Tai (Green) Wingfield, the organization's former vice president of communications.

Likewise, research from the study "Women in the Workplace 2016" by LeanIn.Org and McKinsey & Co. suggests that women of color are the most underrepresented group in the senior and upper ranks of US companies, and their numbers drop steeply at the middle and senior levels. LeanIn.Org is the nonprofit organization founded by Facebook COO Sheryl Sandberg, who also is the author of the *New York Times* and Amazon best seller *Lean In: Women, Work, and the Will to Lead.* Her book soared to the top of international best-seller lists, igniting global conversations about women and ambition. *Lean In* is meant to be an inspiring call to action and blueprint for individual growth. It certainly was a wake-up call for many.

The catchphrase to "lean in" came about after Sandberg encouraged women during her popular 2010 TED Talk to "sit at the table" and to "lean in" to be heard in a business

---

4 *Ibid.*

or boardroom scenario.[5] She stresses that women must "lean in" to whatever role they are playing in an organization. She tells women to bring their chair to the table, sit up straight, and "lean in" to make their voice heard, loud and clear. She encourages women to be audacious ("Lean in, go for it"), and speaks of the need for personal ambition shifts.

The hairs on the back of my neck tend to rise when there are discussions around gender equality and parity, because the focus is usually on majority women's views and experiences in the workforce. There is a difference between women of color in their ascent up the corporate ladder as compared to white women. Both CTI's and LeanIn.Org's reports did reveal that unlike white women, lack of ambition is not the issue for many African American, Latina, and Asian American women. I know for me that was never the problem. I was not unlike many of the women surveyed for the "Women in the Workplace" study, in which 48 percent of women of color said they aspired to be a top executive, compared to 37 percent of white women. At the entry level, only 27 percent of white women said they aspired to be a top executive, compared to 41 percent of women of color. Thus, women of color are leaning in with all their might, but they're still invisible—they're being overlooked.

In the CTI report, the highly credentialed and qualified black women who were surveyed described "being both painfully conspicuous—'unicorns,' as one put it—and manifestly invisible. Or they're seen but not heard: 46 percent of the college-educated black women we surveyed said their ideas aren't heard or recognized," according to Hewlett and Wing-

---

5 Sheryl Sandberg, "Sheryl Sandberg: Why We Have Too Few Women Leaders," TED Talk, December 21, 2010, https://www.ted.com/talks/sheryl_sandberg_why_we_have_too_few_women_leaders.

field. And their experience outside of work falls off the radar of management at work. They are twice as likely as white women to be leaders in their communities—running a school board, leading a youth initiative, heading up a charity or community organization.

"Black women are committed and motivated to attain a powerful position not only in their workplaces, but also in their communities," wrote CTI's Hewlett. "With their vision, commitment, and leadership experience, black women represent a pool of would-be executives that multinational companies can ill afford to underutilize."

I found this research to be quite interesting, since a lot of these findings were being demonstrated by most of the women of color that I knew.

Sitting at the intersection of biases around race and gender, African American women must labor to overcome both. While white women speak of shattering a glass ceiling, women of color describe their barriers to advancement differently. Many women of color who have made it to the executive suite describe the process as breaking through a *concrete* ceiling.

"Let's start by looking at the difference between the materials. While glass is tough, you can shatter it. You can see through it to the level above—and you know that there is something to aspire to. If you can see it, you can achieve it," notes Jasmine Babers, founder of *Love Girls* magazine and a Peace First Fellow, in her *Huffington Post* blog about the corporate environment.[6] "Concrete, on the other hand, is practically impossible to break through by yourself. There is no visible destination, just what seems like a dead end," she continues.

---

6 Jasmine Babers, "For Women of Color, the Glass Ceiling is Actually Made of Concrete," *Huffington Post*, April 20, 2016, http://www.huffingtonpost.com/jasmine-babers/for-women-of-color-the-gl_b_9728056.html.

"This is what women of color face in the workforce: an often impenetrable barrier, with no vision of how to get to the next level."

I have witnessed fellow women of color—my peers in corporate America—chipping away at the concrete ceiling while others were constantly banging their heads up against it. I saw some women who were identified as high-potential talent getting the stretch assignments and the promotions that they truly deserved. Then there was a small group of women and people of color who were almost totally invisible in their organizations. They were buried so deep that they weren't in the line of sight for any decision makers to talk them up in talent review discussions. If they don't know who you are, your name is not going to come up; therefore, you won't be considered for a high-visibility assignment or a promotion. One of the ways I made sure that I was going to be noticed was to consistently do a great job and always raise my hand to be considered for more highly visible projects. I always kept my ear to the ground when it came to projects or assignments that I believed could provide me with a greater level of exposure to demonstrate my talents. If you are able to show you're an exceptional talent, then senior leaders in your organization will come to know about you, or at a minimum they will know your name.

Standing on the Shoulders of Corporate Giants

There are some executives who think that they have "arrived" once entering the C-Suite. I, on the other hand, felt a sense of appreciation and gratitude to have been selected to have a seat at a table where very few people, including women and minorities, were invited to sit. I was going to try my hardest to be the best version of myself at that table.

For many professionals in corporate America, reaching

the C-Suite is not as obtainable as it appears. *C-Suite* is an adjective used to describe high-ranking executive titles within an organization. The letter C, in this context, stands for chief officers who hold C-level positions that are typically considered the most powerful and influential members of an organization (chief executive officer, chief operating officer, chief information officer, chief marketing officer, chief sales officer, chief human resource officer, chief diversity officer, etc.). They set and communicate the company's strategy, and make higher-stake decisions.

What does it take to move within the senior ranks and to ascend to the top of the organizational chart? However bright and ambitious you are, the harsh reality is that only a few will ever reach the C-Suite. Yet, daunting as it may seem, if this is what you desire then you must plot your moves to reach the top. One way to look at is: *Shoot for the moon. Even if you miss, you'll land among stars!* This famous quote comes from the world-renowned motivational speaker Les Brown (Gladys Knight's ex-husband, as many may recall). True, I aimed at the moon and landed on it, but it was not effortless.

I was very clear about the career path I was pursuing. I made it my business to stay abreast of developments within my chosen profession, which meant attending diversity and inclusion conferences regularly to upskill myself and learn about the best practices from other key players in my arena. At a major corporation, a chief diversity officer (CDO) is an organization's executive-level diversity and inclusion strategist. I understood that the path to becoming a CDO was a lot less linear than that of acquiring other executive-level positions. Training, while involving many of the same skills as other executive positions, quite often requires a degree of experience that isn't necessarily obtained simply through traditional academic methods—experience and interpersonal social competence play a larger role. Hence, the tools I developed early on were built around better assessing people and advancing them in their careers. I knew that achieving the status of CDO meant that I needed to have a strong grasp of diversity issues as well as the ability to shape and implement an organization's diversity agenda. As CDO I would need to have a thorough understanding of current laws regarding inclusion, equal opportunity, and discrimination.

CDOs and diversity programs have been in place among major organizations for decades, but "recent growth in diversity roles among major businesses and interest in general seem to have coincided with the start of President Obama's presidency" in 2008, surmises the careers and jobseekers' website Jibe.[7] Diversity initiatives are far more likely to succeed with executive buy-in, notes Jibe. What better way to gain executive buy-in than by having a C-Suite position dedicated to the cause.

For many years, the quest for diversity was very much about affirmative action. Primarily in the seventies and eighties, there was a lot of head-counting of groups of people and individuals. Back then there were some companies that were doing great work in this space, but it was still along the lines of: *How many underrepresented minorities work in the organization? How do we avoid litigation?* There was someone assigned the position of identifying and assessing an organization's current ethnic composition. From where I sat, there wasn't a shift in terms of how diversity was talked about as a business driver until the midnineties. It was no longer an HR-led process;

---

7 Emily Smykal, "Chief Diversity Officer: Do You Really Need to Fill This Position?" Jibe, February 15, 2016, https://www.jibe.com/blog/chief-diversity-officer-do-you-really-need-to-fill-this-position/.

companies were becoming engaged because they saw a shift in consumer patterns as the purchasing power of people of color grew.

It is just within the last two decades that the role of head of diversity or CDO has become a part of the leadership team within the HR division at major corporations. Companies started to hire people who were tasked specifically with managing diversity within the organization. In the beginning, there was still a lot to prove to people. Someone might ask: "So, what do you do? I don't understand, what is the head of diversity? I don't get it. Is this a full-time job?" There was a lot of that kind of discussion. It was still new to some leaders in the company who wanted to know: "What do you do? How do you do it? How does it impact the bottom line of the company?"

Through my actions, they would soon find out. As an advocate for equality and social justice, I have worked tirelessly at refining processes, policies, and programs that support an inclusive work environment.

Beyond understanding the industry and skill set required to reach the top of your respective field, you need to be aware of whose shoulders you are standing on. While I'm not asking anyone to become a history buff, if you want to ascend into the C-Suite as a person of color, you need to be aware of corporate trailblazers.

When I was promoted to C-Suite level as the global head of diversity at Novartis, very few African American women had made it to the top as CEO. Ann Fudge and Ursula Burns were among the first African American women to ever run a S&P 500 company. The first African American to lead a Standard and Poor's 500 Index corporation was John Thompson, at Symantec Corp. from 1999 to 2009. A Harvard Business

School graduate, Fudge built a career in marketing at General Foods and then Kraft, before making headlines for becoming a top-ranking African American woman in the advertising industry when she took the helm as chairman and CEO of Young & Rubicam, from 2003 to 2006. Since 2010, Burns had served as CEO of Xerox, "managing to turn a company once only known for paper copies to a viable and profitable business," according to *Forbes*, which also reported that "in 2015 she helped generate $18 billion in revenue, with adjusted earnings per share of 98 cents."[8] Burns joined Xerox in 1980 as an intern, and worked her way up the ranks to CEO of a publicly traded company. Xerox held the 143 spot on the 2015 Fortune 500 annual listing of the 500 largest US corporations. After six years as Xerox CEO, Burns stepped down in 2016 following the company's split into two public companies: a business process outsourcing company and a document technology company.

Considering only fifteen African American executives have ever made CEO of a Fortune 500 company,[9] her departure offers a dismal outlook for African American women in the corporate sector. Just barely 1 percent of Fortune 500 CEOs are African American. As of 2016, five black men served in that role: Kenneth I. Chenault, CEO of American Express since 2001; TIAA-CREF's CEO Roger W. Ferguson was appointed in 2008; Kenneth C. Frazier became CEO of Merck in 2011; Carnival CEO Arnold W. Donald took the helm in 2013; and JC Penney Co. named Marvin Ellison CEO in 2015. Then there's Craig Arnold, who became CEO of the

---

8   Ursula Burns profile, *Forbes*, September 25, 2017, https://www.forbes.com/profile/ursula-burns/.

9   Ellen McGirt, "Why Race and Culture Matter in the C-Suite," *Fortune*, January 22, 2016, http://fortune.com/black-executives-men-c-suite/.

power management giant Eaton Corporation, which moved its operations to Ireland in 2013, making it ineligible for the Fortune 500 ranking. Chenault is expected to retire from American Express on February 1, 2018. With his departure, the Fortune 500 will have only three black CEOs remaining: Ferguson, Frazier, and Ellison.

There were a mere twenty-two female CEOs among Fortune 500 companies as of December 2015. Only one of these women was a person of color: PepsiCo's Indian American CEO Indra Nooyi; she has held the position since 2006. By the end of the first quarter of 2017, *Fortune* touted thirty-two women leading Fortune 500 companies.[10] The previous record for most female CEOs on the list was set in 2014, at twenty-four. This number stayed unchanged for the next two years, meaning that the percentage of women at the top of the Fortune 500 had been holding steady at 4.8 percent. *Fortune* pointed out that 2017 was a record-breaking year—for the first time ever, more than five percent of CEOs on its list were women, at 6.4 percent.

Notwithstanding these developments, women of color now hold just two spots on *Fortune*'s list. PG&E Corp. tapped Geisha J. Williams, president of electric operations, to lead its clean-energy push as their new CEO and president. Williams, a Cuban immigrant, is reportedly the first female Hispanic CEO of a company of PG&E's size. Women of color represent less than 10 percent of managers and a measly 3.9 percent of senior-level executives, reports Catalyst, the nonprofit research and advisory organization.[11]

---

10 Valentina Zarya, "The 2017 Fortune 500 Includes a Record Number of Women CEOs," *Fortune*, January 7, 2017, http://fortune.com/2017/06/07/fortune-women-ceos/.

11 Catalyst, "Women in S&P 500 Companies by Race/Ethnicity," March 2015, http://www.catalyst.org/knowledge/women-sp-500-companies-raceethnicity.

The truth of the matter is that access to jobs and promotions in corporate America remains a significant conundrum for women of color. Race and gender issues in America continue to be at the heart of a larger systemic problem and a major topic of discussion. During an edition of *NewsOne Now*, a daily African American morning television news show on TV One, journalist and host Roland Martin and his panel of guests discussed "what looks to be the end of an era as it relates to black women running companies in corporate America, what can be done to reverse this trend, and whom diversity is actually benefitting."[12]

NewsOne Now panelist Avis Jones-DeWeever explained, "Diversity has now come in practice to mean white women." The founder of the Exceptional Leadership Institute for Women continued: "If you specifically look at who are CEOs in America and Fortune 500 companies since between 2008 and 2009, we've seen an increase of white women CEOs of Fortune 500 companies by fourfold. At the same time, we've only had one black woman ever in the history of the Fortune 500 and the number of people of color generally has gone down. The problem with our nation's discussion about diversity," she added, "is that when we talk about diversity, when we talk about who is going to get the benefits, we find it is primarily white women, so much so that there is more diversity among male CEOs in Fortune 500 companies than there is among female CEOs."

At a glance, it may appear that very little progress has been made as it pertains to women, especially women of color, in corporate America. Yet, while we remain underrepresented in senior management and the C-Suite, we cannot—we will

12 *NewsOne Now*, "There May Soon Be No Black Female CEOs Among Fortune 500 Companies," 2016, https://newsone.com/3440536/black-female-ceos-fortune-500-companies/.

not—take a backseat to the injustices that continue to prevail. We don't want our employers to feel as if they are taking a risk on us by promoting us into positions of leadership. Women of color deserve a seat at the table. We deserve to lead in our organizations. We just need an opportunity to do so. This is why it's important for us as women to tell our stories and ensure that all our hard work gets acknowledged. All our expertise needs to be shared and all our voices need to be heard. This is my voice. This is my story. This is my journey—my climb to the top.

Key Steps

1. Identify your career goals and interests—what do you envision yourself doing for the duration of your career? Why?

2. Conduct an honest self-assessment of your strengths, weaknesses, and areas for development. Take advantage of training or leadership-development programs.

3. Create a vision board that details your career goals and aspirations. Be strategic about how you plan to achieve both professional and personal life aspirations.

4. Create a personalized "elevator pitch" (no more than one minute in length) describing your aspirations. Recite it aloud and often.

5. Share your career goals and interests with your manager and HR business partner.

6. Allocate specific timelines to accomplish each goal. Have periodic check-ins with yourself (and your mentors) to keep track of your progress.

7. Reinvent yourself if need be, or recalibrate after a

MICHELLE GADSDEN-WILLIAMS ♪ 51

loss (i.e., you were unsuccessful in getting a raise or promotion; a project or an assignment didn't go as planned).

8. "Lean in" to whatever role you are playing in an organization. Don't hold your head down. Be visible. Make sure you aren't being overlooked.

9. Build informal and formal networks inside and outside of your organization and within your industry.

10. Design the strategy that's going to work best for your situation to get the win. Think intrapreneurially and create a job for yourself if you need to do so.

2

PURPOSE, PASSION, POWER

If you can't figure out your purpose, figure out your passion.
For your passion will lead you right into your purpose.
—Bishop T.D. Jakes

B ishop T.D. Jakes, an influential spiritual leader who has a 30,000-member church known as the Potter's House in Dallas, Texas, is highly regarded for his powerful sermons in which he addresses topics such as finding your passion and living a life of purpose. He even delivered an empowering *Oprah Life Class* on these topics, attracting millions of people from around the world. Over more than two decades as a businessman, Jakes has expanded his brand from launching T.D. Jakes Ministries Inc. to establishing TDJ Enterprises LLP, the umbrella under which he produces movies, television programs, and music CDs. What's more, as a best-selling author, he has penned about forty books, selling more than twenty million copies in total.[13]

In his book *Identity: Discover Who You Are and Live a Life of Purpose*, the bishop reminds us: "As you get to know more about yourself—your likes, dislikes, values and triggers—you will have a greater sense of whether or not the life you lead suits you." He insists that having a talent is not the same as living your purpose, speaking of his own musical talents but

---

13 Carolyn M. Brown, "Sowing the Seeds of Prosperity," *Black Enterprise*, April 2012, http://www.blackenterprise.com/business/td-jakes-sowing-seeds-of-prosperity/.

admitting that being a musician was not his calling. He describes passion and purpose as being joined at the hip, and moving together lockstep toward one's destiny. He commands us to connect our passion to our purpose, then set our goals higher than we think humanly possible so we'll find our reward. "Your passion is your conviction about it, your purpose is why you do it, your destiny is where," he declares.[14]

Beyond doubt, I can tell you that throughout my life, purpose is what guides me and passion is what drives me. My passion has always been people, my purpose in life has been championing diversity and inclusion, and my destiny was the corporate landscape. I came into this sense of awareness as a young adult but even more emphatically by the time I decided to obtain a master's degree and attend graduate school at the University of Pennsylvania.

At UPenn, there was a black professor whose class I enjoyed immensely. His name was Elijah Anderson, but he told us to call him Eli. He was one of the more popular professors and his course was quite difficult to get into given its popularity. He taught a class on racism. It wasn't a class about diversity, per se, it was primarily about his research and critical analysis of the black experience in Philadelphia and other cities. Professor Eli addressed racial dynamics, discriminatory practices, how black people responded to racism, and how it showed up in the world.

I decided to take his course because the topic was of interest to me. I had never participated in a class about racial discrimination and I wanted to explore the dynamics of racism among black people. On the first day of this highly anticipated class, I made it my business to introduce myself to the profes-

---

14   T.D. Jakes, "T.D. Jakes on Finding Your Purpose," http://www.tdjakes.com/posts/t-d-jakes-on-finding-your-purpose.

sor and take a seat right in front of the lecture hall so that I wouldn't miss a thing.

It is worth noting that Eli was the only black professor I saw anywhere on UPenn's campus aside from author, TV personality, and radio host Michael Eric Dyson. I tried several times to register for Dr. Dyson's courses, but they were always booked to capacity. Over the years, Eli has written and edited numerous books, articles, and scholarly reports on race in American cities. He's now at Yale University, where he holds the William K. Lanman professorship and directs the Urban Ethnography Project. I am forever grateful for having taken Eli's class, because the course content shaped my views around equity, parity, and fairness.

Discrimination based on race, gender, religion, or any other characteristic is a big part of the study of diversity. But there is so much more to it as a professional operating in this field. Early in my career, I found the subject of diversity to be extremely powerful on a number of levels—not only are you attempting to mirror the composition of the marketplace that you are serving, but you are also designing policies and programs that will impact the personal and professional lives of the people who work for the company, by creating a conducive culture where everyone has an opportunity to realize his/ her potential.

From a corporate standpoint, diversity is strategically important for several reasons: it provides organizations with the opportunity to attract, develop, promote, and retain the best talent; creates an inclusive culture for employees to thrive and, most importantly, addresses the needs and wants of a diverse customer base. There aren't many positions that can have an impact across the critical areas of talent, culture, and customers like those centering around diversity and inclusion.

I spent more than fifteen years working in the pharmaceutical industry and several years in the consumer goods industry, before transitioning to a role in financial services. As I outlined in the previous chapter, I started out my career working in product development and marketing and then moved to human resources. When I went to work for Merck & Co., I assumed various positions of increased responsibility in human resources.

I take pride in saying that my role in human capital management allowed me to make an impact on the business, people, and the culture of the organizations at which I have worked. On a personal note, it appeased both sides of my brain: the human capital side that I love, but also the analytical/business side. I always wanted to do something that filled my soul, something meaningful to me as a professional and an individual. Human capital management filled that void. Fighting for the underdog was something that I reveled in.

In 2008, I was also recognized with an honorary Doctorate of Humane Letters degree from my alma mater Kean College for my personal and professional accomplishments in the field of diversity and inclusion. The formal ceremony took place during the undergraduate commencement exercises at the PNC Bank Arts Center in Holmdel, New Jersey. My family, friends, and mentor Ted Childs were all in attendance.

One of my most notable tributes includes being named the 2010 recipient of the Maya Way Award for Diversity Leadership by the incomparable Dr. Maya Angelou. Dr. Angelou had been a hero of mine for many years. She was an iconic figure to many around the world. She epitomized intelligence, grace, humility, and character. Undeniably, receiving that award in her presence was one of the biggest highlights of my personal and professional life. Also in attendance was

Dr. Dorothy I. Height, a tireless activist for women's and civil rights, who served as the president of the National Council of Negro Women for forty years. To be in the presence of Dr. Height and Dr. Angelou, two legends, was a moment in time that I will never forget.

Clearly, it is very fulfilling to be recognized for your accomplishments. When we are junior in our careers, we strive to fulfill basic goals like getting our first promotion, our first raise. As we ascend up the ranks, we still want the titles and high salaries, but also something a little more satisfying. True joy and true fulfillment in our work is the feeling that we are making a contribution that is even bigger than ourselves. As you become more senior in an organization, you should create new challenges and career goals for yourself, but you should also pursue your purpose—what gives meaning to your life.

Equally important is surrounding yourself with people (friends, peers, spouses) who share your passion and purpose. Diversity officers at other companies can be a tight-knit group, especially people of color because there are so few of us. During my tenure as a senior executive in corporate America, there were about thirty African American chief diversity officers at major corporations. These were people—my peers— who did exactly what I did. We all knew each other since we would often run into one another at roundtable sessions and at the same diversity conferences, such as the annual Diversity and Inclusion Summit. Most of us would show up, so we would see each other on a regular basis. My peers were a part of my power network.

Who's in your circle? It should comprise your industry peers. You never know when their ascension may prove to be advantageous in your climb. It behooves African American women to make every effort to connect with colleagues who are in their same position at other organizations, but just as well those peers who are viewed as trailblazers in their respective fields.

One case in point for me: while I was at Credit Suisse, I didn't have any mentors or sponsors within the organization. I did, however, have an outside advisor, Ted Childs Jr. After a notable thirty-nine-year career, Ted retired from IBM, but during his tenure he was one of the most successful chief diversity officers in corporate America. As a leading workforce diversity expert, he had write-ups in the *Harvard Business Review*, *Fortune*, and *Fast Company*. He was like the godfather of diversity practice. Most of us working in diversity and inclusion roles not only knew who Ted was, we idolized him. When you are a chief diversity officer, you're like a quasi–civil rights leader, meaning some people are threatened by you. Not everyone is going to be supportive of you and your work. Childs was fearless, he was direct as hell in terms of how he communicated with people. Either you liked him or you didn't.

According to *Fast Company*, in one of his speeches, Ted declared: "No matter who you are, you're going to have to work with people who are different from you. You're going to have to sell to people who are different from you, and buy from people who are different from you, and manage people who are different from you. This is how we do business. If it's not your destination, you should get off the plane now."[15] This statement was certainly direct, but it made a lot of sense to many of us. This is how I was going to lead diversity going forward—with conviction, passion, and courage, and with a laser-sharp business focus.

I had the distinct pleasure of meeting Ted at a diversity

15   Keith H. Hammonds, "Difference Is Power," *Fast Company*, June 30, 2000, https://www.fastcompany.com/39763/difference-power.

conference many years ago. Here you had this figurehead on the topic; I simply walked up to him and told him how much I admired his work. I asked him if he would mentor me. He said, "Absolutely."

Ted described diversity work as "constructive disruption," and that always stayed with me. I use this philosophy in many of my talks about diversity. An endeavor, plan, or initiative must be carefully curated or orchestrated. That's the constructive part. The disruption piece is more about the actual activity or the suspension of an activity—changing a way of thinking. When I think and talk about constructive disruption, there should always be a clear desired business outcome. There should always be a clear a vision or a mission that is the anchor to it all.

Through Ted's leadership, IBM broadened its definition of diversity to include sensitivity to cultures, sexual orientation, and age. The company now boasts seventy-two diversity councils and 172 network groups around the world. Without a doubt, Ted was a highly touted corporate executive, a black man who possessed power and influence in my field. I wanted to attain that level of success for myself. So you can understand why I sought him out as a mentor. To this day, I still seek Ted out for occasional wise counsel.

Power and Influence: Who has it? How to Get It

Membership in the corporate elite doesn't come easy. It certainly isn't easy for African American women to obtain. Power in corporate America is defined by an executive's ability to have some bearing on the direction of a company. "There may be different degrees, but if you can influence decision-making at a company, that is power." This is how chief marketing officer Jerri DeVard broke it down during her interview with

Black Enterprise magazine, when she was named one the "50 Most Powerful Women in Business" in its February 2006 cover story. She went on to say, "You can give your input, but that's not influence. You have to have the ability to impact the actual outcome. Power is the result of influence."[16]

DeVard made a name for herself as one of America's top marketing executives, having led prominent campaigns for such powerhouses as Pillsbury, Revlon, and Verizon. Her dynamic career led to a seat at the table on a variety of corporate boards over the years. Currently, she serves as a member of the board of directors of Under Armour and ServiceMaster.

While power may be the ability to direct or influence the behavior of others, Oprah Winfrey's definition of power truly resonates with me. She has described power as the "ability to impact with purpose."

I knew I had arrived when I reached an executive-level position of power with Novartis Pharmaceuticals Corporation. I had been hired as its first African American executive director of diversity and inclusion, where I was responsible for providing strategic direction, leadership, and development of an inclusive environment by integrating diversity practices into all aspects of the business. In addition, I was named co-chair of the internal Executive Diversity Council, where I initiated several affinity and networking groups, and developed the diversity training curriculum for the company. When I was named vice president and global head of diversity and inclusion at Novartis Pharmaceuticals AG, I was the first woman and first African American to relocate to Basel, Switzerland, to serve in such a role; I had a reporting relationship to the

---

16　Carolyn M. Brown, "50 Most Powerful Black Women in Business," *Black Enterprise*, February 2016, http://www.blackenterprise.com/mag/50-most-powerful-black-women-in-business/.

CEO as well as the CHRO of the pharma division.

What does it mean to be first? Women of color often find themselves in the situation of being the only woman and the only minority in the room, or being the first female or the first minority to assume a role. It may be an unfair burden, especially if you feel pressured to be considered a symbol of your gender or ethnic group, and the voice speaking on behalf of your group. But you must move beyond the fear of tokenism, which is defined as the practice of cherry-picking a handful of underrepresented individuals merely to give the appearance of sexual or racial equality within a workforce. Yes, there can be a thin line between tokenism and diversity when organizations make politically correct or symbolic gestures of offering opportunities of advancement to women, minorities, and underrepresented groups. In turn, underrepresented groups often must contend with fitting in as it relates to issues of tokenism and conformity. Among such concerns is additional performance pressure—the never-ending feeling that you are always on stage or under a microscope.

When Rosalind G. Brewer, then president and chief executive of Sam's Club (a business unit of Walmart Stores Inc.), recounted a meeting with a supplier who had no representation of women or people of color on his team during a CNN interview, she spoke out about her efforts to build a diverse team, and the difficulty of often being the only minority and woman in the room.[17] "My executive team is very diverse, and I make that a priority. I demand it within my team," Brewer shared at the time. Immediately, one of the nation's top African American female executives in retail was accused on

---

17   Sara Ashely O'Brien, "Sam's Club CEO Takes Heat for Diversity Comments," *CNN Money*, December 16, 2015, http://money.cnn.com/2015/12/16/news/companies/rosa-lind-brewer-sams-club-diversity/index.html.

social media of displaying a bias against white men.

In the winter of 2017, Brewer announced that she was retiring; this news came after five years with the company and following a tough battle to compete with Costco Wholesale. Brewer's departure is a major blow to the number of African Americans in the C-Suite. Brewer was the first woman and first African American to hold a CEO position at one of Walmart Stores Inc.'s business units. In 2015, she was named one of *Black Enterprise*'s "50 Most Powerful Women in Corporate America." She joined four women, including BET Networks' chairman and CEO Debra Lee (Viacom Inc.), who served as the chief executive of a business unit or a subsidiary of a major corporation. In the fall of 2017, Brewer landed the COO position at Starbucks.

I empathize with Brewer because I know firsthand that workforce inclusion can be a tricky topic to broach. As a woman of color serving in a corporate diversity role at a large multinational corporation, I was working to make managers at all levels of these companies take responsibility for diversity in hiring, promoting, retaining, and mentoring.

Being the first at anything comes with a certain level of responsibility. The constituents that you represent are now looking to you to not only reflect, but advocate for the population that you are affiliated with. Whether you sign up for the task or not, you are now the de facto role model. You are setting the example. All eyes are on you to make intelligent decisions that impact the masses. Women of color should use being "the first" to their advantage. I have learned that you have to meet people where they are, when it comes to topics like race and gender. I have been intentional in using my difference as an opportunity to teach others how I want to be treated and respected as an African American female in the workplace. I certainly used my difference as an opportunity to promote education and awareness of my being a highly capable black female.

When I went to work for Credit Suisse, it was in a sector that I was not familiar with, but I knew that I could stretch and grow. I could do the work that I loved in a different industry and have an impact. I said to myself, *If I can have an impact from a diversity perspective in a pharma industry and consumer goods, maybe I can end my career working for a Wall Street firm and make a change, leaving the place in better condition than when I started.* That was the goal. That was appealing to me—to flex different muscles, learn a new industry, and meet different types of people.

I knew it was going to be a challenge and that's what I was looking for. But to do it on Wall Street . . . when they've been successful without it? *So why would they listen to some black woman from the pharmaceutical industry talk about the business case for diversity and why it's important, why it's a critical business imperative?*

I simply convinced myself: *You know, this is going to be interesting. This is going to be a test of my leadership, but one that I think I'm up for.* I was determined to make the kind of impact that I had in a Swiss pharmaceutical company at a Wall Street firm.

To a degree, a certain level of power comes with a job title. But you can become highly influential through your network too. As founder of the National Coalition of 100 Black Women, Jewell Jackson McCabe made her mark in history as a force to be reckoned with in helping black women gain professional and political clout. McCabe has been quoted as saying: "We hear that behind every great man is a woman. It has been my experience that behind every great effort and achievement in society goes a black woman or a group of black women being unrecognized." She once declared to *Black Enterprise* magazine that black women must recognize the impact of racism and sexism on their career development. She encouraged black women to engage in power networking with prominent business leaders, and to master the traits of corporate leadership defined by CEOs.[18]

Don't overlook your alma mater when it comes to power networking; I highly recommend corporate professionals keep up with their college alumni association. Not simply two months or two years after you walk away with that minted diploma in hand, but as you move further along in your career and your organization. Take advantage of the benefits of being an alumni association member beyond invitations to receptions, sporting events, and special activities. Your alumni association is a vast network of professional contacts.

Meet new people, make connections, and enhance relationships at alumni affairs throughout the year. Consider using your online alumni directory to connect with people who could be great resources for informational interviews or introductions. What's more, consider opportunities to lecture in the classroom or speak at an event. Let the alumni relations staff know who you are—toot your horn. Alumni receive recognition for noteworthy achievements in addition to strong support from their college or university.

Managing your networks speaks to your leadership competence. *Being the Boss: The Three Imperatives for Becoming a Great Leader* is a book that I found invaluable; it was written by good friend of mine and Harvard professor of business administration, Linda A. Hill. In her book, Linda shares a great

---

18   Dawn M. Baskerville, Sherly Hilliard Tuckers, and Donna Whittingham-Barnes, "21 Women of Power and Influence in Corporate America," *Black Enterprise*, August 1991.

deal of her philosophies about leadership style and some other tactics I have used in my own career. Specifically, she focuses on three imperatives—"manage yourself, manage your network, and manage your team"—to achieve the critical goal of influencing others. In speaking about managing your networks, she points out that you must uderstand how power and influence work in your organization, and then build upon mutually beneficial relationships to navigate your company's complex political environment.

When speaking to Roland Martin of *NewsOne Now* about how women of color are MIA when it comes to the highest echelons of corporate America, Barbara R. Arnwine, president and founder of the Transformative Justice Coalition, asserted that blacks in America only achieve progress when they protest, organize, or strategize. She referred to the 2016 appointment of BET CEO Debra Lee to the board of directors at social media site Twitter, making Lee the first African American to hold that distinction.[19] That same year, Roger Ferguson, former vice chairman of the Federal Reserve and CEO of financial services leviathan TIAA, became the first African American elected to the board of Alphabet Inc., the parent of Google. Apple Inc. appointed James Bell, the former CFO and corporate president of The Boeing Co. to its board, making big news in corporate governance circles in the fall of 2015. There may be some truth behind Arnwine's assertions, in that those moves came about after pressure by Rainbow Push Coalition founder and president Reverend Jesse Jackson and other activists.

In an era of increased efforts to diversify corporate boards, it is tempting to think that women of color—Asian, black,

---

19 *NewsOne Now*, "There May Soon Be No Black Female CEOs Among Fortune 500 Companies," 2016, https://newsone.com/3440536/black-female-ceos-fortune-500-companies/.

and Latina—would be highly sought after. But this isn't the case. According to the 2020 Gender Diversity Index, women represented 17.9 percent of the Fortune 500 company boards of directors and 22.3 percent of the Fortune 100 company directors in 2015.[20] In comparison, women of color were 2.8 percent of the corporate board directors in 2015; a quarter of those women of color serve on multiple boards.[21]

It behooves you to know who the top players are in your organization. If your organization lacks board diversity, it is a reflection of senior leadership's commitment to an inclusive environment. When it comes to creating a diverse and inclusive workforce in the twenty-first century, corporations may not be putting up direct barriers or shutting doors to keep out minorities; it's more an issue of removing organizational and cultural obstacles that continue to block minority workers—once hired—from moving up the proverbial ladder in these organizations.

Heed my advice: make a bold move by getting into the same room with women and minority board directors. For example, if you can own shares of corporate stock and attend shareholder meetings where engagement is a priority and you will have the opportunity to be in the same room as your organization's top executives and board members, then do so. If it is true that women of color are invisible in corporate America, then you want to take advantage of every single opportunity to be seen by those at the top, in numerous settings.

The harsh reality is that for much of corporate America,

20 "2020 Woman on Boards," Gender Diversity Index, 2011-2016, https://www.2020wob.com/sites/default/files/2016_GDI_Report_Final.pdf.

21 "Missing Pieces Report: The 2016 Board Diversity Census of Women and Minorities on Fortune 500 Boards," Deloitte and the Alliance for Board Diversity, February 6, 2017, https://www2.deloitte.com/content/dam/Deloitte/us/Documents/center-for-corporate-governance/us-board-diversity-census-missing-pieces.pdf.

racial diversity continues to be a signifigant challenge. As women of color, we must make our presence known. As an executive diversity leader, I pushed to make the companies where I worked more inclusive, diverse, and equitable. I have also taken the gospel of diversity and inclusion on the road. Like other recognized leaders in their fields, I was always eager to speak at conferences to share my knowledge and experiences.

As the cofounder of my own company, I was able to leverage and lend my expertise to several Global Fortune 1000 companies that aspire to amplify their diversity strategies and initiatives, by designing training programs for women and people of color, facilitating executive roundtable discussions regarding race and gender, and conducting keynote addresses about the business case for diversity and executive coaching.

Women of color seek to add meaning and purpose to their lives inside and outside of the office—that is what research tells us. The barriers we face cause many of us to become disengaged, and yet most employees in general are disengaged in the workplace. In fact, a 2014 Gallup report determined that 51 percent of employees were "not engaged" at the office.[22] In other words, they don't feel invested in their work, and they're not getting anything meaningful out of it. Another 17.5 percent of employees described themselves as "actively disengaged."

Self-help author and blogger Mark Manson summed it up best when he said, "Ultimately, what determines our ability to stick with something we care about is our ability to handle the rough patches and ride out the inevitable rotten days."[23]

22   Amy Adkins, "Majority of US Employees Not Engaged Despite Gains in 2014," Gallup, January 25, 2015, http://www.gallup.com/poll/181289/majority-employees-not-engaged-despite-gains-2014.aspx.

23   Mark Manson, "7 Strange Questions That Help You Find Your Purpose in Life," September 18, 2014, https://markmanson.net/life-purpose.

What struggle or sacrifice are you willing to tolerate? This will aid you in identifying what you are truly passionate about.

When you're making career decisions your passion will come into play, along with things like job security, company policies, work conditions, compensation, and location. But if you're focusing on these factors alone, it's unlikely that you'll find long-lasting fulfillment in your work. Following your passion in union with your purpose in life will give you meaning and real satisfaction.

Embracing Pivotal Moments

My pivot from corporate America to pursue entrepreneurial ventures was one of the greatest learning experiences of my life, but it wasn't the easiest turning point. My departure was a well-thought-out plan in that I knew at some point I was going to take a break from corporate America. At the time, Credit Suisse was making changes in leadership at the helm, reducing budgets, and streamlining teams among other major adjustments. I thought to myself, *Now is a good time to get on the off-ramp to take another route and probe a different career path.*

I met with my chief human resources officer in the executive-suite conference room at 7:33 a.m. for one of our typical one-on-one discussions. She thought I was coming in to have the usual *What's happening in your functional area?* kind of conversation. I basically told her that I wanted to do something different, and that difference was me no longer working at the company. She was somewhat stunned and taken aback. But she understood my rationale. Never mind that I'm the kind of person that if it's something I want to do, it isn't a matter of *if* I am going to do it, it is a matter of *when.* She inquired, "Well, what do you plan to do?"

I said, "I'll probably start my own consulting practice focused on diversity. But I don't want to leave you in a lurch. I will stay on board until you identify my successor. I'll stay on for as long as you need me. Perhaps Credit Suisse can become my client." I said it jokingly, but I was also quite serious. Credit Suisse was very supportive when I walked out the door, becoming my first client.

It's about having that clever exit strategy. Now, did I think every single thing through at that point in time? Probably not. In hindsight, there were definitely some things I could have done better from a planning perspective, but the reality was that I wanted to be my own boss. I was happier showing up in my authentic way and helping multiple organizations to reach their potential rather than just one employer. I felt like I was being more impactful by heading my own company.

I used the first ninety days just to reinvigorate, refresh, and reorganize myself. I was exhausted. I held high-powered jobs for many years, and aside from when I was out on medical leave for surgery, I'd never taken a mental or physical break from my career. I was catching up on life. It was more of a staycation. Because I traveled so much, staying home was a luxury. I have a place in New York City and a place in New Jersey, so I commuted between both houses. I spent more time with friends. I watched mindless TV, went to some museums, and took a few classes like kickboxing, Pilates, and spinning. I read books that I'd never had the time for such as Shonda Rhimes's *Year of Yes*, which became one of my favorite books because it validated my decision to focus on me and the things that made me fearful. I could focus on getting back to my better self.

It wasn't just a pivot for me, it was a major transformation for David as well. He was right there with me, and our relationship shifted from simply being a married couple to being business partners. You can be a phenomenal career woman going it alone or a formidable twosome. American culture is entranced with power couples: Will and Jada Smith, Beyoncé Knowles and Sean "Jay-Z" Carter, Kim Kardashian and Kanye West, Barack and Michelle Obama, the list goes on. In its inaugural "Power Couples" list, *Crain's New York Business* describes modern power couples as two halves that independently or at least through their own merits achieve success, create seats of influence, and make an impact at work and in the community. Bonus points were given "if the influence of the couple, when combined, was arguably greater than what either could have achieved alone."[24]

Do I think that David and I are a power couple? We were certainly viewed that way by family friends and the people in our inner circle. No, we weren't the Will and Jada Smith of corporate America. For us, it wasn't about how much we earned and what we could do with that money or how well we wielded our clout when we were top executives. It has always been more about the relationship itself. We have had a solid and very loving marriage, which has always been visible to the people around us. More importantly, David and I have always supported each other's aspirations and choices.

While I was on my staycation, David and I still worked on setting up the LLC and getting a trademark for the name of our company. We decided I would be responsible for business development and conduct more of the client-facing work, whereas David would be the contract negotiator and chief financial officer, among other things. In essence, we were creating something out of nothing.

---

24 "Crain's Power Couples in New York," *Crain's New York Business*, June 26, 2016, http://www.crainsnewyork.com/ny-power-couples.

I started out by wanting to write a blog. But how do you commercialize something like that so that you can actually make money from it? Getting advertisements, subscriptions, or other forms of pay proved to be more challenging than I had anticipated. David and I had received some positive feedback from friends and family who said they liked it. We even started to get a little following, but it was nothing that could really replace a seven-figure Wall Street salary. You have big-name people who don't really make a whole lot of money writing blogs. It takes years and years to develop that. At some point, David and I decided to focus on consulting. I used to always tell him: "Our ecosystem is quite vast. We need to leverage and monetize it a bit more."

Roughly three months after my decision to leave corporate America, I began meeting with other entrepreneurs to get some more tips and tools. I also joined an investment group called Plum Alley to learn from other female entrepreneurs and business leaders about investing in tech start-ups. I wanted to hear about some pitfalls that they may have come across during their start-up days. It was a fact-finding mission of sorts. I was going to lunch with several different women from diverse backgrounds. The one thing that they all had in common was that they were super successful. I was trying to learn as much as I could from these women and leverage my network. Even though my social network is very broad, I wanted to expand my circle a little bit further beyond the industries in which I had labored. I met up with women working in media and entertainment. I spoke with women in the sports arena. Some of the women I reached out to were female founders of tech start-ups, while others were venture capitalists and ran nonprofits. Some of the women were executives from different industries in corporate America. Just a little bit of everybody.

Many of these women were acquaintances of mine. Either I sat on a nonprofit board with them or we had some other type of interaction. I simply phoned, saying, "Hey, I am branching out on my own by starting a consultancy firm, would you mind meeting me for lunch?"

The good news was that no one said no. They all said, "Yes, however I can help." I felt like these were friends, acquaintances, and peers who were really invested in my success. "Anything that you need in terms of support or any help that I can provide," they sincerely offered. They were there for me. I had a good feeling about that.

I have nurtured and kept all my relationships alive, which was the best decision that I could have ever made. One thing is certain: your friends never forget about you. Everyone in my circle was extremely supportive of my new venture and my overall success. As a result, I had a steady stream of client engagements. In all honesty, this is really how Ceiling Breakers got its start.

Being an entrepreneur is tough, it's stressful. It's truly about dancing to a different beat. I had to get used to a different kind of hustle. When I worked in corporate America, the product was based on whatever industry I supported, be it apparel, pharmaceuticals, or financial services. Now, the product was me and the services that my husband and I would provide. You could even say that it was all about turning the product on its head and using myself as the focal point. I had to get used to marketing myself more, because that was the only way I was going to drum up business—selling my services, selling my expertise, selling my intelligence, and selling just who I was as a professional. There are a lot of consultants out there who do what I do. Therefore, I knew that I had to really package myself in a way that was strategic, in a way that was elegant, where I was differentiating myself from everybody else who was doing similar work in the diversity and inclusion space. The good news was that the experiences I had from living abroad and meeting diversity challenges—all of the things that were unique and different about me as a professional—I was able to leverage as an entrepreneur.

There are two sides to Ceiling Breakers. One is our diversity consulting work, where I'm client-facing and David is the back-office support. The second is our media and investment arm. The media aspect came about by wanting to tap into black power brokers, and the way to do that was through entertainment and sports. There is a lot of money circulating in those sectors. To be able to identify more high-net-worth individuals, we had to show up to such events as the Oscars, the Grammys, and the Kentucky Derby. Wherever there was black money, we needed to follow it.

One way for us to enter this space was to invest in diverse projects that were coming to Broadway. We invested in two plays: the first one was a modern adaptation of the timeless classic *Romeo and Juliet*, starring Orlando Bloom and Condola Rashad (the daughter of Phylicia Rashad, the fan-favorite mom on *The Cosby Show*), and the other was a theatrical production of *Black Orpheus*. Our role as investors came about through our relationship with highly regarded African American producers Stephen C. Byrd and Alia Jones-Harvey of Front Row Productions, which has an explicit goal to diversify the Great White Way. Stephen and Alia were the lead producers behind the all-black cast revival of Tennessee Williams's *Cat on a Hot Tin Roof* as well as *A Streetcar Named Desire*, and Horton Foote's *The Trip to Bountiful*. David and I love the arts and of course we love diversity. Accordingly, when we were approached to become investors, we figured: "Yeah. It could be interesting for us to learn more about Broadway, how it works; and to see more people of color and women on stage. Let's get involved." We had the capital to invest and to make an impact.

Interestingly enough, one good thing that came out of writing the blog is that I received some recognition from former *Ebony* editor in chief Kierna Mayo, who was instrumental in my getting the Ebony Power 100 Award.

Now, the Accenture opportunity came out of nowhere. But remember, you must be prepared for opportunities as they present themselves! Accenture was not one of my clients and I did not know anyone on the inside. A New York–based executive search firm contacted me via LinkedIn and asked if I would be open to having a conversation about a new inclusion and diversity executive role at a very successful professional services company. At first I was a bit hesitant because I was not interested in reentering corporate America at that moment. Nevertheless, I opted to have the conversation, since I knew of a few friends who were looking to make career moves and I could pass the information along to them. I received a copy of the position description and it looked quite appealing; I decided to throw my hat in the ring for consideration.

Subsequently, I had two wonderful in-person meetings with the North America CEO, the global CHRO, and a host of other key executives. There was immediate chemistry between myself and the executives whom I met with. The common denominator in these discussions was that everyone saw diversity and inclusion as a key business imperative that would provide them with competitive differentiation. In addition, the company was doing quite well, and I could do the work that I love in a new industry/company and create an impact. I was all about finding meaning at that crucial point in my life.

All the ducks lined up and pointed due east! After several rounds of interviews, an executive assessment, and background checks, I was presented with a job offer within a month.

I was excited about the possibilities of assisting yet another Fortune 500 company with the amplification of their diversity strategy, and integrating the strategy into the business for the long haul; Ceiling Breakers would continue to move forward and thrive with David fully at the helm.

I can honestly say when I wake up every morning that I *love* what I do. My strong advice is to find whatever it is that you are passionate about and integrate that element of passion into your career choices. Life is only a moment in time. There is nothing more devastating, in my view, than to go into a workplace and not like what you do for a living or understand how you got to where you are. This is why I know that I've chosen the right career path—because my profession and purpose do indeed intersect. My passion is my purpose, and it has allowed me to traverse the halls of corporate America and climb higher to positions of power and influence, and to still have an impact—even after closing that door behind me, another door opened.

Key Steps

1. If you are not certain as to what your passion and purpose are in life, seek out the help of a life coach or mentor.
2. Keep in mind that your passion is your conviction about the work you do, your purpose is *why* you do it, and your destiny is *where* you do it.
3. Surround yourself with industry peers who share your passion and purpose.

4. You can become highly influential through your network. Engage in power networking with corporate professionals, business leaders, industry trailblazers, and, don't forget, college/university alumni.

5. You ought to be courageous enough to be vulnerable and different. Don't be afraid to use being the "only one" to your advantage.

6. Get used to marketing yourself more, selling your expertise. Package yourself in a way that is strategic.

7. As you become more senior in an organization, don't just seek promotions, pursue meaningful or impactful work.

8. Explore doing the type of work that you love in different sectors or industries.

9. Don't be anxious of pivot points. These are moments of truths, decisions that you will make that are meant to help transform you and your journey.

10. Always be prepared to seize new opportunities so when one door closes and another one opens, you are ready to enter.

3

TWICE AS SMART, TWICE AS GOOD

There will be times . . . when you feel like folks look right past you,
or they see just a fraction of who you really are.
—Michelle Obama

S honda Rhimes is best known as the creator, head writer, and executive producer of three hit ABC television
series—*Grey's Anatomy*, *Scandal*, and *How to Get Away*
with Murder—under her ShondaLand production company
banner. The political thriller *Scandal* stars Kerry Washington
as the infamous "fixer" Olivia Pope, whose character is based
on Judy Smith, a former George H.W. Bush administration
press aide turned real-life crisis-management expert. In the
third season opener of *Scandal*, Rowan Pope (Joe Morton)
confronts his daughter, who has just been outed as the mis-
tress of the president of the United States.[25]

Olivia is a young African American woman of distin-
guished breeding—an equestrian who attended the finest
boarding school and a top law school. Papa Pope is disgusted
that his daughter is willing to sleep with the most powerful
man in America, only to settle for the position of first lady. In
the infamous jaw-dropping scene: "At the very least, you aim
for chief of staff, secretary of state. First lady—do you have to
be so mediocre?" he screams at her.

During his tirade, he forces a soon-to-be disgraced Olivia

---

25 "It's Handled," *Scandal*, ABC, October 3, 2013.

to repeat back to him the mantra he has instilled in her since childhood.[26] The exchange:

> Rowan: Did I not raise you for better? How many times have I told you? You have to be what?
> Olivia: Twice as good.
> Rowan: You have to be twice as good as them to get half of what they have.

It was one of the most epic moments in television history, because Papa Pope dared to utter what black parents for decades have told their children: in order to succeed in life, in the face of racial and gender discrimination, you must be twice as good, twice as smart, twice as talented. You must perform at a higher standard than your white peers or else you will not be taken seriously, respected, or rewarded for your accomplishments.

Rhimes is a rare breed among African American television showrunners, particularly among females. She made history as the first African American woman to create and executive produce a Top 10 network series with the hit prime-time show Grey's Anatomy. The TV powerhouse is also one of ABC's top-earning executive producers. Rhimes felt the pressure of being a black female showrunner, or what she calls an F.O.D.—a "First Only Different." In her self-help memoir The Year of Yes, Rhimes writes: "When you are an F.O.D., you are saddled with that burden of extra responsibility—whether you want it or not."[27]

Rhimes does not take kindly to reporters grilling her about

---

26 Neil Drumming, "Scandal's Racially Charged Motto: "You have to be twice as good as them," Salon, October 4, 2013, https://www.salon.com/2013/10/04/scandals_racially_charged_motto_you_have_to_be_twice_as_good_as_them/.

27 Shonda Rhimes, Year of Yes: How to Dance It Out, Stand in the Sun, and Be Your Own Person (Simon & Shuster, 2016), pgs. 138–139.

race and diversity. She even expressed being pissed off when she was honored with the 2014 Diversity Award by the Directors Guild of America, since hiring diverse talent should be a given. "You can't be raised black in America and not know," she writes in her book. "This wasn't just my shot. It was ours."

And then she references the memorable moment: the encounter between Olivia and Rowan Pope:

> *I was doing a thing that the suits had said could not be done on TV. And America was proving them wrong by watching. We were literally changing the face of television. I was not about to make a mistake now. You don't get second chances. Not when you're an F.O.D. Second chances are for future generations. That is what you are building when you are an F.O.D. Second chances. As Papa Pope told his daughter Olivia:* You have to be twice as good to get half as much . . . *I didn't want half. I wanted it all. And so, I worked four times as hard.*[28]

Now, I don't recall my parents ever telling me explicitly that I had to be twice as good or to perform at a higher level than my peers. But it was certainly implied. They had high expectations for their daughters, period. They challenged us to keep up, to push ourselves, to strive to do our best, and to compete with the brightest students in the class. And that is exactly what we did.

My father remembers very vividly the time when Monique and I were in third grade and our teacher sent a note home asking that we be placed in a special class. Dad sent a note back to our third grade teacher informing her that he would be at school the next day. When the two of them met face to

28 *Ibid*, p. 139–40.

face, our teacher explained to Dad that because we were falling slightly behind some of the other kids, and our test scores were slightly lower than the other kids, she wanted to put us in special classes. He almost went ballistic.

"Not as long as I pay taxes. I don't care if they are just getting Cs or have different learning styles, I prefer for them to be with the kids that are getting the best grades," he snapped. That was our dad. He simply did not think that we would be better served being in a classroom with students who were subpar.

It goes back to the lack of diversity. There weren't very many black kids in the entire school system at that time. All of the teachers were white. If I'm not mistaken, there was one black teacher among eight or nine different schools in our district. As you can imagine, for a black child who is falling behind, or may not be as quick as the other kids to pick up a lesson, teachers are going to try to throw him or her into a remedial class. *Oh, something's wrong here. We need to put him/her in a lower level.* I think that was the dynamic happening at the time: the perception that the black students weren't as smart as everybody else—the white kids—therefore, they need some special attention. Our parents weren't having any of that.

Dad took issue with what he viewed as prejudice or racial bias whether it was intentional or unintentional. His pet peeve was the way that some educators would speak to us. Several times our teachers, even the vice principal at our grammar school, would refer to us as *you people.* Now that set him off. Dad went to the school to straighten out those educators. He politely yet emphatically told them: "As long as my kids go to this school, their names are Monique and Michelle Gadsden. When you speak to them, you address them as such. They are not *you people.*"

One incident at our elementary school really shook me up. But I never told my parents about it, for fear that they would go stomping up to the school to give that teacher a piece of their minds. Math is not one of my strengths. It's Monique's strong suit. I can safely say that of the two of us, she's probably a lot more cerebral than I am. I had a teacher in the sixth grade who broke my spirit. My confidence waned with this particular teacher.

In my mind, this teacher knew that I was not as strong in mathematics as the other children in the class, but he would make it a point to embarrass me anytime it was my turn to figure out a mathematical problem on the blackboard. I was so nervous to the point that my anxiety got in the way of me doing the work right. I would take a long time at the chalkboard. Then some of the kids would begin laughing. My teacher would say things like, "Okay, today, Michelle." Needless to say, I have hated math with a passion ever since, even though on the job I have grown to appreciate it over the years.

But this is just one of those episodes in my childhood that has been hard to recover from. The shame and humiliation that my teacher projected onto me still haunts me to this day! Even in my adult life, I would have anxiety whenever I had to present an analysis. I had to get over the fear fast. I forced myself to do a perfect presentation, knowing that this was a large part of my role. It's almost like it was both a blessing and a curse. Since then, I've made it a point to always strive to be better than everybody else. I had to go above and beyond, because I didn't want people to laugh at me. I felt like I had eyeballs glaring at me, even in my adult life.

Going above and beyond was an instrumental lesson our father taught us. It wasn't about degrading us, but encouraging us to be competitive. "Always do your best job the first time. Don't think about coming back and doing it a second time. Spend the time to do it to the best of your ability the first time," he counseled.

In most cases, that means sacrifice. He explained that when he first went into computer programming, he used to sleep on the couch in the company president's office at night, because the computer system room was so small. He'd come in and work all night.

The number one thing that my father always told me was that in any job you accept, don't be so restricted that you only learn what you need to know to do your job. "Get in the work environment and be inquisitive," he said. "Learn what everybody else is doing, so that the day might come when someone is not there, and you can step in and do his or her job and be visible to the leadership."

Many of us have come to believe that it is widely assumed that African American professionals in all sectors will not be hired, retained, and promoted in their fields unless they perform at a significantly higher level than their peers. Even America's former first lady Michelle Obama gave her version of the "twice as good" speech to the 2016 graduates of Tuskegee University, a historically black institution located in Alabama. Established by Booker T. Washington in 1881, Tuskegee has produced countless politicians, educators, scientists, artists, and entrepreneurs, all of whom have benefited from Washington's desire to prepare graduates "to become a center of influence," and show fellow African Americans how to lift themselves up by their bootstraps through the pursuit of education.

During her commencement speech, the first lady reminded graduates that their lives would likely be more difficult than their white peers, simply because the playing field was still not level.[29] She spoke about how the army chose Tuskegee as the site of its airfield and flight school for black pilots. While the airmen selected for this program were actually highly educated —many had college degrees and pilot licenses—they were presumed to be inferior, but they did not let that experience of being doubted and discriminated against clip their wings. Instead, they became one of the most successful pursuit squadrons in our military.

Michelle went on to say: "The road ahead is not going to be easy. It never is, especially for folks like you and me. Because while we've come so far, the truth is that those age-old problems are stubborn and they haven't fully gone away. So, there will be times, just like for those airmen, when you feel like folks look right past you, or they see just a fraction of who you really are. Instead they will make assumptions about who they think you are based on their limited notion of the world."

She spoke about having to come the realization that "no matter how far you rise in life, how hard you work to be a good person, a good parent, a good citizen—for some folks, it will never be enough."

She also spoke of a double duty, by acknowledging that for the airmen, one duty was to their country, and the other was to all the black folks who were counting on them to pave the way forward.

In many ways, I was doing double duty, representing black women corporate professionals and paving the way for other young professionals. I was accountable for developing a world-class strategy to identify and retain candidates in 1999 as a senior university relations diversity consultant. I had

29 "Transcript: First Lady Michelle Obama's Commencement Speech at Tuskegee University," *What The Folly?!*, May 12, 2015, http://www.whatthefolly.com/2015/05/12/transcript-first-lady-michelle-obamas-commencement-speech-at-tuskegee-university-part-1/.

transitioned from working in retail and marketing to working in the pharmaceutical industry once I joined Merck & Co. At that time, Merck recruited prospective interns at over one hundred universities across the country. They only hired the best and brightest—about three to four hundred a year at that time. The team that I worked with managed that process.

My job was essentially to partner with the colleges and universities that Merck had an affiliation with through campus or university relations departments. There was a diversity factor in all of this. We would go to a few HBCUs and the Black National MBA Association's conferences, to name a few. It was strategic staffing with a focus and emphasis on diversity. I was the one who would schedule information sessions on campus to talk about what a wonderful company Merck was, bringing an entourage of women and people of color so that the students could see the diversity amongst all of us and how it was the best place to work.

In addition to recruitment, I was responsible for entertaining all the interns to make sure that they had a meaningful experience over the course of the summer. If anyone was not doing well, we provided coaching feedback and counseling. At the end of the internship, the top students would ideally transition to full-time employees. In that role, I managed a $600,000 program budget to develop and implement a comprehensive corporate-wide internship program for 400-plus interns in 2000. And I interfaced with executive management to provide detailed program objectives, project plans, and status reports.

At that point in my career, I was starting to get into the pipeline-development aspect of diversity and inclusion. In addition to the university recruiting side, I was forging partnerships with top-tier schools and middle schools, enticing them to talk about math and science programs like STEM, to foster interest among students of color, and encourage them to pursue careers in the pharmaceutical industry at an early age, before they set foot in college. It was not only a pivotal step but a fulfilling one, because I was designing programs to build relationships with some of the top middle schools across the country; to identify diverse "early talent" and partner with universities to create camps for these students who wished to attend and learn about STEM.

We focused our efforts on eleven-, twelve-, and thirteen-year-olds because we found that it was a situation of *too little too late* to try to identify these students when they were in high school, since by then they might already be falling behind. African American and Latino students weren't rising to the top. Most wanted to go into other disciplines. For instance, someone would say, "Oh, I want to go into marketing, I want to work for Nike," or, "I want to be a sports agent." But if you get to them at an early age and you start talking about the STEM careers in a way that's meaningful for them, you have a much better shot at hooking them and getting them to consider an academic major in STEM or in business.

One of the areas that I knew was a talent of mine was how well I built relationships with people—how well I cultivated and maintained those relationships. At the university level, I took great pleasure working with the interns and witnessing their growth potential.

Working with the interns invigorated me. They were smart, enthusiastic, and optimistic about the future, and exuded the typical millennial archetype by wanting to better understand how they could occupy the C-Suite in the short term.

Like me, most of them knew exactly what they wanted

out of a career. I can recall one occasion when an intern at Merck walked up to the CEO, Raymond Gilmartin, introduced himself, and stated with conviction how he wanted the CEO position someday. You have to applaud the tenacity to tell the CEO of a Fortune 500 company that you are poised to assume his position if given the chance. The interns simply needed some guidance in terms of how to choreograph their careers in a way that would be fulfilling but also purpose-driven.

It made it all worthwhile when someone was hired for a full-time job; I would get that phone call saying: "Hey, Michelle. I just got an offer letter, I'm coming to work for Merck full time." Those were the affection points, meaning those calls made me happy knowing that I helped someone get his or her foot in the door. Some of the interns stayed close to me for a couple of years afterward, but I didn't stay in touch with them for the long term. You know, there were so many of them; we're talking about six hundred young people over the course of that experience.

I really enjoyed working with the interns. They had so much energy, wanting to display their talents and smarts to anyone who would listen, telling us that they aspired to have *our* job someday! I was excited for them, as their futures were bright and promising. All they had to do was continue to work hard and stay the course academically.

Given the fact that Merck's internship program served as a method to attract and hire the best and brightest young talent, the program had a lot of internal and external exposure and prestige for me. There were a lot of company resources assigned to the program by way of teams working on it and funds allocated to it. I led all aspects of the program, from onboarding, program design, ensuring positive intern experience, intern housing allocation, transportation, and so on.

The program consumed my entire life for the ten weeks the students worked at Merck. If someone had an acute appendicitis attack, I was the contact person who went to the hospital to ensure that the student was fine and their parents were contacted. I was the program designer, coordinator, intern advisor, and the occasional medical interventionist. All of this was done in addition to my daily responsibilities in strategic staffing. Yet again, I was working twice as hard, but I was strategically twice as smart as many of my colleagues.

In a relatively short matter of time, I was promoted to Merck's senior manager of diversity programs in 2001. I provided functional leadership and strategic direction for diversity recruitment for all key stakeholders within corporate staffing, corporate diversity, division management, HR business partners, senior management, and other internal and external customers, to ensure that the company approached the employment marketplace with a well-coordinated, one-company approach to diversity branding, sourcing, and recruiting. I stayed in that position another year.

At the time, Merck had a drug in the market called Vioxx, a non-steroidal, anti-inflammatory, and prescription painkiller. Merck was accused of misleading doctors and patients about the drug's safety, fabricating study results, and skirting federal drug regulations. In 2004, Merck withdrew the drug after it was revealed that it had more than doubled the risk of heart attacks. By that point, it was reported that more than 38,000 deaths were related to Vioxx use.[30] But even before that major news broke, many of us working for the company saw the writing on the wall. So in 2002 I decided to join Novartis, a

---

30 Snigdha Prakash and Vikki Valentine, "Timeline: The Rise and Fall of Vioxx," *NPR*, November 10, 2007, http://www.npr.org/templates/story/story.php?storyId=5470430.

multinational pharmaceutical company headquartered in Basel, Switzerland, with offices in New York and New Jersey. I was a few steps closer to getting to the C-Suite.

Pursuing Advanced Degrees to Advance Your Career

What I soon came to learn about my peers in the pharmaceuticals industry was that everyone went to top-tier schools, if not Ivy League institutions. All of my peers—well, except for one or two—had an MBA or some sort of a master's degree under their belt. They were extremely proud of that fact and they talked about it all the time. I went to a very good liberal arts college, but it wasn't Yale, Princeton, or Harvard. I knew that if I was going to make it in the pharma industry—rise up—then I needed to attend an Ivy League graduate school. In doing so, I could at least compete with my peers on that level.

Instead of going to Columbia University in New York City, I decided to drive two and a half hours one way to attend the University of Pennsylvania and obtain my graduate degree. I knew that was going to be the point of differentiation on my resume. I knew that was going to give me the gravitas I needed in the industry. A real incentive was that Novartis offered employee tuition reimbursement. Whatever the cost and wherever you decided to go, the company reimbursed you 100 percent. So, Novartis paid close to $75,000 for me to get my advanced degree from UPenn. What's more, I had competed in track and field at the Penn relays each year in high school; I was familiar and enamored with the school. Ironically, I was getting the chance to return years later as a graduate student.

I drove to Philadelphia two days a week for almost three years. I wouldn't get home until after eleven o'clock at night. But I still got up the next day and arrived to work at 7:30 a.m.

It was just that simple for me. Interesting enough, my boss even said to me: "Why are you driving all the way to Philadelphia to go to grad school?"

My response was: "Because I want to attend the best school, and that's the best school for the program that I want." I needed to check that box. I wanted to be that much better than everyone else.

I reveled in the excitement of being at that university, sitting in those classes, and learning from some of the best and brightest thinkers in the world. It was in a field that I was incredibly passionate about: I was studying organizational dynamics in the School of Arts and Sciences. It was all about organizational development, and how people lead, think, engage, and make decisions—which is what I was doing for a living anyway. I'm proud of my master's degree. It validated my passion for diversity work. It solidified the idea of me wanting to continue the fight for the underrepresented internally in human resources. It confirmed what I already knew—I was in the right profession and had chosen the right field to pursue as a career.

In my view, as an African American woman, knowing how tough it is to compete in the industries that I've worked in—financial services and pharmaceuticals—it is critical that you have an advanced degree—an MBA, an MS, an MA—to be considered for positions of leadership. Pedigree means a lot more than you realize. In pharma, you're working with world-class scientists, physicians, and biostatisticians. It is helpful to have an advanced degree that reflects your intelligence in that arena; it is a key professional credential preferred by most employers.

While holding a graduate degree is not actually a guarantee of ultimate success, it certainly opens many more doors, especially for corporate professionals of color. This has to do with the notion of having to be twice as good, twice as smart. Even nearly two years after I left corporate America, I had companies that courted me, wined-and-dined me to gauge my interest about certain positions. The first thing they would zero in on upon reviewing my resume was my degree from UPenn. I recall some of them saying, "Oh, wow. That's a wonderful school." *Where* you go to school is equally as important as the degree that you obtain.

My advice to any young person is to be very deliberate about both your undergraduate and graduate school choices. I have worked in HR for many years and in various industries; I have some inside knowledge. A lot of times, organizations target specific top-tier schools because they want to recruit the top students. Good or bad, this is commonplace among many corporate employers.

My point is not to say that every person should have an advanced degree or attend an Ivy League institution. I can only speak to my experience. Recruiters look at the rigor of where you went to school. *Why did you go to that HBCU versus going to Columbia University?* I've seen and heard it all. Some of my peers, other African American executives, instill that notion in their children: *You need to go to Brown, Princeton, Harvard, Penn, or Yale.* They know that where you decide to attend undergraduate and graduate school is an indication to an employer of not simply how successful you're going to be, but just how smart you are and whether you deserve to have a seat at the table in that company. Yes, college tuition continues to skyrocket, but if you can get an advanced degree, no one can take it away from you.

My sister Monique has a bachelor's degree, a master's, a law degree, and an education doctorate. We're overachievers when it comes to education. And yet, we are not that different from most college-educated women who view the pursuit of higher education as making an investment in their professional careers. Indeed, US women now lead men in educational attainment for the first time since the Census began tracking the measure in 1940. "Women have earned more bachelor's degrees than men since 1982," more master's degrees since 1987, and more doctorate degrees since 2006, per research from the Catalyst organization.[31]

Studies show that women of color have seen the most advances in educational attainment. By both race and gender, black women are enrolled in college at a higher percentage than any other groups, including white women, Asian women, and white men, according to a new suite of college enrollment stats released by the National Center for Education Statistics. Its findings show that black women earned 67 percent of associate's degrees, 65 percent of bachelor's degrees,[32] 70 percent of master's degrees, and 64 percent of all doctor's degrees[33] awarded to all black students.

It probably goes without saying that these figures don't indicate proof of progress in the pipeline. It is unfortunate that women of color continue to experience setbacks in breaking into more lucrative fields such as math and science, face financial difficulties, and have lower college completion rates in comparison to white women. While women of color have steadily progressed in postsecondary education, those efforts

31 Catalyst, "Quick Take: Women in the Workforce: United States," August 11, 2016, http://www.catalyst.org/knowledge/women-workforce-united-states.

32 "Fast Facts: Degrees Conferred By Race and Sex," US Department of Education, National Center for Education Statistics, *Status and Trends in the Education of Racial and Ethnic Groups 2016*, https://nces.ed.gov/fastfacts/display.asp?id=72.

33 "Indicator 22: Degrees Awarded," US Department of Education, National Center for Education Statistics, *Status and Trends in the Education of Racial and Ethnic Groups 2016*, https://nces.ed.gov/programs/raceindicators/indicator_ree.asp.

do not always translate into equal earnings later down the road. According to Census data, in regard to work/life earnings, regardless of the degree obtained, white women make more money than African American and Latina women among full-time, year-round workers.

The cultural ideas that *You have to be twice as good as other people,* or, *They can be good, but you must be great,* are undergirded by common perceptions that the work put forth by people of color is of low quality and they themselves are intellectually inferior, according to the *Huffington Post* article "Too Smart to Succeed, Too Good to Win—The Plight of Black Professionals and Students" by J. Luke Wood, associate professor at San Diego State University, Frank Harris III, associate professor at San Diego State University, and Joshua Wood, CEO of Region Business. One of the few ways to counter these stereotypes is to be "exemplary." As a result, these men declare, many of us African Americans are tirelessly dedicated to excellence, even to the point of immense self-sacrifice.

"What if your best was too good and set you up for failure? What happens when you become *too* smart to succeed and *too* good to win? You become a target, the center of attention in a bitter (and sometimes unconscious) effort to derail your success or question the standards by which your success is measured, or you become the focus of incessant inquiries surmising that your achievements were ill-gotten," they write.

By no means do they believe that black parents should avoid telling their children to perform at the highest level. But they do think that black children need to be told the full story—that their excellence will not be as valued or welcomed if they are too good or too smart. "Inevitably, we must do so to compete in a system that privileges others," they say. "However, being prepared for the backlash associated with greatness is critical to the success of our community."

Just the same, women have to be strategic about going above and beyond doing great work that will get them positively noticed by influencers in an organization. Lois P. Frankel, author of *Nice Girls Still Don't Get the Corner Office: Unconscious Mistakes Women Make That Sabotage Their Careers*, points out that women tend to believe they have to be twice as smart and work twice as good to be considered half as good, so as a result, women work like ants. Frankel states that it's a myth that people get ahead because they work hard. "The truth is that no one ever got promoted purely because of hard work. Likability, strategic thinking, networking, and being a team player are but a few of the other factors that go into crafting a successful career," she explains.[34]

In every organization, there's a baseline for hard work. When women constantly go over that baseline by working harder than their male colleagues, they aren't always recognized; instead they are given more work, writes Frankel. She cites as an example the story of a male colleague rehashing a Sunday football game with his boss on Monday morning. This type of small talk is leading to that person being tapped for prime assignments. The male coworker is bonding with the boss. Thus, when growth opportunities became available he was picked because the boss was familiar and more comfortable with him. "People aren't hired and promoted simply because they work hard. It happens because the decision maker knows the character of the person and feels confident about his or her ability not only to do the job, but also to do it in a way that promotes collegial team relationships," Frankel argues.[35]

34 Lois P. Frankel, *Nice Girls Still Don't Get the Corner Office: Unconscious Mistakes Women Make That Sabotage Their Careers*, (Grand Central Publishing/Hachette Book Group, 2014), p. 40.

35 *Ibid*, p. 41.

The harsh reality is that yes, as women, especially women of color in corporate America, we must work twice as hard and be twice as smart, because the bar is placed so low for us in terms of other people's expectations. But that's still not enough. We must strive to make the right connections. In essence, you must network your way to the top.

No Second Chances Allowed

Another reality is that when you are a woman or a person of color, you often aren't afforded second chances when you mess up. I carried that message with me throughout my career. I adhered to it when I was working as a staffing and diversity manager at Wakefern Food and I was selected to help the CEO and the COO create a presentation for the co-op members. We would have these all-member forums; these are the owners of ShopRite Supermarkets who would get together quarterly. The CEO and his direct reports would conduct a "state of the union" address to its membership. I was chosen to work with the CEO and his team to put together this major presentation. We're going back a number of years, so PowerPoint was fairly new to this company and it was also very new to me—although I did not tell them that. I wanted to knock the cover off the ball. I said to myself, *Okay, I can't screw this up; this is my time to shine.*

I was putting together the presentation based on information that was given to me and something wasn't going right. I remember that I was having a technical problem and I wasn't making any headway because of this glitch. I don't recall at this moment exactly what the problem was, but I got up out of my bed and I went to the office. I basically stayed there overnight and worked with the IT team to fix whatever this problem was so that the CEO and the COO would have a successful presentation. I stayed there until five in the morning after arriving around ten that night. I was determined to do whatever it took to make sure that this presentation was up and running seamlessly, and that things were going to go well at the end of the day.

I never even told my boss about the technical problem. I just showed up and said, "Here's the presentation," and he delivered it without a hitch—it was flawless. Afterward, I got the biggest thank you and handshake from the CEO and several of his direct reports. I was a star. I really felt like I went above and beyond my job. I felt ten feet tall despite my short stature. Let's just say, that was definitely a proud moment for me.

I made a point to use that opportunity to show senior and executive management that I was committed, that I had grit, and that I was going to do whatever was required of me to produce excellent results and make them look good—not just my boss, but also my mentor in HR.

Like Rhimes, I knew that second chances are a rarity when you're a person of color. I felt compelled to get it done and get it done right, the first time out. During an interview, the late legendary artist Prince shared how the comedic actor, writer, and producer Chris Rock once joked: "Leonardo DiCaprio can make one bad movie after another, and he just keeps going. Chris Rock makes a bad movie, and he doesn't work again. Black people aren't allowed to make mistakes."[36]

Notwithstanding, I have witnessed a few of my white male counterparts fail in an epic way and still rise above the ashes to a position of greater responsibility. Why is it that they re-

36 "Prince: Black People Don't Get Second Chances," the *Guardian*, February 25, 2014, https://www.theguardian.com/music/2014/feb/25/prince-black-people-dont-get-second-chances.

cover seamlessly without reprisal, while others—women and minorities—seem to go up in smoke?

A new working paper from the National Bureau of Economic Research on Discrimination and Worker Evaluation reports that when it comes to getting and keeping jobs, "African American employees tend to receive more scrutiny from their bosses than their white colleagues."[37]

According to Gillian B. White, "The NBER paper, authored by Costas Cavounidis and Kevin Lang of Boston University, attempts to demonstrate how discrimination factors into company decisions, and creates a feedback loop, resulting in racial gaps in the labor force." The two conclude that because "black workers are more closely scrutinized, it increases the chances that errors—large or small—will be caught." These errors will lead to poor performance reviews and lower wages. Furthermore, "it's more likely that a black employee would be let go for these errors than a white one. Thus, another way of looking at the findings, Lang says, is that blacks simply don't get a second chance."[38] Just to keep a job, black workers must meet a higher bar.

The researchers also found that "only in instances where black workers are monitored and displayed a significantly higher skill level than their white counterparts would they stand a significant chance of keeping their jobs for a while. But even in instances where the productivity of black workers far exceeded their white counterparts, there was still evidence that discrimination persisted, which led to lower wages or slower promotions."[39]

---

37 Gillian B. White, "Black Workers Really Do Need to Be Twice As Good," the *Atlantic*, October 7, 2015, https://www.theatlantic.com/business/archive/2015/10/why-black-workers-really-do-need-to-be-twice-as-good/409276/.

38 *Ibid.*

39 *Ibid.*

Recent studies show that African American profession-als and managers in corporate America stand a 30 percent chance of being discriminated against at work.[40] Race-based grievances and complaints remain the same: minorities have been passed over for promotions even though they were qual-ified, moved from a key assignment, stuck in dead-end lower positions, and placed as managers over mostly minority-filled de-partments. While the playing field is still far from level, prov-ing intentional job discrimination is difficult. "In 2014, the US Equal Employment Opportunity Commission received 31,073 charges alleging race-based discrimination, but dismissed 71.4 percent of them due to a lack of reasonable cause."[41]

In *Nice Girls Still Don't Get the Corner Office*, Frankel states that one major mistake women make is pretending that the workplace isn't a game. "Many women view the whole idea of the game of business as something unpleasant, dirty, and to be avoided at all costs. But the workplace has rules, boundaries, strategies, winners and losers," she explains.[42] Among the advice that Frankel offers is that playing the game in business means being competitive; it means that you are aware of the rules and develop strategies for making them work to your advantage. "Not only is business a game, but the rules of the game change from organization to organization and from department to department within an organization," she suggests, further noting that what works with one boss may not work with the next one.

Indeed, each organization within a given industry will have its own culture, and for you to thrive within that organi-

---

40 Cora Daniels, *Black Power Inc.* (John Wiley & Sons, 2004), p. 17.

41 Tanzina Vega, "Working While Brown: What Discrimination Looks Like Now," *CNN Money*, November 25, 2015, http://money.cnn.com/2015/11/25/news/economy/racial-discrimination-work/index.html.

42 Lois P. Frankel, *Nice Girls Still Don't Get the Corner Office*, p. 18.

zation, it is essential that you determine as best you can what that culture is, and if it's a good fit for you.

Before you can even begin to seriously address the advancement of your career from your present position, you have to assess how your performance will be perceived and rewarded in the company, says Keith R. Wyche, author of *Good Is Not Enough: And Other Unwritten Rules for Minority Professionals.* Among his key points of advice is to "refuse to remain in a role, department, or company that, after you have demonstrated you can achieve, will not recognize and reward your achievements."

My advice to corporate professionals is: before you make such a move, be sure you have done all you can on your end to build upon relationships with your colleagues and senior-level managers on a regular basis. It is extremely important for aspiring professionals of color to pay close attention to how influence is measured. Stop thinking that being political means selling out or selling your soul. Business is all about relationships fostered and nurtured, both inside and outside of the office. Be mindful not to take yourself out of the social-networking loop, because this could put you at a severe disadvantage. Not only do you want to make sure that you are in the room, make it a point to get noticed.

This is why the back of the classroom was not the place for me. Even now, I don't sit back and wait for things to happen. Be aggressive. Ask questions. Always participate. Like my father, I come from a background of making things happen. I learned from him that when you walk into a room, you don't have to know my name, but you will by the time I walk out the door. He was taught that principle by his granduncle who used to tell him: "People don't have to know you, but they will know about you by the way you carry yourself."

If rewards and promotions come from being recognized and liked by key players within the organization, then you must establish a bond with those individuals, and a rapport with your boss. Having company advocates keeps you from working twice as hard in a vacuum or void. The more people who know you, know your strengths and abilities, know your value to the organization, and know some of your ambitions, the more likely your name will be discussed when opportunities arise.

The keys to success cited by many professional women of color in the corporate arena include: exceeding performance expectations, communicating effectively, connecting with mentors, building positive relationships with managers and colleagues, and using one's cultural background to enhance job performance. If *best* is possible, then *good* is simply not enough!

Key Steps

1. Use your F.O.D. (First Only Different) to your advantage. Flying stealth or below the radar is not an option.
2. Sit up front and raise your hand, but do so for high-profile, high-impact assignments.
3. Be better than good. Be that "go-to" person who your colleagues, peers, and superiors will call on when they are looking to build a high-performance team.
4. Discover sets of strategies and unwritten rules in your organization to develop and advance in your career. Having mentors will help you understand company culture and decipher the right codes of conduct.

5. Continue to sharpen your skills by attending conferences, taking educational classes on an annual basis, or participating in leadership training and executive development programs to enhance your performance and your position.

6. Do whatever is necessary to differentiate yourself from the masses. If that means driving a hundred miles per day to attend the best graduate school in the area, then make the sacrifice.

7. Do things right the first time! Treat every assignment and position as if it were your last. Remember: no second chances.

8. Cultivate meaningful relationships with your colleagues, peers, and superiors. Join professional associations.

9. Hard work alone won't cut it. Likability, strategic thinking, and networking are all significant factors in your advancement.

10. Know your value! Don't stay in a role, department, or company that will not recognize and reward your achievements.

4

TRIED & TRUE ANCHORS: MENTORS VS. SPONSORS

The mediocre teacher tells. The good teacher explains.
The superior teacher demonstrates. The great teacher inspires.
—William Arthur Ward

My father was one of the few black male executives in our Edison neighborhood, so he was the go-to person for a lot of my friends and peers, who would seek his counsel and support as it pertained to their careers. Dad told it like it was and didn't hold back: "This is what the challenge is going to be. This is how you're going to be perceived, and this is how you need to get around some of those challenges."

In the beginning of my career, I didn't go to my father for a lot of guidance. I wanted to prove that I could do it myself and that I could make my own connections. I didn't want him picking up the phone and calling on favors for people to employ me right after college. In hindsight, this was probably an immature decision on my part since many of my classmates relied heavily on their parents to make meaningful connections for them to advance their careers, or at least land their first *real* job opportunity right after graduation.

In my first full-time job, I was part of Bamberger's Executive Training Team, an acceleration program that planned training in the major disciplines of the retail business. As trainees, we received classroom instruction and participated in workshops in addition to on-the-job experience. I had a sponsor (advocate) named Beth Morris. She was a very tough leader; she expected a lot from herself and from those who worked for her. When I joined the program, I didn't have a lot of interaction with her, but she saw something in me that even the person I was directly reporting to didn't see—I had potential and was willing to learn. I was willing to roll up my sleeves and do what was required to get the job done.

Beth gave me visibility within the organization, and because of that, I was promoted fairly quickly from assistant department manager to running my own department, which had more revenue generation. I was able to cultivate a relationship with her. Although she was feared by my colleagues, and I must say I was a little intimidated by her myself, I think her bark was worse than her bite. In the end, she was willing to support me as a young woman of color. Beyond Bamberger's executive training program, I have benefitted in my career from programs that tap high-potential employees for leadership development. This, in turn, has enabled me to tap career mentors.

There is an undeniable truth that a mentor is invaluable to anyone's career journey and success. Thinking about mentorship in a broader sense, I learn from everybody. Whether it was a teacher, a coach, a family member, a fellow colleague, a boss, or even the nighttime office cleaning crew; I give praise to all the people in my life who have played a major role in helping me realize and reach my full potential. As someone who strived to be a leader, I experienced how mentors not only help you excel in your current position but also assist you in getting to that next job or career level.

I believe there are significant benefits for women of color to have multiple mentors. In its report "Optimizing Mentoring Programs for Women of Color," Catalyst research revealed that racially and ethnically diverse women with more than one mentor have higher promotion rates than those with just one.[43] Diverse women stand to gain a great deal from organizations that have mentoring programs, especially those that facilitate multiple mentorships by offering a combination of venues such as mentoring circles and one-on-one mentoring pairs, the report states.

However, it's not just about quantity but quality. Catalyst research shows that while the number of racially and ethnically diverse women with mentors has grown over time—from one-third to one-half—one distinct difference when compared to white women is that women of color are more likely to have mentors who lack power.[44] Based on data from Catalyst's studies on "Women of Color in Professional Services," "62 percent of diverse women with mentors cited 'lack of an influential mentor or sponsor' as a barrier to advancement compared [to] 39 percent of white women." If women of color lack powerful mentors, then they're more likely to lack access to sponsors or advocates who can influence decision makers, and get high-visibility assignments and senior-level promotions.

What's more, reports Catalyst, diverse women with influential mentors are more likely than those with noninfluential mentors to experience advantages in the workplace (e.g., greater satisfaction with career advancement) and the organization (lower intent to leave and higher organizational commitment). Even diverse women who reported having influential mentors lagged behind their white women counterparts in several areas, including overall satisfaction with the

43 Katherine Giscombe, "Optimizing Mentoring Programs for Women of Color," Catalyst, December 5, 2012.

44 Deepali Begati and Katherine Giscombe, "Women of Color in Professional Services," Catalyst, July 15, 2007.

relationship, trust, and mutual understanding, according to Catalyst.

Fortunately, that was not the case for me. When I started working at Wakefern Food Corp., I approached the head of HR who I have previously mentioned, Ernie Bell, who was also African American. I walked into his office one day and asked if he would be my mentor and he said yes. As a result, I had more exposure than most young professionals in that company—white or black—to the CEO, COO, and chairman of the board. So, Ernie turned out to be more of a sponsor than a mentor. He took me under his wing and provided me with feedback on my performance. In a lot of ways, he put his own reputation on the line to ensure that I had the right kind of exposure to the decision makers. He also recognized my desire to have a bigger role at Wakefern. I was treated like his protégé. We would meet once a month and it was incredibly helpful to have his ear and his support.

How you manage a mentoring relationship is critical. It is important to be open and up front with your mentor about advice he or she may give you, which you may or may not choose to follow. Always show appreciation for his or her counsel. When I accepted a position at Merck, Ernie was upset, and rightfully so, at the fact that I didn't tell him until I resigned that I was leaving Wakefern. I didn't come to him first before I announced it to my direct manager and other people who were invested in my career. I was so nervous at the thought of talking about my leaving because he had given me so many opportunities to shine and get in front of leadership. And yet, he was also the one who encouraged me to seek other opportunities. He was simply disappointed that he wasn't the first to know that I was moving on. I regret that decision to this day. I should have done the courteous thing and let him know before speaking to anyone else. He called me on the carpet about my actions and I apologized profusely. This experience sure taught me a lesson about being transparent with not only those who invest in my career, but others as well.

I was hired at Merck by a black woman, Angela Knight. From the moment I accepted the job offer, Angela provided me with a great level of support. She taught me things I probably needed to know about the culture and the climate of the organization. She was helpful in my navigation through the company. She was my direct boss, and unbeknownst to her, she was my informal mentor. Since there were so few people of color in leadership roles at Merck at that time, we looked out for each other. If you weren't doing your job to the best of your ability, people would strategically intervene by pulling you off to the side to say, "You need to do this a little bit differently and here's what I would suggest."

What was equally nice about Angela? She was a soror. Like me, she was a member of Alpha Kappa Alpha (AKA). My twin Monique was an AKA as well, but she pledged undergrad at an HBCU with 101 line sisters, whereas I pledged a grad chapter in 2002. It was a *great* sisterhood. I liked the idea of having one of my sorority sisters as a mentor. More importantly, it was nice to know that someone was looking out for me.

There were instances where some colleagues would watch their peers go in a downward spiral and just say to themselves, *Mm-mm, that's too bad.* These were rare occasions.

Now, bear in mind that career coaches, mentors, and advocates are not the same thing. For me, mentors are people who come to know who you are as a person—your core values, needs, and wants. They understand your strengths and weaknesses. But more importantly, they hold a mirror up to you and give you candid feedback. They hold you accountable if you fall short and fail to do what you said you would do. They will describe to you where they see opportunities for your career development. They're the ones whose shoulders you can tap for years to come.

Sylvia Ann Hewlett, the author of many career books, including *Forget a Mentor, Find a Sponsor*, is president and CEO of the Center for Talent Innovation. She notes: "Mentors act as a sounding board or a shoulder to cry on, offering advice as needed and support and guidance as requested; they expect very little in return. Sponsors, in contrast, are much more vested in their protégés, offering guidance and critical feedback because they believe in them."[45] Hewlett is also the co-director of the Women's Leadership Program at the Columbia Business School.

In the article "Mentorship and Sponsorship: Why Both Are Crucial for Women's Career Success," Hewlett shares some of the key attributes of a sponsor. Most notable is that "your sponsor needs to be in a powerful enough position to be able to open doors for you"; "your sponsor needs to believe in your value as a professional and be willing to go to bat for you."[46] "Women with sponsors take as many risks as men with sponsors, because if you have a powerful person backing you, you can risk falling flat on your face. There's someone there to pick you back up," Hewlett writes.[47]

To underscore the importance of sponsorship, Hewlett re-

---

45 Silvia Ann Hewlett, "Mentors Are Good. Sponsors Are Better." the *New York Times*, April 13, 2013, http://www.nytimes.com/2013/04/14/jobs/sponsors-seen-as-crucial-for-womens-career-advancement.html.

46 Tricina Elliker, "Mentorship and Sponsorship: Why Both Are Crucial for Women's Career Success," *Everwise*, November 18, 2015, https://www.geteverwise.com/career-success/mentorship-and-sponsorship-why-both-are-crucial-for-womens-success/.

47 *Ibid.*

counts the story of Larry Summers and Sheryl Sandberg: "He sponsored her like crazy when she was in her twenties. She delivered like crazy for him, in return, and he took her with him to the Treasury as his chief of staff. He opened doors for her in Silicon Valley too."

Then Larry Summers was up for consideration as head of the Federal Reserve in 2013. Sandberg went to bat for her old sponsor, even breaking ranks with other female leaders who were lining up behind Janet Yellen, according to Hewlett. "And in a way she was then sponsoring him," she adds.[48]

If you are a person of color it is even more important for you to obtain both mentors and sponsors. CTI research shows that "the vast majority of women (85 percent) and multicultural professionals (81 percent) need navigational help." A study of women professionals reported that just 11 percent of black women in their sample indicated that they had a sponsor, compared with 13 percent for white women.[49]

These findings are in keeping with studies by Stella M. Nkomo, a professor at the University of Pretoria. Her internationally acclaimed research on race and gender in organizations, leadership, human resource management, and managing diversity appears in numerous journals. Nkomo is also the coauthor with Ella L.J. Bell Smith, a professor of business administration at Tuck, of the 2003 Harvard Business School Press book *Our Separate Ways: Black and White Women and the Struggle for Professional Identity*. What they discovered is that more African Americans reported that they had no access to mentors and were often *ghettoized* in staff positions with little decision-making power. The black women Nkomo in-

---

48 *Ibid.*

49 Dan Schawbel, "Sylvia Ann Hewlett: Find a Sponsor Instead of a Mentor," *Forbes*, September 10, 2013, https://www.forbes.com/sites/danschawbel/2013/09/10/sylvia-ann-hewlett-find-a-sponsor-instead-of-a-mentor/#664dda571760.

terviewed perceived their relationships with their supervisors less positively than their white counterparts. White bosses were afraid to give their black female employees honest feedback, reportedly for fear of being called a racist. This, in my view, is an excuse white bosses use to not have an open and honest conversation with their subordinates of color.

Broaden Your Network Beyond Your Reflection

CTI discovered that it is not uncommon for female sponsors to be careful not to choose female protégés for fear it might look like they're playing favorites and choosing gender over merit. Hewlett's advice to women: "Most of the people at the top are white men, and you should pursue them as your sponsor."[50]

In all honesty, women of color don't have to be mentored only by other women. Nor by other people of color. Personally, I have no problem being mentored by white men or women. To tell the truth, I've found that having mentors who are different from one's self—race, nationality, gender, sexual orientation, etc.—is a great way to gain a new perspective in one's career. I wanted to surround myself with top-notch people who genuinely cared about me and my career development; people who would listen to me about my dreams, goals, and aspirations—and not belittle them.

While Angela was my direct boss at Merck, she reported to Mark Streifer, a white male who influenced my advancement within the organization. He reported to another white male, Howard Levine, who was the big boss—he served as the vice president of human resources for our division. Howard was an openly gay man whom I thought was the most courageous person in the company. Not only was he a genuinely nice and kind person, but he came out at a time and in an

50 Elliker, "Mentorship and Sponsorship."

industry where a lot of people were not out of the closet.

He would often ask me what I wanted to do long-term and short-term. He made it a point to get to know me. We lived in the same town and he would invite me over to his home. I met his partner. It was very nice. We would just talk about life, work, a little bit of everything. Because he was the big boss, I had to keep my relationship with him private. I was very discreet about my interactions with Howard. He really extended himself to me in a casual way, and it was genuine. I really had a fondness for him. Once I decided to leave Merck, he was disappointed but he understood. Mark and Angela understood too.

Mentors can help you grasp the unwritten rules of an organization and provide a map for navigating the uncharted corridors to power. But most importantly, by assisting you with both organizational insights and self-assessment, mentors can help prepare you to attract sponsors. Keith R. Wyche, author of *Good Is Not Enough: And Other Unwritten Rules for Minority Professionals*, explains it this way: "The person giving you career advice is a mentor and *not* your sponsor." He adds, "A sponsor is a person who doesn't just speak with you—they speak [favorably] about you. It's someone who wields power and helps position you for that next step in your career."[51] In other words, sponsors put you on the radar screens of key influencers at your company—and within your industry.

Many people's perceptions about you happen when you're not in the room, explains Wyche, who racked up over thirty years at major corporations including Ameritech, AT&T, IBM, and Pitney Bowes. He rose to become a division president and one of the highest-ranking African American exec-

51 Keith R. Wyche, *Good Is Not Enough: And Other Unwritten Rules for Minority Professionals* (Penguin, 2008).

utives at a Fortune 500 company. "While advice is helpful, it won't get you that promotion you are hoping for. Simply put, a mentor stands beside you, while a sponsor stands in front of you helping to propel you forward," writes Wyche.

When I was at Novartis, Sally Cunningham was the head of human resources. Sally, who was white, was one of the few women who sat on the executive committee of the pharma division. Every day was a struggle for her simply because that environment was incredibly tough, since it was very male dominated. Despite that, Sally was incredibly elegant and smart. She was a real role model for a lot of women in the organization.

On one occasion I was invited to present some information to the executive committee about diversity and employee resource groups. We were also talking about the results of the employee opinion survey, which revealed that the African American population at Novartis was not quite as happy as the rest of the employees in the organization at that time.

When I walked into the room, I took a seat—not at the boardroom table, but in one of the chairs lined up against the wall behind it. Sally turned around and said, "Michelle, you don't sit in the back of the room, you sit here at this table."

I thought you had to be invited to sit at the boardroom table. She told me: "You sit right here next to me."

The CEO and other leaders were trying to wrap their heads around why the African American talent was so unhappy and wanted to know if anybody had any data to support or substantiate the findings of the survey. I spoke up and said something along the lines of: "We really need to take a deeper dive and look into this population because I think that there may be some fear in the system and some challenges in the organization, in terms of why they're not as happy as other groups, and we really need to investigate." I knew what I said was impactful because the CEO nodded in affirmation, and Sally was smiling.

Then we started talking about employee resource groups—also known as ERGs, affinity groups, or business network groups: employees who voluntarily ban together in their workplace based on shared characteristics or life experiences. Senior management wanted to know why the black ERGs at Novartis were struggling more than everybody else—women, Asians, Latinos, and other ERGs.

I wasn't invited to speak, I just started talking. I hit them with: "You have to understand the history of this group; in the past when they would get together, they would be looked upon negatively, as if they were trying to cause trouble in the company."

I explained how it didn't feel like a positive dynamic that this resource group existed, so there was fear associated with being a member of it. They didn't want to be perceived as doing something disruptive or nonsensical and not working, when ERGs do actually work, because they tackle issues or challenges and come up with solutions.

I had everyone's undivided attention in that room. I continued: "There needs to be some additional education and awareness more broadly throughout the organization, so people understand and support all employee network groups and not just some of them."

My presentation in the boardroom that day went so well that afterward, when I saw some of my peers and senior leaders in HR, they showered me with praise: "I heard you did a wonderful job and Sally was raving about you." At that point, I felt ten feet tall. Some months later I told Sally I wanted a mentor.

When she asked, "Who are thinking about?"

I told her: "Paulo Costa."

She inquired: "The CEO?"

Not missing a beat, I responded, "Yes."

You must understand, that was a bold move on my part. One might exclaim, *Michelle, you've got a lot of nerve making that request!* You bet and I did, unapologetically. *Why would someone junior in the organization ask for the CEO of Novartis Pharmaceuticals to be her mentor?* We talked through the why.

I said, "Because he's smart, I like the way he leads, I can learn a lot from him, and he can learn a lot from me." She spoke to Paulo about me, sharing my background with him. He graciously agreed to serve as my mentor.

Paulo was one of the best leaders I've ever worked for— brilliant, compassionate, cultured, and firm but fair—all the great qualities a leader displays. During our first mentoring meeting in his office, there was a picture of a little house on his desk. It wasn't quite a shack but it was a very modest home. I just asked him point blank: "What's this picture of?"

He said, "This is the home that I grew up in and I always keep it on my desk to remind me of where I came from." He came from humble beginnings in Brazil. He was well educated, a Harvard MBA among many other fine attributes.

Every quarter I would meet with him. We would talk about my career—challenges I might be facing in the organization or other issues that needed to be addressed at his level. He was a trusted advisor, professional in every sense of the word. Novartis is a global health care company based in Basel, Switzerland. I really wanted to work in Switzerland. Aside from Sally, Paulo was one of the first people I told about my desire to go global. He was willing to work with me to get me closer to my goal. From that very first meeting, Paulo was generous enough with his time to explain to me what was important to him about leading and engaging with people, even on a casual level. He didn't have to do it. He was extremely busy but he made the time for me. I am thankful for that. We still stay in contact to this day.

I had two more sponsors at Novartis who were white men. One was the person to whom I reported directly to, Thomas Ebeling. He was the CEO of the pharma division globally. A very powerful German guy, he built the entire pharma division from the ground up. He was a brilliant businessman, and had a memory like an elephant. He expected a lot from people, and your best was never good enough. He always pushed you to do more because he knew that you were capable. Most of us thrived under his leadership. The other person was Alex Gorsky, who is now chairman and CEO of Johnson & Johnson; he was another exceptionally talented leader who I learned a great deal from. He became CEO of Novartis Pharma once Paulo retired. I developed a wonderful relationship with him. I was the head of diversity for the company; he relied on me and he trusted my judgment. I consider Alex to be a dear friend.

I make it a point to touch base with all of my mentors and sponsors at least once per year. I owe a lot of my success to these individuals. They are all exceptional leaders who saw things in me that I did not even see in myself. I feel honored to have been able to cultivate relationships with these individuals and to call each of them a friend and trusted advisor in every sense.

Find a Seat at the Table

I am forever grateful to Sally for teaching me an ever-important lesson about sitting at the table. You should never sit in one of the chairs lined up against the wall. Don't make the mistake of leaving seats at the table for people whom you think are more important or more deserving. Snap at the chance to make a presentation before senior management. It's not only an opportunity for you to shine, but also to build upon your relationships with the movers and shakers in the company.

One way to broaden your connections and build valuable networks of influencers is to serve on community or nonprofit boards, which tend to attract accomplished, interesting people, suggests Alice Korngold, president and CEO of Korngold Consulting. Korngold provides strategy advisory services, and facilitates leadership strategy retreats for board members and executives from multinational corporations and NGOs.[52] Serving on a nonprofit board helps to round out your resume, and by working on issues that you care about and earning a good reputation in the process, you'll build valuable relationships with fellow board members and the organization's donors. Nonprofit board members gain expertise on salient issues such as economic development, education, housing, health care, and the environment.

I have had the honor of serving on the boards of several nonprofits. I sat on the See Forever Foundation board of Maya Angelou's charter school. I was also a member of the Harvard Women's Leadership board and the S.L.E. Lupus Foundation board. Most of these organizations had heard of me and my work, and invited me to join. There is a process for serving on a nonprofit board; you must go through a series of interviews, talking about your strengths and weaknesses, and what you can bring to the organization.

For over ten years I have been a board member of the Jackie Robinson Foundation. Its mission revolves around rais-

---

52 Alice Korngold, "Nonprofit Boards: Bootcamps for Corporate Executives," *Huffington Post*, April 20, 2012, http://www.huffingtonpost.com/alice-korngold/nonprofit-leadership_b_1287793.html.

ing funds and building bridges for students of color who are academically gifted but do not have the financial means to attend college. We provide scholarships and support services to minority students. Rachel Robinson, the baseball legend's widow, founded the organization in 1973. She is what I call one of my many *Sheroes*.

Before I joined the board, I had raised a significant amount of money for their annual gala. They were impressed with what I'd been able to accomplish for them on my own time. A couple months later, Della Britton, the CEO and president, asked if I had an interest in serving on the board and I said, "Are you kidding? The Jackie Robinson Foundation, really?"

It's a who's who that sits on that board. There are company presidents, C-Suite individuals, entrepreneurs, lawyers, celebrities, you name it. It's an honor for me to serve on this board, as Jackie Robinson was one of the many heroes who my grandfather would talk about while my sisters and I were growing up.

Serving on nonprofit boards has been invaluable for me. From a leadership and developmental perspective, I have gained a strong knowledge base. I've also gained exposure to various leadership styles, organizational cultures, and business models. By joining a nonprofit or community board, you have an opportunity to expand your personal and professional networks by meeting executives from other industries and interacting with and understanding complex board dynamics. You get to view a number of organizational issues through a very different lens.

I would advise anyone who is interested in joining a nonprofit board to do your homework! Conduct research on a number of organizations that you might have an interest in. Make sure the board's mission and core values align with your own principles. Ensure that the focus of the board is on a topic you are passionate about and truly committed to. You will spend too much time on these boards and committees for the subject to be less than engaging for you.

As you rise up in your organization, it is equally important to mentor others along the way. Remember, mentoring is a two-way street. So you too have something to gain. There are several ways that you can benefit from being a mentor, including sharpening your skills. Mentoring talent that you can retain in your organization can go a long way toward making you more of an asset. It gives you added value. The experience you gain by mentoring someone else can facilitate your own professional growth. It definitely helped to strengthen my leadership skills by working with individuals from various backgrounds.

I've had as many as eight protégés at one given time. It was a real melting pot. This allowed me to learn from various cultures and understand different experiences. I would rarely say no if someone asked me to be a mentor. I tried to orchestrate and formulate a career plan for my protégées. Some might have issues with a tough manager who they didn't get along with, or there was a perception issue. I would give them advice on how to turn that situation around. I would sit in meetings where talent was being discussed in terms of job openings or promotions. I could sit in a room and talk about specific people that I had cultivated a relationship with and I could say, "This is the person that should be in that job and here's why."

For sure, mentorship and sponsorship relationships played a critical role to my success over the years on both the receiving and giving end. As the recipient of mentoring, I was able to navigate my way through the organizational culture, build a relationship with a senior leader, strengthen a number of technical skills that were key to my development, build confidence, and learn to take total control of my career.

Who's Got Your Back? Closing the Sponsor Gap

Now in its twelfth year, the *Black Enterprise* Women of Power Summit is touted as a business event that attracts more than a thousand mid- to senior-level managers, C-level decision makers, HR officers, diversity officers, executives, and professionals. The annual conference is designed especially for women of color, to explore all the ways they can achieve their professional and personal goals. This summit is by far the largest black women's professional summit in the US—likely in the world. I was unable to attend for years, given competing priorities and a hectic travel schedule. When I finally attended for the first time along with a client of mine in March of 2016, I was extremely impressed with the content, caliber of speakers, the various topics, and above all, the seamless coordination of shepherding thousands of black women in and out of plenary and breakout sessions for three to four days. *Black Enterprise* CEO Earl "Butch" Graves Jr., WOP editorial director Caroline Clarke, and Team *BE* are deserving of all accolades as this is not an easy feat to pull off!

At the 2016 WOP Summit, the women talked about the importance of having influencers in your corner while climbing in your career. AT&T's chief diversity officer Cynthia Marshall, during the "Who's Got Your Back: Addressing the All-Important Sponsorship Gap" panel discussion, used a sports analogy to break it down: "A mentor is your personal trainer and a sponsor is your agent."[53]

Thanks to great bosses, mentors, and sponsors, Marshall has received invaluable guidance for growth in her career. She

---

53 Courtney Connley, "How to Solve the Sponsorship Gap in Your Career," *Black Enterprise*, March 10, 2016, http://www.blackenterprise.com/event/how-to-solve-the-sponsorship-gap-in-your-career/.

went on to share that a sponsor is someone who is willing to put his or her professional representation on the line to advocate for you. *Black Enterprise* magazine honored Marshall as one of the "50 Most Powerful Women in Corporate America" in 2015, for the vital role she plays in AT&T's diversity efforts.

Marshall, along with panelists Tracey Travis and Sharon Brogdon, spoke candidly about why a mentor is not enough in helping you to reach the next level.

"Mentors are important, but sponsors are the ones that get your career going," said Travis, who serves as executive vice president and chief financial officer for Estée Lauder.[54] Shedding light on how both sponsors and mentors have helped them to reach success, the panel also advised a roomful of leading women on how they can go about getting a sponsor to speak on their behalf.

Brogdon, who at the time was director of strategic capability at Intel, encouraged the women to be deliberate about who they want to be their sponsor and to examine how the relationship can be a two-way street, where both parties benefit from each other.

"My protégés are constantly providing me with new information, sending me articles, and letting me know about events I may be interested in," asserted Travis, while augmenting Brogdon's point.[55]

Under the direction of Carol Fulp, who served as moderator, the WOP Summit panelists and attendees were charged with conducting an accountability exercise and thinking about an action item that they could commit, to help seal the sponsorship gap, as noted in *Black Enterprise*.

---

54 *Ibid.*

55 *Ibid.*

It is problematic when African American women tend to get a late start in strategically positioning themselves for advancement in areas such as securing P&L (profit and loss) positions and operating roles, as well as developing the important relationships that provide guidance, strategy, and feedback, according to the "Black Women Executives Research Initiative" published in 2008 by the Executive Leadership Council (ELC) and Institute for Leadership Development and Research. The study was conducted by the consulting firm Springboard Partners in Cross Cultural Leadership, to examine the facilitators and impediments to black women executives in reaching the C-Suite. Among the dynamics covered in the study were the importance of relationship building, solidifying mentorship and sponsorship, identifying opportunities for risk-taking, and cross-cultural competence in a global work environment.

Springboard once again partnered with the ELC in 2014–2015 to reinterview nearly 80 percent of the black women executives from the original study. While sponsorship is not a new phenomenon, mentoring was a much more prevalent topic in the 2007 interviews. Black women executives in the 2014–2015 interviews reported much higher levels of sponsorship, though it was eye-opening that many black women executives were less confident about the strength and effectiveness of their sponsorship relationships.[56]

ELC's report revealed that black women executives suffer from the lack of comfortable, trusted, and strategic relationships at the senior level with those who are most different from themselves—most notably white males. Black female

---

56 Pamela G. Carlton, Alexis Smith, Marla Baskerville Watkins, and Morgan Carven, "The Black Women Executives Research Initiative Revisited," Executive Leadership Council and Springboard—Partners in Cross Cultural Leadership, 2016.

executives often don't have the opportunity to showcase the breadth of their skills and experience to the higher levels of an organization.

One way you can fill the sponsorship gap is by taking advantage of the relationships that you have built. "Don't be afraid to connect the dots among people in your network," suggests *Nice Girls Don't Get the Corner Office* author Lois P. Frankel. She points out that men rely on relationships to open doors for them, and unlike women, they don't view it as taking advantage of anyone.[57] She stresses that there's a difference between name-dropping and using a relationship to open a door: "Don't be afraid to ask for permission to use a colleague's name when you're trying to get the attention of someone." Ask for introductions if there is someone with whom you want to connect. In kind, introduce people in your circle with like interests or needs. It is these very connections that can lead to your gaining mentors and sponsors. Frankel reasons that as opposed to guilt by association, it's success by affiliation.

I concur wholeheartedly: you must be courageous about approaching people to be your mentor or catching the eye of a potential sponsor. Many people, especially people of color, are very hesitant about breaking the rules or talking directly to the CEO. I think that many of us struggle with, *What's that conversation starter? Do I simply say, "Hello, my name is . . . and I want you to be my mentor?"* No, it must be a little bit more strategic than that. You must do your homework—you must understand who this person is, where they went to school, if there's some information about their personal lives out there, what's important to them, and what keeps them up at night.

You're dealing with senior leaders, and so your credibility

---

57   Frankel, *Nice Girls Don't Get the Corner Office*, p. 63.

and your career may be on the line. One false move and that could be it for you. Practice before you go in the room; write everything down; have a formal agenda. Be clear about the objective of the relationship. What do you want to get out of it? Anybody can meet with a senior leader. But what is your objective as a protégé? How are you going to make it interesting enough that he or she is going to continue to want to meet with you and not see it as a waste of time?

I learned from the very best, including three CEOs of major multinational corporations. I made it a general rule of thumb to always surround myself with incredibly smart people. And I maintained my relationships with all of them. That's one of the things that I'm most proud of achieving. Anyone who has mentored me or served some sort of a role in my career success over the years, I still keep in touch with. I thank him or her regularly for the critical role they've played and continue to play in my professional career.

Key Steps

1. Be clear about your needs for a mentor and sponsor. What do you want to get out of the relationship? What can you offer in return? Remember, it's a reciprocal relationship.
2. Create a list of leaders whom you would like to have as a mentor and as a sponsor—a mentor can possibly lead a sponsor to you. This list should have a diverse mix of people.
3. Work through your internal network to propose the "ask" for mentorship. Clearly articulate why you selected this individual.
4. Be prepared in the event that the person you are asking to serve as a mentor declines the opportu-

nity. This could very well happen. Ask for feed-back as to why the individual declined and move on to the next person on your wish list.

5. Prepare for your first meeting by having a clear agenda, establish and agree on the frequency of the meetings and rules of engagement; discuss roles and responsibilities, expectations, and the duration of the relationship.

6. Use your time wisely! These leaders are very busy and you want to maximize the time you have with them.

7. Thank your mentors and sponsors for their will-ingness to serve in such a capacity.

8. Beyond the relationship, keep in touch with these individuals even if it's only a call or e-mail ex-change once or twice per year. Gratitude will take you a long way!

9. Be active. Most people who are successful in their organizations are successful elsewhere, such as trade groups, community organizations, or non-profit boards.

10. Groom others. Be a mentor to someone else in your organization as you move up.

5

GET WHAT YOU WANT, GET WHAT YOU DESERVE

Ask for what you want and be prepared to get it.
—Maya Angelou

On May 4, 2017, at five thirty p.m. in the rotunda of New York City Hall, I bore witness to a milestone. On that day, New York Mayor Bill de Blasio signed into law a bill that prohibits both public and private sector employers from inquiring about or relying on a prospective employee's salary history. The mayor was joined by senior administration officials, elected officials, and advocates—of which I was one. He used my pen to sign it. It was my first time meeting Mayor de Blasio; we shook hands and exchanged hellos. I had received an invite to attend the ceremony from one of the mayor's staffers; she was a senior policy advisor for the Commission on Gender Equity.

The bill (Intro. 1253) was sponsored by Public Advocate Letitia James, the first woman of color to hold a citywide office in New York City. There were a lot of women of color there in the room that day for the signing. While I didn't get to see her, the first lady of New York City, Chirlane McCray, commented in a press statement that "NYC is abolishing a practice that subjects people, especially women and individuals of color, to discriminatory procedures before they are hired."[58] This legis-

---

58 "Mayor de Blasio Signs Bill Prohibiting All NYC Employers from Inquiring about Salary History of Job Applicants," May 4, 2017, http://www1.nyc.gov/office-of-the-may-

lation is considered to be a major step toward achieving pay equity for New Yorkers.

Regrettably, we have all heard the stories about why women make less money than men. The pay gap is due to occupation, hence, even though there are more women in the workforce, they tend to go into fields where salaries are lower or they perform lower-paying jobs. Women don't know how to negotiate, leaving money on the table. Women interrupt their careers to have children, suffering a loss in wages as a result. They lack confidence. They don't speak up. We have all been fed these jaded messages—that if we would just change our behavior, we could shrink the pay gap between men and women.

Truth be told, inequality in pay stems from workplace gender and racial bias, according to the latest research data. I am struck by the fact that when white women speak of parity they continue to cite statistical data as it relates to the gender gap in pay, but often avoid discussing unequal pay between themselves and women of color. It takes twenty months for a black woman to earn the same wages a white man earns in twelve months. Black women are still expected to make do with less. Black women have also experienced a stagnation in wages.

A report by Valerie Wilson and William Rodgers of the Economic Policy Institute (EPI) shows that the equity pay gap is widening for black women in the workforce. Not only are black women's salaries grossly unequal to those of white men, black women's wages are falling further behind white women's wages. Wilson states that over the last 35 years, "we have lost ground in closing racial and ethnic wage gaps while gender

or/news/285-17/mayor-de-blasio-signs-bill-prohibiting-all-nyc-employers-inquiring-sala-ry-history-job#/0.

wage gaps have unquestionably narrowed. But this has largely been the result of falling men's wages rather than improve- ments in women's wages."[59]

In 1979, for instance, white women's wages were 62 per- cent of white men's wages, compared to 58 percent for black women relative to white men—a racial difference of four per- centage points between white and black women in the work- force.[60] Phrased differently, white women and black women earned sixty-two cents and fifty-eight cents, respectively, for every dollar that white men earned.

While the pay figures vary slightly, Pew Research Cen- ter analysis of US Bureau of Labor statistics likewise shows that white women fare better, earning eighty-two cents on the dollar as of 2015, in comparison to African American women earning sixty-five cents and Hispanic women earn- ing fifty-eight cents.[61] BLS data shows, however, that Asian American women follow roughly the trajectory of white women, making eighty-seven cents on the dollar earned by white men in 2015.[62] The BLS report "Women in the Labor Force" cites education as the reason for Asian women's advantage.

Asians are stereotypically considered a "model minority," notes Georgene Huang, Fairygodboss's Chinese American

59 Valerie Wilson, "Black Women's Wages Are No Longer Gaining Ground on White Men's, and They're Falling Further Behind White Women's," Economic Policy Institute, August, 17, 2016, http://www.epi.org/publication/black-womens-wages-are-no-longer- gaining-ground-on-white-mens-and-theyre-falling-further-behind-white-womens/.

60 Valerie Wilson and William Rodgers III, "Black-White Wage Gaps Expand with Ris- ing Wage Inequality," Economic Policy Institute, September 20, 2016, http://www.epi. org/publication/black-white-wage-gaps-expand-with-rising-wage-inequality/.

61 Eileen Patten, "Racial, Gender Wage Gaps Persist in US Despite Some Progress," Pew Research Center, July 1, 2016, http://www.pewresearch.org/fact-tank/2016/07/01/ racial-gender-wage-gaps-persist-in-u-s-despite-some-progress/.

62 "Women in the Labor Force: a Data Book," US Bureau of Labor Statistics, December 9, 2016.

CEO and cofounder.[63] "While there are relatively few Asian men or women in leadership positions in corporate America, it's a cohort that's often believed to achieve a disproportionate amount of professional success due to a combination of cultural upbringing and educational privilege," she writes in the *Fast Company* article "How Data on Race Shapes Women's Workplace Experiences May Surprise You."

Typically speaking, Asian Americans tend to earn more than other ethnic groups in the US workforce and hold more advanced degrees. Asian Americans are 50 percent more likely to have bachelor's degrees and nearly twice as likely to hold PhDs, JDs, MBAs, or MDs. Yet, even so, when stacked up against Asian American men with the same level of education and work roles, Asian American women only make seventy-eight cents on the dollar.[64]

Accordingly, gender bias remains the dominating factor in pay inequalities. "You can't negotiate your way out of discrimination," as put succinctly by Lisa Maatz, vice president of government relations at the American Association of University Women (AAUW).[65] Just because a company is owned or controlled by men of color doesn't mean there will be fair pay and equal treatment of female employees of color.

When it comes to handling pay inequality, let's just say that my experience reflects the times, and reinforces some common perceptions around women and salary negotiations. Of which, the big three are: women don't ask for more money,

63 Georgene Huang, "How Data on Race Shapes Women's Workplace Experiences May Surprise You," *Fast Company*, November 17, 2016, https://www.fastcompany.com/3065717/new-data-on-how-race-shapes-womens-workplace-experiences-may-surprise-you.

64 "The Wage Gap and Asian Women," The National Law Center, March 2017.

65 Women in the World Staff, "Today Is "Equal Pay Day," the *New York Times*, April 12, 2016, http://nytlive.nytimes.com/womenintheworld/2016/04/12/today-is-equal-pay-day-when-women-have-finally-earned-what-men-did-in-2015/.

women don't know how to ask in a way that benefits the entire organization, and when women do ask, they negotiate with shortsighted information about their monetary value. Over the last twenty years, the market has been flooded with reports to substantiate these assessments.

Take the widely popular book *Women Don't Ask: Negotiation and the Gender Divide* by Linda Babcock and Sara Laschever. In a study of the salaries of male and female MBA graduates from top schools, the authors found that about 7 percent of women attempted to negotiate, while 57 percent of men did. Respondents who said they negotiated their job offers increased their salary by over 7 percent. Babcock and Laschever surmised that unlike men, women don't often ask for raises and promotions, or better job opportunities. The takeaway: women have low expectations.

In the article "Ask and You Shall Receive? Gender Differences in Negotiator's Beliefs About Requests for a Higher Salary," Lisa Barron, an assistant professor in organizations behavior at the Graduate School of Management at the University of California, Irvine, references research conducted with MBA students. The study examined differences in the amounts of salary requests, and beliefs about those requests. The findings revealed that both male and female respondents negotiated for more money, so the women weren't afraid to ask. But the men wound up receiving significantly more, because they believed they were entitled to earn more than others, while the women asked for what they perceived as fair. Whereas 85 percent of the men felt comfortable measuring their worth in dollars, 83 percent of the women were uncomfortable and unsure of their monetary value.[66] The takeaway: women don't know their worth.

---

66   Lisa A. Barron, "Ask and You Shall Receive? Gender Differences in Negotiator's Beliefs About Requests for a Higher Salary," *Human Relations*, 2003.

Authors Claire Shipman, an ABC News reporter, and Katty Kay, a BBC World News America anchor, assert that women suffer from self-doubt in their book *The Confidence Code: The Science and Art of Self-Assurance—What Women Should Know*. Having interviewed some of the most influential women in the nation, they found that relative to their male competitors, women don't consider they're ready to be promoted until they've met 100 percent of the qualifications; they routinely underestimate not just their abilities, but also their performance. The takeaway: women lack confidence.

Admittedly, I didn't necessarily have the confidence to advocate for my own salary early on in my career. I didn't feel confident enough to negotiate in my twenties right out of college. On top of that, I thought that I was being treated fairly and trusted the people and process on the inside. So, I just didn't make it a point to try to ask for more money than what was being offered to me. As is the case with many students entering new jobs, I took the first offer of pay. If my peers made attempts to negotiate a higher starting salary, I was totally unaware of it.

One of the main reasons that I never really negotiated or tried to be hard-core when it came to my salary was that I didn't know what the salary bands were—whether I was at the low, middle, or high end. I had no idea where I fit in the equation. The hope for me was that the staffing team and hiring manager were not lowballing me. A lot of times, when I would leave a company to go to another company, there was a salary increase. But again, if you think you're doing well, you don't realize that you're underpaid. So, you're basically playing fierce catch-up by going to another company and asking for a higher salary. If you're already on the low end, how much does it really matter with a bump in pay, in terms of pay inequality? You're still at the fifth or tenth percentile.

When I graduated from college thirty years ago, making $25,000 in my mind was a decent salary. *I'm doing great.* Needless to say, if I could give my younger self advice, knowing then what I know now, I would have a direct conversation about salary. I would ask, *What's the salary range you normally pay for this position,* or, *What do you consider this position to be worth?* I would benchmark salaries in my field or industry to negotiate with as a baseline pay, a starting point. I would be more deliberate in my negations during those first job offers, ready to make counteroffers. I would negotiate the entirety of the compensation package to make sure that my needs were met.

I did start to barter back and forth as my corporate positions became more senior. At that point, my thought process was, *Okay, we're going to negotiate this. I want the following items.* I basically learned as I went along—with some outside guidance and assistance. I also had my father and husband coaching me from the sidelines and saying, *Okay, you need to ask for this, that, and the other thing.* On my own, I wasn't quite as confident in the beginning of my corporate career.

The confidence didn't come with asking for more money until I was in my midthirties. That is when I cultivated my voice. It was then that I knew, *Don't take what they give you, you don't have to be happy to have a job or happy with whatever they offer you. There's an opportunity to negotiate.* I would say to myself: *There's some bandwidth to ask for, and apply 10 percent more than the initial offer. Instead of five weeks of vacation, ask for ten. What's the worst thing that can happen? Ask for stock options, ask if they're going to buy those out from the former company that you worked for and if they are going to roll over the IRA. Ask for a sign-on bonus.*

I started to ask for more than just higher pay. Working

in HR, I had the chance to see people ask for and receive all these perks and fringe benefits. And I began to want those things too. I saw my counterparts, especially white men and women, asking for all sorts of personal benefits, from car service to a dog sitter. I thought, *Okay, well, either I'm just a novice at all this and these people know what the hell they're doing, or I need to be more brave in these conversations and ask for what it is that I really want.*

When I would sit across the table from my bosses for my performance appraisal, merit increases, and bonuses, if there were things that I just didn't agree with—I would speak up. I didn't let fear about how I would be perceived hinder me. Now, I have no problem with asking for what I want and getting what I believe I deserve.

What's ironic is that I could advocate and negotiate for other people, but for myself, that was hard to do at first. Yeah, I could champion and go to bat for my team—for the people who worked for me—asking for certain things. I could do that like nobody's business, but when it came to myself, I found it to be a lot more difficult. It just took a lot more time and effort to muster up the courage to do so.

Apparently, I'm not alone. According to Hannah Riley Bowles, a senior lecturer in public policy at Harvard's John F. Kennedy School of Government and faculty chair of its Women and Power program, "Women do substantially better negotiating for others than for themselves."[67] She points to research that shows that women perform better when their role is to advocate for others as opposed to negotiating for more pay for themselves.

---

67 Glynnis MacNicol, "Three Ways Women Can Negotiate Better on Behalf of Themselves," *Elle*, April 21, 2014, http://www.elle.com/culture/career-politics/advice/a14179/three-ways-women-can-negotiate-better/.

Interestingly enough, when I was still building up my confidence to advocate for a higher wage, it was brought to my attention, in some cases by C-Suite executives, that I was paid less than my counterparts, particularly the white men and women at the company. One CEO I used to report to pointed out the inequity in my pay. He gave me a substantial salary increase because of the shortfall. I never realized this because, of course, you don't know what you don't know. When you don't see everyone's salary or you don't know what the salary bands or ranges are, you don't know that your pay is unfair. I thought it was really terrific of him to even think to say to me: "Look, Michelle, we've got to bump up your salary because I don't know who did this or how this was done, but in comparison to your peers, you're grossly underpaid."

In another instance, it was brought up to me by the head of HR at one of the companies I worked for. He said, "You know, Michelle, your salary is really low." He brought that to my attention when I was at an executive level. Then when I became a global vice president living overseas, during my year-end performance review, which is when you hopefully get a merit increase, the CEO basically said to me: "You are grossly underpaid in comparison to your peers, so I gave you a substantial increase." It was very honest and very human of him.

I departed Novartis in 2010, and it should be duly noted that in that same year a US jury ordered Novartis to pay more than $250 million in punitive damages to current and former US female employees who alleged widespread gender discrimination. At the time, it was the largest case to go to trial and the biggest award in an employment discrimination case in US history, according to the plaintiff's law firm, Sanford Wittels & Heisler.[68] The case involved 5,600 women and Novartis reached a deal by agreeing to pay $152.5 million to settle the lawsuit. As part of the settlement, Novartis reportedly agreed to distribute money to eligible class members and spend an additional $22.5 million over three years to improve its personnel policies.

Five years later, the pharmaceutical giant was hit with another lawsuit—a $110 million claim against Texas-based medical company Alcon, which was acquired by Novartis in 2010. Alcon had routinely denied female employees equal pay and promotion opportunities. *Stat News* Pharmalot columnist Ed Silverman took note of how the lawsuit gained notice, in part because the women claimed the company fostered "a boys' club atmosphere and mentality that [was] hostile to women, and [restricted] access to leadership positions […] The lawsuit charged that women comprised less than 15 percent of senior Alcon management positions," which contributed to the discrimination. "The women also claimed companywide metrics were used to assess job performances that were 'subjective and used to downgrade the performance ratings of female employees,' because final decision-making authority [was] given to Alcon managers who [were] primarily male."[69] Novartis agreed to pay $8.2 million to settle the sex discrimination claim.

If you know you're a victim of pay discrimination, there are ways that you can fight back. During his term in office, President Obama made strides to strengthen equal pay laws,

---

68   "Novartis Pharmaceutical Gender Discrimination Class Action—$253 Million Jury Verdict; $175 Million Settlement," Sanford Wittels & Heisler, 2010, https://sanfordheisler.com/case/novartis-pharmaceutical-gender-discrimination-class-action/.

69   Ed Silverman, "Novartis Agrees to Settle Sex Discrimination Suit for $8m," *Stat News*, January 4, 2016, https://www.statnews.com/pharmalot/2016/01/04/sex-discrimination-novartis/.

including the very first piece of legislation he signed: the Lilly Ledbetter Fair Pay Act. It amended the Civil Rights Act of 1964 so that unfair pay complaints can be filed within 180 days of a discriminatory paycheck—the 180 days resets after each paycheck is issued. The law makes it easier for employees to effectively challenge unequal pay. It is named after a woman who discovered that her employer, Goodyear Tire & Rubber Co., was paying her less than her male counterparts, who were doing the same job. Ledbetter took her complaint all the way to the US Supreme Court.

In 2016, the Obama administration launched the Equal Pay Pledge to encourage businesses to take action to advance equal pay by conducting audits, reviewing processes, and embedding equal pay efforts into other initiatives. More than a hundred companies, including Amazon, L'Oréal USA, PepsiCo, Spotify, PwC, the Gap, and American Airlines, signed the pledge to report pay by race, gender, and ethnicity.[70]

Taking it a step further, the Obama administration sought novel methods to close the gender pay gap by unveiling seven "Hack the Pay Gap" apps to help women address disparities. One app was called "What's My Pay Gap?" and helped women see how the gender pay gap affected them individually depending on their race, occupation, and age. Another was the "PowerShift" app, a tool to help women negotiate their pay offers by providing clear, useful salary breakdown and range data on what men in a similar situation were making, and legal info about fair pay.

Apps like these allow anyone with a smart phone, tablet,

---

70 Diana Doukas, "Over 100 Companies Sign the Equal Pay Pledge," The White House, December 7, 2016, https://obamawhitehouse.archives.gov/blog/2016/12/07/over-100-companies-sign-equal-pay-pledge.

or computer to find tips on topics from typical pay ranges and skill level requirements for certain jobs to how to negotiate salaries, and more. I encourage any woman to seek out and utilize these kinds of tools.

Likewise, the American Association of University Women (AAUW) offers a resource: its Work Smart interactive workshop teaches women to craft and perfect persuasive salary pitches. Since 1881, AAUW has been promoting education for women and girls, and working hard on many fronts to close the gender pay gap. AAUW's key efforts include urging companies to conduct salary audits to proactively monitor and address gender-based pay differences, and pushing congressional action with such legislation as the Paycheck Fairness Act. AAUW has also been empowering women to know their professional worth and encouraging them to learn strategies on how to better negotiate a fair salary.

Stay on top of what you're worth by benchmarking as much information as you can about what others are earning based on your job field, location, industry, and company. To learn current market rates for the job, you can also use calculators like those found at Salary.com and Monster.com, which offer pay ranges for thousands of job titles in almost every industry. Recruiters also have access to information on salaries in various fields and industries.

The bottom line is to honor your worth! Speak up and be honest with your employer about your salary needs. Don't make demands per se, but be specific about what you want and have the market data to substantiate your request. *If you don't ask, you don't get.* The worst thing that can happen is they say no. In turn, this will give you a greater sense of where you stand in the company.

There Is No Place For Self-Doubt

I always found it fascinating when some of my male counterparts over the years would have reservations about giving their female employees feedback for fear of a lawsuit or other problems. I found this comical. Every individual deserves to receive some sort of feedback no matter what role they are in. To withhold that kind of information for fear of hurting someone's feelings or the threat of litigation is no excuse in my view. Feedback is a gift and everyone deserves to receive it—the good, the bad, and the ugly.

Research shows that there is a big difference in how men and women respond to receiving feedback from their peers. In other words, there is also a gender gap in feedback and self-perception. Published in the *Academy of Management Learning and Education*, Margarita Mayo, a professor of leadership at IBE Business School in Madrid, conducted a study that involved MBA students around the average age of thirty and with six and a half years of work experience.

"At the beginning of the one-year MBA program, students were assigned to learning teams of five or six members"[71] to discover how they would react to feedback they received about their leadership competences from one another. After the end of the trimester, the members of each team rated each other on leadership skills. Looking at the feedback over time, Mayo found that while all the students started off by rating themselves higher than they were rated by their peers, women adapted to their team members' perceptions of them much more quickly than men did.

For example, a female MBA student might give herself a

---

71 Margarita Mayo, "The Gender Gap in Feedback and Self-Perception," *Harvard Business Review*, August 31, 2016, ttps://hbr.org/2016/08/the-gender-gap-in-feedback-and-self-perception.

4.5 out of a 5-point rating scale of leaderships competencies, while her peers might rate her a 3. That female student would then become more likely to give herself a lower rating such as a 3.5 or a 3. In comparison, a male MBA student would rate himself a 5 but with a peer rating of 3, he might adjust his self-rating to 4.5 or 4.[72]

Put in another way, the women more quickly aligned their self-awareness about their leaderships skills with peer feedback, whereas men continued to rationalize and inflate their self-image about their leadership qualities over time. Mayo further notes that the results for the study demonstrate women have a greater sensitivity to social cues.

There is a stark contrast between how women view themselves versus how others perceive them. Writing in the *Harvard Business Review*, Mayo points out: "Women's alignment of their self-image to reflect what others think of them increases self-awareness, which is the first step for learning."[73] Thus, "Women should be motivated to seek out training and advice to develop their leadership competencies and improve their chances of promotion," writes Mayo, who teaches authentic leadership, change, and work/life balance.

"When assimilation of negative feedback involves doubts about one's competence and lower confidence, it can discourage women to take on new challenges," Mayo explains. In contrast, when men preserve their positive self-views, this "can encourage them to seek out new challenges and take advantage of opportunities." Even when women are self-confident and do seek out a promotion and higher compensation, research shows that negotiating women are 30 percent more

---

72 Margarita Mayo, Maria Kakarika, Juan Carlos Pastor, and Stéphane Brutus, "Aligning or Inflating Your Leadership Self-Image? A Longitudinal Study of Responses to Peer Feedback in MBA Teams," *Academy of Management Learning and Education*, July 20, 2012.

73 Margarita Mayo, "The Gender Gap in Feedback and Self-Perception."

likely than men to receive negative feedback; they're either "intimidating," "too aggressive," or "bossy."[74]

Women are punished and are not given pay increases when they try to negotiate—pretty much no matter what they ask for or how they ask—per Harvard Kennedy School's Hannah Riley Bowles, who has been studying gender effects on negotiation through laboratory studies, case studies, and extensive interviews with executives and employees in diverse fields.[75] Her research has demonstrated that both men and women will consider the consequences for asking for more money, but women tend to worry more about how they will be perceived—and rightly so, it seems.

In 2015, then Reddit CEO Ellen Pao became a game changer and an international symbol for gender imbalance in Silicon Valley when she lost a landmark sex discrimination lawsuit against a former employer, the venture capital firm Kleiner Perkins Caufield & Byers. Pao's lawyers argued she was an accomplished junior partner passed over for promotion because the firm she worked for used different standards to judge men and women.[76] Pao claimed she was fired when she complained about discrimination.

After around eight months on the job as CEO, Pao resigned from Reddit following user backlash against the firing of a well-liked employee. Pao reportedly even received death threats from users angry at her handling of the situation even

---

74   L.V. Anderson, "Managers Are Afraid to Give Women Negative Feedback—Until Women Ask for Promotions," *Slate*, September 28, 2016, http://www.slate.com/blogs/xx_factor/2016/09/28/managers_are_afraid_to_give_women_negative_feedback_until_women_ask_for.html.

75   Maria Konnikova, "Lean Out: The Dangers for Women Who Negotiate," the *New Yorker*, June 10, 2014, http://www.newyorker.com/science/maria-konnikova/lean-out-the-dangers-for-women-who-negotiate.

76   "Jury Says Silicon Valley Firm Did Not Discriminate Against Ellen Pao," NBC News, March 27, 2015, https://www.nbcnews.com/news/us-news/jury-reaches-verdict-ellen-pao-gender-discrimination-lawsuit-n331626.

though there were no specifics on the dismissal of Victoria Taylor, the director of talent who managed the site's "Ask Me Anything" subreddit (discussion area). Pao issued an apology to users for shutting down the popular subforum, yet she too was forced out. Remember, *no second chances* for women who mess up. Nevertheless, Pao is known for having highlighted women's issues and eliminating salary negotiations at Reddit to help female employees achieve parity with men in pay.

In the *PBS News Hour* story "Ask the Headhunter: Women Don't Cause the Pay Gap. Employers Do," Nick Corcodilos boldly declares that the media and experts should "stop blaming women for the gender pay gap [...] Employers should change their behavior."

Employers who pay unfairly do so for obvious reasons— because they can get away with it, claims Corcodilos, who started headhunting in Silicon Valley in 1979 and has answered over thirty thousand questions from the Ask the Headhunter community over the past decade. "I've been a headhunter for a long time. I've seen more job offers and observed more salary negotiations than you'll see in a lifetime," he shares. "I've observed more employers decide what salaries or wages to pay than I can count. And I am convinced the media and the experts are full of baloney about the pay gap between men and women."[77]

The times are changing; recent research supports Corcodilos's point. Over the years, surveys did show that the top reasons women quit their jobs included: dissatisfaction with the boss and work/life balance. But researchers now note that motherhood and family are not the reasons thirtysomething

---

77 Nick Corcodilos, "Ask the Headhunter: Women Don't Cause the Pay Gap. Employers Do," *PBS News Hour*, April 12, 2016, http://www.pbs.org/newshour/making-sense/ask-the-headhunter-women-dont-cause-the-pay-gap-employers-do/.

women are leaving organizations. They're leaving chiefly because they're tired of making less money than their similarly (or less) qualified male coworkers, according to a special report on millennial women from the International Consortium for Executive Development Research.[78]

"Our research shows that the top reasons why [millennial] women leave are not due to family issues. The top reasons are due to pay and career advancement," states the ICEDR report's coauthor Lauren Noël.[79] The report itself quotes women under thirty saying that the number one reason they quit is: "I have found a job that pays more elsewhere."

Millennial women (ages nineteen to thirty-five as of 2016) are "the generation of female workers that has figured out that they're not the problem. Unlike their older peers, per the report, they've figured out that when they're not getting paid what they want" or what they deserve, "they quit and go to work for an employer who will pay them more."[80]

Much like Ask the Headhunter's Nick Corcodilos, turning all of the previous analysis on its head is the Catalyst report "The Myth of the Ideal Worker: Does Doing All the Right Things Really Get Women Ahead?" by Nancy M. Carter and Christine Silva, which tackles persistent notions about the gender gap. Career advancement strategies used by women and men were compared, to determine if using the same strategies ultimately leads to the same career outcomes. The findings revealed that when women did all the things they have been told will help them get ahead—using the same tactics as

78　Lauren Noël and Christie Hunter Arscott, "What Executives Need to Know About Millennial Women," International Consortium for Executive Development Research, 2016, https://www.icedr.org/research/documents/15_millennial_women.pdf.

79　Nick Corcodilos, "Ask the Headhunter: Women Don't Cause the Pay Gap. Employers Do."

80　Ibid.

men—they still advanced less than their male counterparts and had slower pay growth.

The Catalyst report showed that the "men were significantly more likely than [the] women to have countered their first post-MBA offer by asking for a higher salary (50 percent of men, [compared to] 31 percent of women)."[81] But the authors discovered that women were more likely than men to ask for career-building experiences and training, and just as likely as men to negotiate for higher compensation or job placement during the hiring process for their current job. Yet the men in the study (which followed the career paths of 3,345 MBA graduates from around the world) made more money and advanced further and faster than their female counterparts.

When asked whether they had specifically negotiated for a higher-level position or greater compensation during the hiring process for their current job, Catalyst found no significant difference between the approaches of women and men overall. The study revealed that "47 percent of women and 52 percent of men reported that they had countered" their initial offers "during the hiring process by asking for a higher salary." Furthermore, "14 percent of women and 15 percent of men had countered by asking for a position at a higher job level."[82]

Such data raises some insightful questions: "Maybe it's not that women don't ask, but that men don't have to? Are men being rewarded without even having to ask? Do women have to raise their hands and seek recognition to an even greater extent than men do to receive the same outcomes?"[83] The an-

81 Nancy M. Carter and Christine Silva, "The Myth of the Ideal Worker: Does Doing All the Right Things Really Get Women Ahead?" Catalyst, October 1, 2011, http://www.catalyst.org/system/files/The_Myth_of_the_Ideal_Worker_Does_Doing_All_the_Right_Things_Really_Get_Women_Ahead.pdf.

82 Ibid.

83 Ibid.

swer to all of the above is yes. Which chiefly boils down to the point that women are being evaluated according to different criteria, even if the person doing the evaluation doesn't realize it. Not all discrimination in the workplace is the result of bias against women. Sometimes it's actually bias in favor of men. In such instances, it doesn't matter what personal characteristic we're talking about—gender, race, social background. Meaning, men have a tendency to reward their own, which allows white male privilege to prevail in corporate America.

We should applaud the efforts of advocates who are trying to level the playing field for equal pay. If you are among the countless working women who feel as if they're not getting the credit they deserve, especially when it comes to pay and promotions, it is time to act. So, yes, the first step toward successful negotiating is making the decision to negotiate in the first place; knowing that you have the skill set, knowledge, and experience for the job, so you don't have to be grateful for any salary offered.

Negotiate the whole package. If you settle for a compensation package that doesn't meet your needs and wants, you won't be satisfied in the long run. Create a list of must-haves and nice-but-not-necessary benefits, advises the Five O'Clock Club. For three decades, the Five O'Clock Club has offered a targeted, strategic, research-driven approach to career development.[84] "Always let the employer make the first bid so you have a starting point for your counter-negotiations."

A question that the Five O'Clock Club often hears is: "How long should someone stay at a job?"[85] The response

---

84 "Salary Negotiation and the New Age of Interviewing," Five O'Clock Club, September 22, 2016, https://fiveoclockclub.com/blog/salary-negotiation-new-age-interviewing/.

85 "Will You Actually Get Promoted, or Are You Simply "Promotable?" Five O'Clock Club, September 23, 2016, https://fiveoclockclub.com/blog/will-actually-get-promoted-simply-promotable/.

varies. "In certain industries, such as entertainment [...] job hopping is to be expected." But in other industries, employees are expected to be more stable. "If you're learning new skills that increase your marketability and fit" your vision, "or if you are set to get a promotion, you should stay." Bear in mind that "there's a big difference between being 'promotable' and being in a position where you are actually about to be promoted." Likability is relevant, but at the same time, don't be a people-pleaser or allow yourself to be a scapegoat—taking the rap for others' mishaps. Be a team player but don't take on dead-end assignments just to help a coworker so you can be perceived as a nice person.

Five ways you'll know that you are promotable per the Five O'Clock Club:

1) You are "invited to meetings where your peers are not included."
2) You are privy to company information that your peers are unaware of.
3) You are "asked for input on major decisions."
4) You are "assigned to important task forces" or special projects.
5) You are "given more responsibility, including tasks for which your boss is responsible."[86]

"Even if you work hard and are valued, your boss may still keep you right where you are." You might even be undermined by your boss if he or she dislikes you. All the more reason to be "clearly visible in the power structure to get promoted." On the other hand, you may be doing well but your company is not, which also could deter your chances—and anyone else's

---

86 *Ibid.*

for that matter—of moving a rung up the ladder.

The 2016 "Women in the Workplace" study by McKinsey & Company and LeanIn.org revealed that "for every 100 women promoted, 130 men are promoted." Moreover, "Almost twice as many men are hired from the outside as directors and more than three times as many are hired as SVPs." The study also found that "only 29 percent of black women think the opportunities go to the most deserving employees, compared to 47 percent of white women, 43 percent of Asian women, and 41 percent of Hispanic women."[87]

As women of color, we must *step into our power*. This is played out in the film *Hidden Figures*, adapted from Margot Lee Shetterly's book *Hidden Figures: The American Dream and the Untold Story of the Black Women Mathematicians Who Helped Win the Space Race*, which focuses on three real-life African American female pioneers: Katherine Johnson, Dorothy Vaughan, and Mary Jackson. These female pioneers were part of NASA's team of women that had the job of a *computer*. Before the electronic computers that we're familiar with today, this group (essentially mathematicians) calculated by hand the complex equations that allowed space heroes like Neil Armstrong, Alan Shepard, and John Glenn to travel safely to space.

Six months after the attack on Pearl Harbor, the National Advisory Committee for Aeronautics and Langley began recruiting African American women with college degrees to work as human computers. While they did the same work as their white counterparts, African American human computers were paid less, and relegated to the segregated west section of the Langley campus, where they had to use separate

---

87 LeanIn.org and McKinsey & Company, "Women in the Workplace," https://womeninthekworkplace.com/.

dining and bathroom facilities. They became known as the *West Computers*. Despite having the same education, they had to retake college courses they'd already passed, and were often never considered for promotions or other jobs within NACA.

In December 1943, Vaughan joined NACA's segregated West Area Computing Unit—a group that she would run six years later as NACA's first black supervisor, thanks to her mathematical prowess and leadership tenacity.[88] Albeit, the film takes liberties with timelines and events; one of the film's three narrative threads follows how Vaughan (Octavia Spencer) avoids becoming obsolete, and her pursuit of a formal promotion to supervisor.[89] Despite her successes and capabilities, she is constantly passed over for promotions. She then learns that her entire department of human computers will soon be replaced by an electronic computer—an enormous IBM mainframe that's being installed. A gifted technician, Vaughan seeks out a book from the local library (a segregated library from which she's been thrown out); she soon learns the programming language FORTRAN and becomes NASA's resident expert programmer.

She had the foresight to learn the language and teach it to the other women in the computer pool, and in turn helped the agency transition from human to IBM computers.

It is a fact that Vaughan was one of the first on the job to master computer programming and coding languages like FORTRAN.[90] Her leadership and programming skills made

---

88 Margot Lee Shetterly, *Hidden Figures: The American Dream and the Untold Story of the Black Women Mathematicians Who Helped Win the Space Race* (William Morrow, 2016), pgs. 36, 172–73.

89 *Hidden Figures*, directed by Theodore Melfi (2016; 20th Century Fox).

90 Margot Lee Shetterly, *Hidden Figures: The American Dream and the Untold Story of the Black Women Mathematicians Who Helped Win the Space Race* (William Morrow, 2016), pgs. 204–206.

her an invaluable instructor. Vaughan's work was integral to the success of the space race, as well as the Scout Launch Vehicle Program that started in 1961. The stories of Vaughan and the other "hidden figures" is exemplary of how women can be more diligent and vigilant in terms of how they manage their own careers. The takeaway here is to look for different and unique opportunities to highlight your strengths and showcase your talents. Figure out how to differentiate yourself from the masses. Think broader about the role that you play and the impact that you have.

The best way for women to bargain for more pay and a promotion without blowing themselves up or face pushback is by linking up with their tried and true anchors. This is where mentors and sponsors come into play to help you up your game. Remember AT&T CDO Cynthia Marshall's sports analogy: your mentor as your trainer will show you how to maneuver within the organization, and your sponsor as your agent will help broker the best deal on your behalf.

I have to reiterate how crucial sponsors are in giving you real career traction and putting you on the path to power and influence by affecting three things: pay raises, high-profile or stretch assignments, and promotions. Based on focus group research, CTI discovered the following:

> When it comes to asking for a pay raise, the majority of men (67 percent) and women (70 percent) resist confronting their boss. With a sponsor in their corner, however, nearly half of men and 38 percent of women will make the request— and the focus group research suggests that they will succeed in getting the raise. When it comes to getting assigned to a high-visibility team or plum project, some 43 percent of male and 36 percent of female employees will approach their man-

ager to make the request. With a sponsor, the numbers rise to 56 percent and 44 percent, respectively.[91]

CTI's research further shows that "individuals who are most satisfied with their rate of advancement are individuals with sponsors."

What does all this empirical data mean? Simply this: it is not enough for women to just ask, they must understand organizational structures and recognize race and gender stereotypes. While it's difficult to change workplace bias, discrimination, favoritism, or white male privilege, women at all levels of the corporate ladder can benefit by learning to negotiate in ways that will render the best outcome. This is in accordance to each woman's own situation—from where she stands in her organization. It is a disservice to talk of pay and promotion as a zero-sum game.

Key Steps

1. Don't be afraid to ask for what you want and get what you deserve. Just be aware of your company's culture and how you're being perceived by decision makers.
2. Remember that hard work alone will not pay off. Don't simply put your head down.
3. Position yourself for a promotion by getting assigned to task forces or special projects. Raise your hand for high-visibility assignments.
4. Always be prepared to show you have a track record of success. Maintain self-confidence in your capabilities and performance. There's no place for self-doubt.

---

91 Schawbel, "Sylvia Ann Hewlett: Find a Sponsor Instead of a Mentor."

5. Work with a starting point—a base pay—for your salary negotiations. Know your monetary value. Don't lower your expectations.

6. Role play if necessary to prepare in advance for a conversation over pay if you have some trepidation about salary negotiations.

7. Use a strategic and research-driven approach to your career advancement. Benchmark your industry, your company, and your line of work.

8. Leverage your mentors and sponsors to assist with salary negotiations and promotions.

9. Rely on your sponsors and network to help you gain visibility in your organization's power structure in order to gain upward mobility.

10. Be sure your employer values you and your work, otherwise you are unlikely to move up.

6

GOING GLOBAL AND UPWARD MOBILITY

One must travel to learn.
—Mark Twain

A s a young girl, I loved geography. I would point to the world map and tell my parents: "Someday I am going to visit Europe, Africa, and Asia. I may even choose to live there!" I always had a fascination with different cultures. At age seven I had a vision of what I wanted to be, what I wanted to do, and where I wanted to go in life. Little did my parents know, I was prophesizing my future.

As previously discussed, in 2000 I went to work for Novartis Pharma, the subsidiary of the Swiss pharmaceuticals company Novartis AG. I came in as a director of diversity, working for the US head of diversity, and was promoted after two years to be executive director of diversity. Then after another year, I was promoted to vice president of diversity, and then the global chief diversity officer. It was during this period of my career that I began traveling overseas more.

I could travel with ease, without worries; I didn't have the kind of responsibilities at home as some of my colleagues. Yes, I had my husband David and my five-pound toy Yorkshire terrier, Myles Davis, but that's different than having two or three kids at home waiting for you. Therefore, I wasn't missing birthday parties, basketball games, dance recitals, graduations, and all those kinds of family events—special moments—or dealing with those specific work/life-balance issues. From a managerial standpoint, my home life opened some doors for me and made it easier for me to take advantage of international assignments. If I had to travel to another continent—Europe, Africa, South America, or wherever—senior management wasn't overly concerned about my family obligations. One of my career goals was to have a bigger job with more responsibilities on a global level.

Making myself so readily available and approachable, in part, falls in line with the desire to be twice as good and work twice as hard. So, yeah, I was always the first one in the office, always the last one to leave, always the first to raise my hand for that stretch assignment. The division CEO would have these roundtable discussions, where he would bring high-potential talent together to talk about career opportunities. This one time during a luncheon talk he asked everyone sitting around the table: "Who's interested in potentially moving to Basel, Switzerland, for an assignment?"

Basel, that's where the global corporate headquarters for Novartis was located and that was where he worked as well. I was the first person to raise my hand. As a matter of fact, of the fifteen people who were sitting in that room, I was the *only* one who raised a hand. I blurted out, "I'll go."

Somewhat surprised, he replied, "You would?" in his German accent.

Without hesitation I answered, "Sure I would."

For some company employees, it's just not plausible to work and live abroad. On top of that, there are those colleagues who question your willingness to leave the United States and relocate to some foreign country where you don't speak the language, you barely look like the people native to that country, and it's a totally different culture—

all of that change just for the sake of a job? Absolutely, yes!

I was very clear about my intent. I had my hand raised high in the air, because I knew it was what I wanted. I knew that with respect to working for this particular multinational pharmaceutical company, if I wanted to get to the next level, going global was something I needed to do. Once again, I had to check that box.

Less than six months later, the head of HR for the pharma division called me and said, "We have this opportunity for you in Basel. You raised your hand in that room, are you serious about taking on this job?"

Again, I replied with an emphatic, "Yes!" I went home and spoke to David about it. I've always talked about living abroad over the years, even before I worked for a global company. I was thinking, *Wow, I'm going to live in Europe!* It was part of charting the course and trajectory of my career.

When I got the call from HR, David was a seasoned professional, managing a multimillion-dollar business product for AT&T. He had been there close to twenty years, but would not rule out doing something different in his career. I didn't hold back as I told David about the phone call. "Look, if I get this job, it's a big job. Are you going to retire? What's going to happen?" I asked him.

David didn't bite his tongue; one of the first things he said to me was: "I will only consider moving if you are guaranteed a promotion. We will not move and have me give up my career for you to take a lateral position. Because you want to be vice president, it has to be a step up from where you are. Yeah, I'll just retire."

We nodded our heads in agreement. At that point, David was embedded in his career, but he was willing to leave his job for the betterment of mine.

For David, the timing was right too. During this period, AT&T's aim was to become a communications giant with interests in the telephone business, cable television, and wireless communications, and as such, the company was doing a significant amount of reorganizing and right-sizing. AT&T had announced the sale of its cable business to the Comcast Corporation and there were ten thousand layoffs over two years—2001 and 2002—in the company's business, consumer, and corporate units.[92] About two thousand of those employees who were laid off worked in New Jersey, where many of the company's operations were based. Most of the layoffs affected employees working in management, like David.

It was under these circumstances that David also said to me, "Chelleton," his nickname for me, "if you are guaranteed the promotion and all the ducks line up in terms of your relocation package, the next time a downsizing is announced, I will volunteer." So when he went in to resign, he actually had to wait, because he wanted to get a payout. AT&T was offering buyouts, it seemed, every six months or so. David later told me his support manager asked him three times if he was sure that he wanted to leave the company and move abroad. David wasn't concerned with finding employment in Switzerland because of his skill set, education, and the major corporations there that would undoubtedly have to staff roles to which he was accustomed. His support made it easier for me to leave and on top of that we didn't have to go home and talk to kids and say, *Guess what, Mommy and Daddy* . . . I just had one person I had to answer to and that was my husband. David understood that this wasn't just something that I wanted

---

92 Seth Schiesel, "AT&T to Cut About 5% of Work Force," the *New York Times*, January 7, 2003, http://www.nytimes.com/2003/01/07/business/technology-at-t-to-cut-about-5-of-work-force.html.

to do, it was something that I *needed* to do. If I wanted to have the big job and sit in the big chair as the global chief diversity officer, I had to move to where the CEO was—in Basel, Switzerland.

I had developed an affinity for Switzerland. I adored its beautiful landscapes and architecture. Besides, David and I had almost six months to marinate on it. So I knew that if they asked me the question I was going to say yes, and pack up our house, the dog, my husband—and leave. And that's exactly what we did. David took the buyout, and relocated with me and Myles Davis to Basel, Switzerland, in 2006.

A lot of the traveling spouses of expats were content not to work again, but David always wanted to make his own money. That was important to him. So, during a brief downtime upon his arrival, David used his passion for golf to write a children's book called *I Want to Play Golf,* which is a conversation piece for children and their caretakers. It offers several inspirational messages for children to not only navigate their way around the sport but also through life.

After having settled in Switzerland for almost two years, David then decided that he wanted to reenter the corporate workforce, and he began working for Syngenta AG, a global Swiss agribusiness that produces agrochemicals and seeds.

In my role as global chief diversity officer, I reported directly to the CEO of the pharma division with an additional reporting relationship to the corporate head of HR. I also had exposure to the chairman and CEO of the entire company. I had the big job; I had the top diversity job. I was responsible for providing strategic direction and guidance to the chairman, board of directors, divisional CEO, executive committee, as well as a host of other key stakeholders, to ensure that all divisional diversity practices, strategies, and change management initiatives were globally aligned and linked to the business strategy of Novartis. Plus, I developed meaningful and cost-effective strategies that supported all aspects of Novartis' local and global diversity objectives, outreach activities, and initiatives. I managed a multimillion-dollar annual budget and a team of twelve direct reports, along with a global infrastructure of 107 diversity champions in key markets and seventy-three countries. What's more, my team and I designed a comprehensive global governance model for thirteen employee resource groups at Novartis.

The Novartis campus in Basel is probably one of the largest employers in Switzerland. Conceived by the famous Italian architect Vittorio Magnago Lampugnani, Novartis' headquarters had been transformed from an industrial complex to an ultramodern campus of innovation, knowledge, and encounter. On that corporate campus were thousands of people from ninety countries, representing over ninety nationalities. Thus, you heard different languages every day—mostly German—and you saw different types of people every day—mostly Europeans, Americans, Asians, Australians, and Africans.

I felt at home. Why not? Studies show that Switzerland is not only a thriving center for business but a good place for ambitious individuals ready to jump-start or jettison a career. Actually, Switzerland is ranked the best place for career advancement, according to HSBC's survey "Expat Explorer: Balancing Life Abroad," which looks at the finances, career progression, and cultural experiences worldwide of over twenty thousand expats (short for *expatriate*, a person residing in a country that is not their native homeland). More than half of the expats surveyed found their work to be more fulfilling in Switzerland than back at home.

Additionally, expats saw an improvement in their financial well-being by living in Switzerland. The three main financial benefits: receiving a higher salary than at home, enjoying greater disposable income, and being able to save more. Life is about more than just the salary in Switzerland. Seven in ten reported an overall improvement in their quality of life after moving there, compared with the global average of 53 percent.[93]

Not only did we enjoy a better quality of life, David and I treated our move to Switzerland as if it were an adventure. It was easier for me to adjust to a new way of living because I had already been traveling to Basel quite a bit in my previous position. I was falling in love with the place. I enjoyed the rich culture, the food, and the people who I found to be very friendly. Our home in New Jersey was in the suburbs, where there was a lot of farmland. So, when we decided to move to a different country, we wanted to immerse ourselves in a totally different experience. That meant getting an apartment in the city, which was the best decision that we could have made. We could take the tram, a rail system much like San Francisco's BART. When there were jazz festivals, Christmas bazaars, and different things that were happening in the city, we were right in the heart of the place. What's more, we had family and friends who visited Basel regularly.

We had such a terrific time based on the locale and who we networked with; we were quite comfortable in our surroundings as expats. We had our weekly routine down: David found an Italian barber who knew how to cut his hair as good as, or even better than, some of the previous barbers back home in the US. I even found a great Dominican hairstylist who coiffed my hair for me every Saturday afternoon. As a woman of color, you know how our hair is as important as our wardrobe. It had to be done well!

---

93 "Expat Explorer: Balancing Life Abroad," HSBC Expat, 2015.

Just as important, we developed a nice network of diverse friends who were African, Chinese, British, French, Indian, Swiss, and German. We extended ourselves to different people from all walks of life. It was an amazing experience getting to learn all about their cultures and getting to hear stories of what it was like for them growing up. We met other African Americans from the States—artists, dancers, a guy who was an opera singer from San Francisco—who felt like they could make it there in Switzerland.

I remember sitting on the tram going to work one morning, and there was this Swiss couple who started talking about me in German. They were trying to figure out my nationality—was I American, African, Middle Eastern? As I exited the tram, I said to them: "*Adieu, ich wünsch Ihne e schöne daag,*" which is *Goodbye, have a nice day,* in German. They looked at me like I had three heads and eight legs. So, yes, we learned the language. You know that when individuals come to America, they typically speak English to everybody whether they really know the language or not. There are expectations in the USA that you should know some English. Well, in Swiss society, that's what they assume about Americans—when you go there, you'll speak German or French. They almost force you to learn; in most cases, they're not going to speak to you in English unless they absolutely must.

Not only did David and I learn to speak German, but even our dog Myles understood both English and German—even some French—because all his sitters were multilingual. A major plus for us was that the Swiss, as is the case with many European countries, were much more dog friendly than Americans. Meaning, we could carry Myles practically anywhere we went. He could go with us to the post office, bank, a department store, and even into most restaurants and cafés.

He could ride on the train. Not to mention, Myles loved all the surrounding trees and having free access to the parks throughout the city. Unlike here in the States, we didn't have to contend with people snarling and telling us: "Oh, don't let your dog in the grass." So Myles didn't mind leaving New Jersey behind; he was now living carefree in Switzerland.

Behind the Glass Border

To put things into perspective, roughly eight million Americans live and work abroad in 160-plus countries, not including military personnel, per the US State Department. "That makes them equivalent to the combined populations of Chicago, Los Angeles, Philadelphia, and Tucson," notes the Association of Americans Resident Overseas.[94] This also means that the world is a wide-open job market from North America to Europe, Asia, Africa, Australia, and South America.

Not only did living in another country challenge me to learn more about myself, it also made me a more marketable employee down the road. For those of us working at multinational companies, the ability to work and lead across cultures proved to be a necessary skill. As with many people, I discovered that a willingness to take on an international assignment and relocate to another country benefited my upward mobility in a global organization—not only Novartis, but Credit Suisse as well—when presented the opportunity. What's more, understanding how a company operates internationally is key to understanding its overall business and strategy. Besides, there are employers who have made investments in high-potential employees, to develop an international mind-set and gain international experience. The thinking is that some of these

---

94 "8.7 million Americans (Excluding Military) Live in 160-Plus Countries," Americans Helping Americans Abroad, https://www.aaro.org/about-aaro/8m-americans-abroad.

high performers could one day ascend to the C-Suite.

And yet, not everything is rosy. While some employees see the benefits of international assignments, others face both personal and professional challenges with the destination country, such as not receiving adequate cultural awareness training, losing touch with the parent company, or strained spousal or personal relationships, as family members struggle with culture shock, reports Communicaid, a leading provider of English and foreign language courses, intercultural training, and global communication skills.[95] Relocating abroad also comes with a whole new set of cultural norms, attitudes, and behaviors. You must be able to integrate your new cultural surroundings with your own unique cultural background. Your peak performance is impacted by your having the cultural skills to adapt to, and understand, new customs and traditions. It's also imperative that you pay a little attention to the economic, political, and cultural differences.

I was more fortunate than many of my female counterparts. Just as there is talk of a glass—and concrete—ceiling, women are also held back behind glass *borders*. PwC's "Developing Tomorrow's Female Leaders" report discovered that 69 percent of female millennials desire "to work outside of their home country during their career."[96] In fact, 63 percent of female millennials see international experience as critical to career advancement. Yet only 20 percent of current international assignees are female. That's particularly impactful, given PwC's prediction that the number of workers who will

95 Matthew MacLachlan, "The Best (and Worst) Things About an Expat Assignment," Communicaid, November 9, 2016, https://www.communicaid.com/cross-cultural-training/blog/living-and-working-abroad-the-expatriate-experience/.

96 "Next Generation Diversity: Developing Tomorrow's Female Leaders," PriceWaterhouseCoopers, 2014, http://www.pwc.co.za/en/publications/next-generation-diversity.html.

take on global assignments will rise by 50 percent over the next decade. This situation begs the question: is it because women aren't being considered for the international assignments, or because they aren't taking them?

In a report titled "Misconceptions About Women in the Global Arena Keep Their Numbers Low," Catalyst tried to find those answers by interviewing more than a thousand women and men, including current and former expatriates, their spouses, frequent fliers, and human resources executives. Survey respondents believed that women were not as "internationally mobile" as men, "yet 80 percent of women expatriates (working abroad) have never turned down relocation, compared to 71 percent of men." Some respondents believed clients outside the US were "not as comfortable doing business with women as they were with men." Yet "76 percent of expat women said being a woman had a positive or neutral impact on their effectiveness overseas."[97]

Culture is another perceived barrier for women. Some cultures are less supportive of women, so organizations will avoid sending women there, for fear that they cannot be effective. The report concluded that misconceptions about women's abilities to handle international assignments and their willingness to accept these assignments are key barriers to women getting selected for the global business arena.

What's more, research shows that people of color face another set of challenges if they work for a multinational corporation and try to move up the ladder. Whereas international assignments "are considered an important ticket to get punched for upward mobility, there is a gap between the

---

97 Catalyst, "Misconceptions About Women in the Global Arena Keep Their Numbers Low," http://www.catalyst.org/media/misconceptions-about-women-global-arena-keep-their-numbers-low.

number of minorities on expat assignments and the number of nonminorities on expat assignments," especially white men, a study by ORC Worldwide (now Mercer) revealed.[98] "Over 80 percent of the companies surveyed believed that global assignments are key to upward mobility in their company. Yet, only 14 percent of those companies make special efforts to ensure diversity in the expatriate ranks."

"In other words, women and minorities aren't receiving these international assignments commensurate with their representation in middle to senior levels of management, and they continue to be underrepresented at these levels to begin with," per this report.

This is the reason I raised my hand in the first place. This is why I spoke up about my willingness to reside in Basel. That move paid off for me. Even before relocating, a significant benefit was the chance to experience a different culture first-hand, develop a broader worldview, and travel extensively to another country or countries. One thing I had in common with other expats is that global assignments can increase one's management and leadership skills by helping you become more patient, tolerant, flexible, adaptable, and humble.

On the other hand, many expats in the ORC study complained about receiving little to no preparation and support by their companies prior to, during, and upon their return. Knowing more about the culture, history, language, thinking style, work approach, lifestyle, and values of the host country were all mentioned, as well as more information about the actual package, what to expect and what not to, and the process for returning once the assignment was over. Again, David

98 Patricia Pope, "Going Global: Will an International Assignment Benefit Your Career?" *Diversity MBA*, September 13, 2009, http://diversitymbamagazine.com/going-global-will-an-international-assignment-benefit-your-career.

and I had traveled to Switzerland, thus we equipped ourselves for what to expect and to transition smoothly once we made the move. Novartis was very good about handling key items during our stay, like our taxes.

Another challenge mentioned by ORC was the importance and difficulty of maintaining relationships with mentors and sponsors in the US while on international assignment. *Out of sight, out of mind* was the reality for a significant number of respondents who noted that they bore the burden to proactively work at keeping and building relationships with influential executives in their home country.

My thoughts on this are: While you should size up opportunities for an international move within your organization, you can't just dive right in. Do your own due diligence. Meaning, you need to research the cultural norms, learn the languages, and understand the nuances of that country. Don't rely on assumptions. The ORC report cited a case study where a Chinese American, who accepted an international assignment, thought that he would have a positive experience living and working in China because of his heritage. But it proved to be quite the opposite. He explained that in most cultures, a white American will have the rites of passage an ethnic minority won't. In China, he noticed, there was a near preferential treatment of whites. He felt that Chinese people were very hospitable to whites, but treated each other relatively harshly. On a personal note, his family fit in better because they didn't have to worry as much about standing out physically as in the USA.

ORC concluded that anyone who is different, and has been the outsider in a society, can easily adapt to a global assignment. Minority expats tended to be more conscious of the environment and respectful of others in the host country, which helped them fit in and adapt. And for some, being the only black person in the room proved to be an advantageous dynamic. ORC further suggested that women have coping/interpersonal skills which are useful in conflict resolution and building relationships on global assignments.

Several of the women and minority professionals surveyed ultimately ended up leaving their companies because their success wasn't acknowledged or rewarded. However, despite initial disappointment, each of them moved forward in their careers, working for other corporations in more senior-level positions. In the end, they still managed to leverage their international experience and their career advancement. The same could be said for my own experience—and then some. That promotion to global chief diversity officer and my relocation to Basel was, in fact, my entry into the C-Suite.

Since preplanning is crucial, I would advise anyone to consider joining groups on LinkedIn to get the inside scoop on what the industry landscape is like abroad. Read foreign trade magazines to stay abreast on the latest developments. In actively pursuing an overseas post, think of it as a recognizance mission, whereby you gather information by observing. I know from experience that the best way to learn about a new place is to spend as much time as you can with the local residents.

If the company you work for has offices around the world, plan to take your next vacation in one or more of those cities. Visit your company's offices while there and meet up with colleagues—some of whom you may have spoken to on the phone or exchanged e-mails with. Learn to speak the language—even if it's just a few conversational phrases. By building a strong network within your company, by connecting with international colleagues—you never know when they might be able to open a door for you in another part of the business. Just as you should research a company before you go for an interview, demonstrate you understand how your industry works in another country, and show your employer that you can fit in.

Take the opportunity to mix it up with your working environment and have new experiences. While on vacation, your primary interests might be food, fashion, and culture, but for a work assignment your primary concerns are safety, job opportunities, and wages. Utilize reports and surveys about your potential new homeland overseas. For instance, Switzerland, Sweden, and the Netherlands are the top three countries in terms of career rankings, offering a balance of career advancement and job security without making expats compromise on their home life, the HSBC survey "Expat Explorer: Balancing Life Abroad" showed. That balance reflects a common trait in these countries of a rewarding but stable work environment; Sweden and the Netherlands also rank second and fifth for their willingness to embrace diversity in the workplace.

The HSBC survey further revealed that the benefits of working in these countries did not come at the expense of an expat's personal life, as each of these destinations rank in the top five countries globally for the best working culture. Even career-driven expats in Switzerland find it relatively easy to strike a balance between work and life. Around three in five, or 59 percent of expats, "report a better work/life balance after moving to the country," meaning expats can advance their careers without sacrificing their social or family life.

I had the same workload as I did back in the States. But for me, yes, the Swiss did have the whole work/life-balance thing figured out. They work hard like Americans do, but they take their rest days. On Sundays, all stores are closed because that day is considered family time. Actually, we had to get accustomed to the fact that the stores weren't open twenty-four hours. Almost everything shuts down at five p.m.

People would work part time and full time, but they weren't staying till midnight or sleeping in an office on a couch. Folks worked hard and they often worked late, but I didn't see any of the extremes that I witnessed in New Jersey. No, people would log in their work time, then they would go home at night, have dinner with their families, and put the kids to bed. You would start to see some activity at night or in the evening, but that's about the extent of it. They weren't sitting in an office or having nannies raise their children.

As with most Swiss, I would take the entire month of July off for summer vacation every year. The Swiss take anywhere between four and six weeks of vacation at one time. I was not accustomed to taking such an extended vacation and it felt great! I was able to switch off, recharge, and reboot. It was the best cultural experience and probably the healthiest lifestyle I ever had. Also, when the Swiss take vacations it is truly a vacation experience for the entire family.

Now, in terms of standard of living as far as the cost of things, it was very expensive to live in Switzerland. The country is almost as famous for its high cost of living as it is for its ski slopes. On the other hand, cost-of-living surveys show that Swiss salaries and living standards are also among the highest in the world. To give you a sense of how expensive it was: going to the grocery store and getting a pack of Kraft cheese slices would have cost about four dollars back home, which was about ten Swiss francs. A combo meal at McDonald's was about fourteen francs and a gallon of milk was a little over five francs. In fact, the cost of living in Switzerland is currently 61.96 percent higher than in the United States (not including the average cost of rent), according to data from the research site Numbeo.com. Rent in Switzerland is 41.71 percent higher than in the United States.

Kiss, Bow, or Shake Hands

As the global chief diversity officer, I traveled to wherever there was a Novartis office. I was in Dubai, Singapore, China, Ethiopia, and Brazil. I went all over Europe, from the Nordic countries like Sweden and Norway, to England. I had to learn how to navigate different customs and immerse myself in a different culture each time I would travel. An invaluable resource on how to handle common business interactions is the book *Kiss, Bow, or Shake Hands: How to Do Business in Sixty Countries* by Terri Morrison, Wayne A. Conaway, and George A. Borden. It gives you a quick but deep insight into the minds of citizens in different countries. Any person who would report to me, I recommended that they read this book to learn about culture, etiquette, and business protocol.

The genesis for the book dates back to the nineties, when Morrison first created a digital database on doing business in sixty countries.[99] Some of the first users of this database included Booz Allen Hamilton, AT&T, and DuPont. In 1994, that database was the foundation for the first *Kiss, Bow, or Shake Hands* book, which is still very popular among international business executives and professors as a reference guide or even bible of international culture and business etiquette.[100] In addition to outlining acceptable conversational icebreakers, each country profile includes information about various

---

99 Adam Wooten, "International Business: 'Kiss, Bow, or Shake Hands' Is a New Guide for International Sales and Marketing," *Deseret News Business*, December 30, 2011, http://www.deseretnews.com/article/705396512/Kiss-Bow-or-Shake-Hands-is-a-new-guide-for-international-sales-and-marketing.html.

100 *Ibid.*

issues, including perceptions of punctuality, work schedules, and greetings (in other words, whether to kiss, bow, or shake hands).

More than a decade after establishing itself as the number one book on international business etiquette, the second edition of *Kiss, Bow, or Shake Hands* was fully revised to reflect the profound global transformation that had occurred since its debut. In this new edition, author Terri Morrison—the leading expert in this field—includes: comprehensive updates for each of the book's sixty-plus country chapters; several brand-new sections, like cultural IQ tests, "Know Before You Go" tips, and alerts on international security; and additional chapters on Austria, Belize, Ireland, South Africa, Vietnam, and the Vatican.

The book gives you the cultural norm of nearly every country on the planet. If you were going to Kuala Lumpur, the capital of Malaysia, and you didn't know the proper greeting, it tells you that it's a handshake between men, but a nod and a slight bow between men and women. I would read the chapter on the country I was visiting before I would set foot there. If I was going to Saudi Arabia, I knew that I needed a head scarf. I did my homework before I even got on the plane. It was my trusted guidebook. Of course, *Kiss, Bow, or Shake Hands* doesn't tell you *everything* you need to know about a country, but it tells you enough; you're not going to make some crazy mistake in Abu Dhabi like shaking the hand of a Sheikh—I made this mistake once. My colleague was very polite about it but I was mortified. He used this as an opportunity to teach me the rules of engagement between men and women. You simply cannot afford to not know the practices, customs, and philosophies of other countries.

Global assignments are not necessarily meant to be life-long career changes. Typically, with international assignments, you have a three- or five-year stint in another country. As I was approaching my seventh year living in Basel, it was either stay or go back to the United States and do the same job I had been doing before I relocated. Another possibility was to localize and officially become a Swiss citizen. I wasn't going to do that. Giving up my US passport, living in Switzerland for the rest of my life like the iconic Tina Turner, was not an option—or at least it wasn't something David or I ever intended to do.

So, I scheduled a meeting with the head of HR for my division and inquired, "What is next for me? My contract is coming up for expiration. I don't want to localize; what are my options?"

He wasn't giving me a straight answer. His response went something like: "Well, you have time and don't worry."

Yet, I was worrying. If I was going to move back to the States, I wanted to know what was going to happen to me in terms of being a company stakeholder.

I forced the issue. I declared: "I would like to have a bigger job. I want to do this and something else—can we broaden the scope of the role a bit? I want to be the head of diversity globally, but I also have an interest in talent management."

There was nothing available in talent management at the time. He also did not appreciate my forcing the subject. "Michelle, you're making this hard for me. I can't create something that is not available. We can't push someone out of a job to give you that responsibility," he told me.

I let it go: "Well, okay."

No doubt, I was disappointed. I felt like not only had I made my mark at the Novartis Basel campus but I had left a distinguishable impression. In the beginning, I was viewed as an anomaly, because a lot of the people working there had never seen a woman, let alone a woman of color, reporting to the divisional CEO. I was the first woman of color in that position in the history of the company—so it was unprecedented. The women looked to me like, *Wow, Michelle is here and she's going to help us get to where we want to be, and help make this place better for us.* That role came with a lot of responsibility and expectations; everyone was looking to me to be a savior of sorts, because the company had a very Swiss German culture, meaning that mostly men were in charge, and the voices of the women there were not as pervasive.

I worked hard, I fought for the things that I felt were right, and I was not afraid to speak up for things that needed to be talked about. Taking risks was never really an issue or a problem for me. I managed to cultivate relationships with a lot of my peers and superiors who did not look like me. I served as a trusted advisor to many of them. I would mentor them in some ways on certain career topics; in turn, they would mentor me in terms of my survival and being a black woman living in a foreign country. I had a wonderful network of people who cared about me. They really were invested in my success.

Yet my career was trapped in a holding pattern. It all started to change after the CEO, who had supported me, left the company. Novartis was becoming a more difficult workplace. My safety nets were disappearing. Those who I trusted and relied heavily on for mentoring and support were leaving the company. Although my colleagues had the same level of leadership support, many of us still felt like we were hanging out there on a wire by ourselves. David attended some of the company dinners with me. The new executive team that came in wanted to embrace me. They wanted me to feel like I was one of the guys, but it was clear to me and David that

I was not. It was largely due to the role itself. Diversity is not considered a profit center. Diversity practitioners are not really making money for the company. You're *spending* money for the company. Thus, some of my peers did not see it as a credible role that had any kind of benefit or linkage to the business strategy.

When leadership in your organization shifts and you discover that you no longer have the same level of support or your status drops a peg, it's time to leave. It doesn't have to be right away, but you need to start planning your exit strategy.

Opportunity knocked and I readily answered the door when a headhunter came calling about a chief diversity officer role available at Credit Suisse's financial headquarters in Zurich, Switzerland. I went to speak with the recruiter. I got on the train to Zurich and met with several executive committee members at Credit Suisse. I went through many interviews and a psychological assessment.

It was exhausting; I had to keep going back in, and I had to say the same things over and over again. It was due diligence behind the rapid-fire questions that went line by line on my resume: *What made you decide to leave this position? Why did you move to Switzerland?* Those were the preliminary high-level interviews. Then, once they got serious about hiring me and actually had my paperwork processed, they brought me back and asked additional questions like, *How do you lead? Can you work in different scenarios? What do you want to do? Where do you want to be? Would you want to move to Zurich?* Those questions were more centered on professional growth. The leadership at Credit Suisse really wanted to get to know who I was. So they kept hammering away. But I understood what was at stake, and that this was a significant move for the person bringing me into the organization, as she too was an African American woman.

A few weeks later, I got the job and resigned from Novartis. Credit Suisse had made a very appealing offer, which was basically: "If you stay in Switzerland for at least one more year, possibly two, we will repatriate you back to the United States and you can work in New York City."

I said, "Okay, great."

I was thinking, *At least that's my ticket going back home, because I know I eventually want to go back home to my family.*

In January of 2011, I went to work for the Credit Suisse Group AG as the managing director and global head of diversity. Credit Suisse provides private banking and investment banking services in Switzerland and internationally. It operates through Swiss Universal Bank, International Wealth Management, Asia Pacific, Global Markets, and Investment Banking and Capital Markets segments. In that role, I provided strategic direction and guidance to the chairman, CEO, executive committee, HR executive committee, HR management committee, and other key stakeholders to ensure that all divisional and regional diversity practices, strategies, and change-management initiatives were globally aligned and linked to the business strategy. I also developed meaningful and cost-effective strategies that supported the bank's regional and global diversity objectives, outreach activities, and initiatives. I provided overall facilitation and organizational development to support the development of four regional diversity councils sponsored by the regional CEOs. I designed a comprehensive global governance model for thirty-eight regional employee resource groups.

David, Myles Davis, and I moved back to the States two years after I accepted their offer. I would remain in that position and at Credit Suisse for the next two years. Going global—taking an international assignment—did indeed benefit my career as well as enrich all of our lives.

Will going global be a benefit in advancing you in *your* career? For those who are reluctant, I would say go for it, because the impact on your personal life will be immeasurably positive. Even if you don't see the return on your move right away. You simply must be prepared before, during, and after for any glitches you may encounter. You and your family will benefit for the rest of your lifetime if you can be flexible and adaptable to the challenges—professional, personal, and social—in the new host country.

Key Steps

1. Make your career—and global—aspirations known to your manager, HR, mentors, sponsors, and network.
2. Network with individuals who have already had the expatriate experience, to get a sense of what life is truly like overseas.
3. Use your vacation time to meet and talk with your global colleagues, to get a feel for that country during your on-the-ground research.
4. Do your homework and due diligence long before the opportunity arises in your organization.
5. Talk things over with your spouse/partner to ensure that he or she is fully on board with the idea of moving overseas. Also, have these talks with your children using what-if scenarios.
6. Be prepared to say yes. The opportunity may not present itself again if the timing is not convenient for you. These assignments are expensive for the company and may be rare.
7. If you're on the fence about taking an assignment

overseas, the best thing to do is not waver. Take a leap of faith.

8. Familiarize yourself with the cultural norms and learn the language of the host country where you intend to work.

9. Make sure that you have a clearly articulated career plan (that you agree with) in place for reentry or when your overseas assignment concludes.

10. Maintain relationships in your home country to ensure you aren't forgotten, and make sure to deliver results in your global assignment.

7

HAVING IT ALL—THE BOLDFACE LIE

"Shonda, how do you do it all?" The is answer is this: I don't.
—Shonda Rhimes

MGadsden-Williams @mgadsenwilliam 30 Aug 2016.
Twenty years ago today I married my best friend David Jamal Williams @high55lander. Looking forward to
growing old with you!

That was the tweet I sent out on our twentieth wedding
anniversary. Yeah, David and I are each other's confidant.
We talk about work and life—communication is one of our
strong points. We are very, very close. We've done everything
together. We've always traveled everywhere together. After
all, we practically grew up together. We were young when we
first met—I was just twenty-one years old. We got engaged at
twenty-four, and married three months after my twenty-seventh
birthday. So we've known each other a long time, during some
formative years in our lives. Many of our friends and family
would characterize us as having the perfect marriage. I think
those perceptions are mostly based on how David and I support each other; we've always been there for each other.

I am very fortunate that with everything I have gone
through in my career and my life, David has had my back.
In this regard, I couldn't have chosen a better mate. And to
think that it started with a blind date. All thanks to David's
coworker at AT&T, Reginald Rufus.

My mother and I were in David's office building; Mom, who is an entrepreneur, was delivering merchandise to a client at the AT&T headquarters in Basking Ridge, New Jersey. I had no real interest in going with Mom to see her client. So I decided to have a seat in the lobby and wait for her to return from her meeting. Not to mention, I had just broken up with my boyfriend a few weeks prior, and as such, I was in no mood to meet or greet anyone.

David was traveling out of town and his buddy Reginald decided to play matchmaker. He thought, *Oh, she's a nice-looking woman, let me go over and chat her up.* Reginald was fair-skinned, clean-shaven, short-statured, nicely dressed, and very soft-spoken. He approached me and introduced himself: "Hello. How are you? I'm Reginald Rufus. Are you waiting for someone?"

I was slightly intrigued: "My mother is in the building meeting with a client, and I'm waiting for her to return."

We continued with the small talk and he continued to pepper me with questions: "Are you a recent college graduate? What school? Where are you from? You look like a nice girl. Are you seeing anyone?"

"No," I said, slightly irritated.

He then told me: "I have someone I'd like you to meet if you're open to it."

At first I politely declined. I had just gotten out of a bad romance and was not interested in pursuing another relationship.

In the back of my mind, I was wondering if he was making up this story so that he could ask me out on a date, when I noticed that he was wearing a wedding ring. Of course, I gave him the side-eye, because I was not about to get involved in a relationship with a married man. Reg convinced me that he did in fact have a colleague by the name of David Jamal

Williams, who was a manager, from East Orange, New Jersey, very single, and traveled to Manassas, Virginia, frequently on business.

Finally, I figured, *What the hell.* I had nothing else to do with my free time and nothing to lose. *What's the worst thing that could happen?* I still had some reservations. *If David's such a great guy, why is he single? What's wrong with him? Does he come with a lot of baggage? Is there some crazy ex-girlfriend who still has feelings for him; who could potentially harass me once she found out he was dating someone else? Or what if he's some deranged axe murderer waiting to kill me and dispose of my body?* All these scenarios were running through my head. I decided to just go along with it and see where the conversation took me. He ended up giving me David's phone number, which I dialed soon after. Reg was telling the truth! David seemed like a nice guy. We just talked. We spent hours on the phone together and got to know a lot about each other before we even met. It was about two weeks of telephone conversations before we set up the first date.

It was December 1991. We met at the Olive Garden in Springfield, New Jersey, on Route 22. We agreed to meet at seven p.m. For our date, I decided to drive my mother's BMW to impress him. I arrived about thirty minutes early, parked my car right near the entrance, and sat, watching everyone as they entered the restaurant. About fifteen minutes later, I saw a red Audi pull up. I slouched down in my seat, so as not to draw any attention to myself. David had arrived. He walked inside the restaurant and sat down in front to wait for me. He was a very good-looking guy—everything that he described himself to be. I checked my makeup, teeth, and hair in my rearview mirror and decided that I was ready to make my grand entrance.

I walked straight up to the front desk and announced, "Yes, I'm here for dinner with Mr. David Williams."

He stood up and said, "I'm right here."

He was even more handsome up close. He was well dressed in a suit and tie. The suit accentuated his muscular physique. He smiled; it was nice, friendly. I was pleased with what I was seeing. Reg was on point!

We took a booth. I ordered a house salad with balsamic vinaigrette to start, followed by a pasta dish. David ordered the same. One thing he immediately learned about me was that I'm a take-charge kind of gal. I told him: "If you're not happy with your meal, you make sure you send it back. Make sure that it comes out the right way, the way you requested it." Even then, my mind-set was very focused. Besides, I wanted to make sure that David was happy on the date, and that he got what he wanted.

We spoke, we ate. Right after our meal we drove around, and continued the conversation in the car. The red Audi he drove was actually his. At the time, we were facing similar experiences in our love lives. We were both looking for something serious—we weren't about playing any games.

During that one-hour drive, we talked about kids, but we didn't go too deep into it, because we were still trying to feel each other out. It was more about, *Okay, kids will come, but what's the status of our careers? How much money do we have in the bank?* We talked about our goals, our values, and our commitments. David was very easy to talk to. He was a great listener, engrossed in conversation, very well versed on topics that I also had a passion for, like current events, business, and the arts. He was also very genuine with his thoughts and opinions.

David told me: "Everything that you're saying, I'm actually thinking it." For him it was like divine intervention. In his mind, he was thinking, *Yup, this is the right one.* I shared with David that I wanted to be a vice president of a major corporation by the time I was thirty. He thought that was very admirable, considering at that point I was still working part-time at Bamberger's. I was basically fresh out of college and still trying to find my footing, and figure out the career path that I wanted to pursue.

I was adamant in our discussion: "I want to get here. I want to be at this level. I want to manage people. I want to be successful. I want to travel. I want to go global." I didn't know what that looked like or how it would take shape, but I was clear about what I wanted. David found that intriguing.

I am a strong believer that mapping out your career and planning your life with a partner go hand in hand. One of the most important decisions you can make in your career success is your choice of a mate. Make no mistake about it, your work life impacts your home life and vice versa. Your climb is going to be that much more difficult if your significant other does not have your back. He or she will either make it easier or harder for you to achieve your goals. If your dreams and desires should shift over time, your partner has to be able to handle such an adjustment.

From the onset, David and I were on the same page in terms of how we saw our careers developing. David went to work for AT&T right out of high school. He cut his teeth in customer service. It was an entry-level position. He wanted to ascend that corporate ladder as far and as fast as he could, but at the same time, he realized that he still needed to earn his college degree since he hadn't taken the traditional route. David knew it was going to be a little tougher for him, but he was up for the challenge. He saw AT&T as a great company to work for that would allow him to take a different career path, and assume different positions to get the experience he needed to excel. Since AT&T paid 100 percent reimbursement for education expenses, David ended up working his way through school, and obtained a bachelor's degree summa cum laude in business management from the University of Phoenix, and other professional certifications through accredited universities.

David and I had the same understanding about how we wanted to grow as a couple, a partnership, and as husband and wife. We met in 1991, got engaged in 1993, and married in 1996. Naturally, it was a long courtship and engagement. We spent that time learning more about each other—and eventually started living together. You learn a lot about a person when you cohabitate. My parents are ol' school. Hence, I got pushback from my mother: "What's the point of him marrying you if you guys live together already?"

I was thinking, *Whatever.* But I tried to reassure her: "No, it's going to be fine."

David and I always felt like we were doing the right thing. We were in no rush. We were going to take our time so long as we were committed to each other. We told ourselves, *Let's wait and get it right the first time.*

What's more, we wanted to be practical out of the gate. We weren't going to let our emotional states take over our financial situation. Historically, the father of the bride absorbs all or a huge chunk of the wedding expenses. As with other modern-day couples, David and I were going to bear the responsibility of paying for at least half of our wedding, reception, and honeymoon expenses. As we were planning our wedding, we were determined to stick to a budget, which was going to be well under the typical $26,645 price tag in the US. We didn't want saying *I do* to cause us to go broke over a one-day celebration—something all too familiar for many newlyweds. Anyways, David and I wanted to make sure that we had enough savings for a lovely honeymoon in Italy. We were to spend ten glorious days in Rome.

From the beginning, David and I steered and engineered how we saw our lives developing, which meant putting money toward our priorities every time—items that we were going to appreciate, and items that would provide us with a firm ground to stand on.

By the time I was in my early thirties, I had a brand-new house, a husband, and a dog, but not the proverbial 2.5 kids. In our society today, if you have a spouse, kids, and a career as a woman, you are perceived to be living a full life. Whereas, if you are missing one of those elements as a woman, your life is half full. For as long as I can remember, or at least while I traversed through the halls of corporate America, there have been convoluted conversations about women *having it all.*

The popular thinking is that the term is meant to be empowering, allegedly adopted by the women's movement and used by feminists like Gloria Steinem, who promised women they could have it all by balancing the demands of career with the demands of motherhood.[101] But in the article "The Complicated Origins of 'Having It All,'" the *New York Times Magazine* traces it back to *Cosmopolitan* editor in chief Helen Gurley Brown. The then-sixty-year-old magazine editor had been bringing "her mix of workplace confessionals and candid sex tips to a growing demographic of single working women," reported the *Times,* when she came out with her book *Having It All: Love, Success, Sex, Money Even if You're Starting With*

---

101   Jennifer Szalao, "The Complicated Origins of 'Having It All,'" the *New York Times Magazine,* January 2, 2015, https://www.nytimes.com/2015/01/04/magazine/the-complicated-origins-of-having-it-all.html.

Nothing, published in 1982. Here's the irony: Brown didn't like the title. In fact, according to the *Times*, she conceded to her editors' choice for the title, but not before emphatically reiterating her objections: "*Having It All* sounds so [expletive] cliché to me," she said.

So, Brown's book exclaimed that women could have it all—"love, sex, and money"—and Madison Avenue ad men and women's magazine editors have since spun it as women could have it all with a rewarding career, loving marriage, and happy children. Women have felt the pressure from this catchphrase for more than thirty years. As Facebook COO Sheryl Sandberg sees it: "Having it all is the worst. No matter how much we all have and how grateful we are for what we have, no one has it all, because we all make trade-offs every single day, every single minute."[102]

For African American executive women, the trade-off has been marriage, if you take to heart various studies and surveys. "Professional women find maintaining love relationships a major challenge, and as a result many executive women remain unmarried or in a committed partnership. In fact, only 57 percent of women over thirty in corporate America are married, compared to 83 percent among high-achieving males," reports *Madamenoire*, the digital black women's lifestyle guide.[103] The *Harvard Business Review* reports that "nine out of ten high-achieving married women have husbands who are employed full time or self-employed. Only a quarter are married to men who earn more than $100,000 a year."[104]

---

102 Sheryl Sandberg and Sonia Sotomayor, *Oprah's Next Chapter*, Season 2, Episode 217, Oprah Winfrey Network, March 24, 2013.

103 Ann Brown, "Waiting to Exhale? Men Reveal the Challenges of Dating an Executive Black Woman," *Madamenoire*, September 29, 2015, http://madamenoire.com/589473/waiting-exhale-relationship-challenges-executive-black-woman/.

104 *Ibid.*

Apparently, when we aren't stressing over being powerful working women in (or out of) a relationship with a significant other, we are trying to cope with being powerful working women and mothers. As women continue to balance working careers with family responsibilities, the idea of *doing it all* has become a valued social norm. Shutting down this concept, Shonda Rhimes gave the 2014 commencement address at her alma mater, Dartmouth College, where the screenwriter and producer delivered a powerful speech about the fallacy of doing it all:[105]

> *"Shonda, how do you do it all?" The answer is this: I don't. Whenever you see me somewhere succeeding in one area of my life, that almost certainly means I am failing in another area of my life. If I am killing it on a Scandal script for work, I am probably missing bath and story time at home. If I am at home sewing my kids' Halloween costumes, I'm probably blowing off a rewrite I was supposed to turn in. If I am accepting a prestigious award, I am missing my baby's first swim lesson. If I am at my daughter's debut in her school musical, I am missing Sandra Oh's last scene ever being filmed at Grey's Anatomy. If I am succeeding at one, I am inevitably failing at the other. That is the trade-off. That is the Faustian bargain one makes with the devil that comes with being a powerful working woman who is also a powerful mother. You never feel 100 percent okay; you never get your sea legs; you are always a little nauseous. Something is always lost. Something is always missing.*

---

105   Shonda Rhimes, Commencement Address, Dartmouth College, June 8, 2014, http://www.dartmouth.edu/~commence/news/speeches/2014/rhimes-address.html.

My own awakening occurred in May 2008. David surprised me with a luxurious vacation to Monaco. We had talked about visiting this fabulous country and how we'd go the next time we had an opportunity. David planned a five-day excursion and we stayed at the elegant five-diamond Hôtel Hermitage. I was ecstatic! We wined, dined, shopped, and did a lot of sightseeing. The only problem was that I brought my BlackBerry on vacation with us. At the time, I had a lot of competing priorities at work. I was making and receiving calls; answering e-mails for the entire first day of our vacation. At first, my working was not problematic. But when David would speak to me, I was so ensconced in my work that I did not respond immediately. He was so annoyed with me that he snapped: "Are you here on vacation with me or are you planning to work the entire time?"

His remark completely shocked me. I was torn. I had a lot of work on my plate and wanted to do a good job since I had been recently promoted, and I wanted to prove to my employer and myself that I was worthy of the role. Here it was, my loving husband took the time to plan this beautiful and expensive vacation for us and I was practically ignoring him. I could see the hurt and disappointment in David's eyes.

It was at this point that I decided to delegate the work to my team, turn off the BlackBerry, and give David 100 percent of my attention. I was so angry at myself—that I had allowed my work to get in the way of my marriage. I was succeeding at work and failing at being a wife. It was right then and there that I made a promise to David, and myself, that although my career was important, I would make sure that I carved out time for us, and not work as much. Granted, the BlackBerry still went on vacations with us. But I set a ground rule for myself—I would only check it twice per day: once in the morning and again in the evening. I had to make a choice. It was impossible to give 100 percent of myself to both my marriage and my career. I chose to put David first and my career second.

Most couples' career moves during their marriage involve trade-offs, notes Meg Whitman, chief executive of Hewlett Packard Enterprise, in her book *The Power of Many: Values for Success in Business and in Life*. "Sacrifice is not such a terrible thing when someone you really love wants something," she writes.[106]

Ambitious women often marry equally ambitious men, a combination that can create dangerous roadblocks for women's high-powered careers, according to Joan S. Lublin of the *Wall Street Journal*.[107] The problems that career couples often face revolve around relocation, promotion, frequent business travel, and conflicts of interest. In *Earning It: Hard-Won Lessons from Trailblazing Women at the Top of the Business World*, Lublin points out: "Two-career couples struggle with figuring out how both partners can get ahead without derailing their relationship."[108] In other words, one spouse might feel his or her career must take priority over their spouse's career.

David and I did not have mismatched expectations about our lives and our careers. We were always fully supportive of each other's endeavors. He did not become insecure when I was at Novartis and started making more money than him, especially with my bonuses. Pharmaceutical bonuses were blowing telecom bonuses out of the water. He couldn't keep up at that point. But David will tell anyone he didn't have a

---

106 Meg Whitman, *The Power of Many: Values for Success in Business and in Life* (Crown Business, 2010), p. 134.

107 Joan S. Lublin, *Earning It: Hard-Won Lessons from Trailblazing Women at the Top of the Business World* (Harper Business, 2016), p. 158.

108 *Ibid*, p. 160.

hang up about that at all since what I was doing, I was doing for the family, and that's all that mattered. Maybe that
made us a curiosity, perhaps a scarcity. This links back to the
idea of finding a partner or spouse who has similar aspirations,
dreams, and goals.

Much like David made sacrifices for my career when he
took the buyout from AT&T and relocated to Switzerland
with me, he changed lanes with me when we shifted from career couple to business partners. It was a huge adjustment for
the two of us in several ways. When we were gainfully employed, we did our equal share of fun-filled spending. We both
like nice things. David and I like fast cars, nice vacations. I
love fashion. I enjoy looking the part. Meaning, if you're an
executive, you dress like one. I worked in industries where all
the women dressed to impress, especially on Wall Street. These
women wore Chanel, Tom Ford, YSL, or Christian Louboutin
every day. In the beginning, I wanted to hire a public relations
rep to help snag business. David snarled, "Well, we can't shop
in Louis Vuitton right now if you plan to do that."

Consequently, we had to get to know each other's management style, how we attack projects and solve problems.
There are challenges that come with building a business with
your spouse. It put a strain not only on the business, but on
our relationship too, with respect to our finances. We were
no longer living off large corporate salaries. We were chas-
ing down invoices, making sure clients paid. We were charged
with ensuring that we had enough clients not only to sustain
our lifestyle, but also to feed the business.

The reality of life is that there are hits and misses in a
career, love life, and parenthood. There are compromises and
trade-offs, be it your professional or personal life. A guilt trip,
or beating yourself up, is not warranted. One might easily

imagine OWN media mogul Oprah Winfrey bellowing this. I know for sure marriage and motherhood are not for everyone. While I embraced my role as David's wife, I too came to understand that motherhood wasn't for me.

The Empty Womb: Motherhood Is Not Womanhood

Admittedly, when I moved to Switzerland, there were times that I felt subpar as a woman, because Swiss life can be characterized by a strong sense of motherhood. I saw firsthand that in Swiss culture, a woman's primary role is a domestic one. If you're not doing that, then the attitude is like, *What the hell's wrong with you?* Whereas with my American colleagues back in the US, I didn't undergo much societal pressure to have kids—but with the Swiss, anytime I met or saw someone, they were like, *You don't have children? Why?* There was always a question about it.

If you're a woman in your childbearing years, there is a high chance that family and friends will pressure you to have children. Women are often not considered whole or worthy until they bear offspring. If you believe that this antiquated way of thinking no longer exists, think again. Women are still shamefaced about wanting to live child free.

Our society in general equates womanhood with motherhood. But the two are not synonymous. As women, we can choose to have a child. If we desire to give birth, it is a personal decision not a public debate. We are aware of the wonderful, glorious life force in the world that is the act of motherhood. Yes, motherhood is a gift to mankind. But if we choose not to have a child, there is nothing mentally wrong with us; we are not selfish human beings, and our lives are not meaningless.

Children were not a top priority for me or David. I had decided long ago that I did not want to be a mother and David respected that decision. But as we were getting older, we started to give more thought to our legacy and the idea of raising a family. There was a period, long before we moved to Switzerland, when I did feel guilty and selfish. The pressure came when my mother would constantly ask me: "When are you guys going to have kids? You've been married a long time and you don't have any children. You would give a child a nice home." That kind of background noise started to make me rethink my decision about not having children.

I was in my thirties and I had some reproductive health issues as result of fibroid tumors on the walls of my uterus; I also had endometriosis, which is a disorder in which "tissue that normally lines the uterus grows outside the uterus."[109] One doctor advised us: "You guys need to probably start now if there's any chance, because endometriosis is only going to get worse—and if the fibroids continue to grow . . ." I understood that I would be putting myself at risk for other complications during pregnancy.

I knew that if I waited any longer, childbirth would become much more difficult for me. There would be no turning back. In all candor, David and I did try to have children, to no avail—I couldn't get pregnant. What were our options? We chose surrogacy (assisted reproduction), which entails having another woman carry and give birth to a baby. We knew couples who had used surrogates. I was referred to an attorney named Melissa Brisman who specializes in reproduction, and partners with a fertility group that is considered one of the best in New Jersey. Melissa has been a pioneer and leader in the field of reproductive law. She was doing groundbreaking work in that space; drafting legislation and arguing before

---

109   Mayo Clinic Staff, "Endometriosis," http://www.mayoclinic.org/diseases-conditions/endometriosis/home/ovc-20236421.

state Supreme Courts; setting laws and protecting parental rights for children born through assisted reproduction. Melissa knew a lot of women who were having difficulty having their own natural childbirths. As a matter of fact, she too used surrogacy on her own personal journey to parenthood.

Surrogacy is legal in some US states, and countries including India, Russia, and Ukraine. States have different laws with respect to surrogacy and the legal rights of the intended parents. There are two main types: gestational surrogacy and traditional surrogacy. A traditional surrogate mother is the baby's biological mother, since it's her egg that gets fertilized by the intended father's sperm. Gestational surrogacy may take a few forms, but in each form, the child is genetically unrelated to the surrogate mother. Gestational surrogacy is more commonly used in the US than traditional surrogacy, and is considered less legally complex. That was the route we took. David and I thought gestational surrogacy was a great way to go if we were going to start a family. It would be my egg, David's sperm, and our child that would be carried by somebody else. It made perfect sense to us.

In places where surrogacy is legal, couples may enlist the help of a third-party agency to oversee the process of finding a surrogate, entering into a contract with her, and recommending fertility centers for insemination—generally via in vitro fertilization. These agencies can help make sure that surrogates are screened with psychological evaluations and other medical tests to ensure healthy deliveries. They also facilitate all legal matters concerning the intended parents and surrogate.

In addition to her reproductive law practice, Melissa owns the surrogate mother agency Reproductive Possibilities. Our first in-person meeting with Melissa was to go over the legalities of surrogacy. David and I took the ninety-minute car ride to North Jersey. We were both a little nervous. I admit that I had some anxiety about the meeting. I just held onto David's hand for comfort as we walked into her office. She was interviewing us and we were grilling her as well. She wanted to know why we chose to travel down this road. If she was going to represent us, she had to make sure we didn't have a whole bunch of baggage—psychological issues. We were in her office for about ninety minutes. After that point, we had more conversations with her team. There was so much to digest in one sitting. Afterward, I began to do more research.

David and I went for an initial orientation to learn more about surrogacy and what it involved. Reproductive Possibilities would manage the process of selecting the women based on their criteria; and later present the profiles to the women for review and consideration. These surrogate women are oftentimes wives and mothers.

There was a long questionnaire that David and I had to fill out, about geographical location, age, race, etc. You know: *Can the surrogate be an African American student at Spelman or could she be a fifty-year-old mom living in Wisconsin?* We wanted someone who was younger than I was at the time. We wanted someone who was well educated, a college graduate. We preferred a woman of color but she didn't have to be African American, because at the end of the day, the sperm and egg came from us, so the baby would ultimately be ours. We wanted someone who shared our cultural and family values. The surrogate had to take good care of herself, with an appreciation for health, wellness, and fitness. This was important to us; this person was to carry our child. We wanted her to be within driving distance—New York, New Jersey, Pennsylvania. You can't monitor every move that the surrogate mother makes every hour, or every minute of the day, but it was certainly going to be harder to keep track of her if she were in Florida or somewhere else thousands of miles away.

Surrogacy is a long process. You must go through these batteries of tests, both the intended parents plus the surrogate, just to find a carrier who is both medically and psychologically suitable. There must be trust established between the intended parents and the surrogate mother. I knew that I really wanted to be part of her pregnancy. I wanted to be part of the birthing process. I wanted to witness all the things that she was doing that I couldn't do for myself.

After the child is born, the surrogate gives the child to the parents, often without any further relationship. But not us. After the baby was born, I wanted to still maintain some sort of a relationship with the surrogate mother, because quite honestly, she was giving us a precious gift. I didn't want to completely cut her out of the picture, so I decided that this woman would bring a child into the world for us and not be extricated from our lives.

Once we were approved for surrogacy and we signed the paperwork, Melissa's team put together profiles of women whom they had screened and interviewed who were deemed a good match, having met our criteria. After combing through a book of profiles, David and I came across a woman in Pennsylvania—Lisa. She was African American and Native American. My father's side of the family is part Cherokee Eastern Band, so I liked the fact that we had ancestral roots in common. She had one child. She was a single mother. She wanted to be a surrogate to help another family. "Oh, she sounds great," we cried out.

Everything that was done, including the conversations, was monitored. Members of Melissa's team were on the telephone to make sure that there were no misunderstandings or unpleasant altercations without them knowing about it. Our first call with Lisa lasted for about forty-five minutes. It was awkward at first. I was very nervous and really did not know what to say to this woman. She was extremely pleasant and eased our fears about working with her almost immediately. It was a three-way conversation between Lisa, David, and myself. But it really was mostly Lisa and me doing all the talking. She was trying to feel me out. She asked what I did for a living, what were my likes, what were my hobbies, how would I treat the child, why at this stage of my life was I interested in having a baby. In turn, I asked her about her upbringing, spiritual background, etc. It was a real getting-to-know dialogue on a visceral level.

David and I liked Lisa a lot. She was poised. She was bright. When I asked her why she was interested in surrogacy, she told me that it wasn't about the money, it was more about her being able to help another woman. That struck me, because we recalled as we looked at other surrogate's profiles that when answering the same question, some said, *Well, this will help me out financially*. Lisa's response tugged at my heartstrings. David agreed and we notified the agency: "We'd like to meet her, talk to her more, get to know her a little bit better. But she sounds terrific." The deal was done, we were moving full steam ahead.

David and I were fortunate in that we were both gainfully employed and had disposable income, enough money saved up to pay for assisted reproduction. It may seem alluring, but surrogacy is not cheap. If you want to save money, you can handle the surrogacy arrangement on your own using a lawyer, but it will still cost you about $50,000, per the American Academy of Assisted Reproductive Technology Attorneys. The cost of hiring a full-service agency to walk you through the process step by step can run upward of $150,000, which includes doctors, psychological screenings, counseling, attorney fees, medications, travel expenses, and compensation for the surrogate. You must pay all medical expenses associated with becoming pregnant, pregnancy living (i.e., maternity clothes and prenatal care), giving birth, and recovering after childbirth.

We spoke with Lisa over the phone for weeks. I liked that she talked about how she enjoyed motherhood and all the things that come along with pregnancy and childbirth. She was very articulate in the way she described certain experiences such as having a C-section, which meant that the likelihood of her having a C-section for our child would be greater. The thought didn't bother Lisa. But I was scared for her and couldn't help but think, *This is major surgery. What if she dies?* I even babbled to David: "This woman wants to put her life at risk for us."

Now, another major financial and legal consideration for expecting parents is what to do if the surrogate gets pregnant with multiples—twins or triplets. Do you just want the one baby? Is it okay if she has six babies? The likelihood that the surrogate, through the egg implantation process, has multiple babies is high. You need to decide with your spouse or partner to say, "Okay, if she gets pregnant and she has triplets, we're going to keep all three," "I don't want three. I just want two," or, "I just want one." David and I were emphatic: "If Lisa gets pregnant with triplets, we'll take all three. It's our children." It didn't matter to us what the outcome was going to be, at that point, we just wanted children.

I became very close to Lisa in a couple of weeks. One weekend, we tried to reach Lisa on her cell phone but she was completely out of pocket. No response, which was unusual for her because normally she would either call you right back or call you the next day, but you would hear from her. We were talking just about every day or every other day, so when she disappeared for an entire weekend, David and I thought it was odd. We didn't know what the heck happened to her and frankly, we were nervous.

Finally, the following Monday, I called her and this time she answered the phone. I asked, "Hey, what happened?"

She was nonchalant: "Oh, well, I went to see my boyfriend in Texas."

I was taken slightly aback: "Well, first of all, you never told us you had a boyfriend, and second of all, you didn't return our calls till like three days later." Now I'm upset, rightly so. "Is that how this is going to be? You're going to become pregnant with our child and just run off to Texas or somewhere for a weekend and I don't know what you're doing or who you're doing it with or what you're eating and drinking?"

We kind of got into it after that. I wasn't upset that she went to visit her boyfriend, but she could have just told us that. I had an issue with the mere fact that she just didn't say anything. It was almost like she was hiding something, which made us wonder, *Well, what else is she keeping from us?* I called our lawyer: "Should we be concerned about this?"

"Yes, you should," was Melissa's reply.

David responded right away: "You know what? Let's leave her. Let's find somebody else to do this."

We were both very disappointed. At that stage, we were preparing for the egg extraction and then the egg implantation. We—David, Lisa, and I—were starting to work together as a unit. Okay, Lisa was out. Back to the drawing board. Based on the profiles, we came across another woman from Georgia, a student at Spelman, a person of color. She needed the money to help pay for her college tuition. She was a talented and gifted student. She came from humble beginnings. She simply couldn't afford to continue to go to college. When we spoke to her on the phone, she came across as extremely knowledgeable; she did her homework. She called us often. We called her often. It was a great relationship that was just starting to form. Then I got the job offer in Basel, Switzerland.

Now, what was I supposed to do? Melissa informed us: "You can't be a surrogate family out of the country and then take the baby out of the country, there's a lot of legalities involved. It would be too complicated." Then she tried to reassure us: "If you come back and you're still interested, we're here for you."

In any case, it was going to be challenging to have a baby with us, starting new careers and a new life, in a different country. We wouldn't have our immediate family around us to help with the childrearing. At first, David and I were thinking, *We're going to Switzerland and we'll revisit having a baby at some later date.* But eventually, we both agreed that it wasn't the right time. We had waited too long, and by the time we made the decision to move to Switzerland, it just didn't seem like it fit.

In all honesty, I personally was a little bit relieved. I still wasn't feeling very maternal. In hindsight, I was trying to have a baby because it was expected of me. I've got to say, I was a little jealous of the surrogate women; although I treated them nicely, these women were doing something that I couldn't. So, to listen to them, to hear them talk on the phone about what's going to happen to their bodies with the baby . . . they were the ones who would experience the whole thing. Sure, they could send me videos of sonograms and ultrasounds, but it's not like being there and it's not like me experiencing it.

By the time I turned forty, I had had four surgeries to remove fibroids over the course of ten years and a hysterectomy the last go-round. On more than one occasion during a physical exam, I learned that I was extremely anemic. I was feeling lethargic and my menstrual cycles were heavy. It became a quality-of-life issue as I could not function, not to mention I was at risk for heart failure. My doctor told me I had two options: do nothing or get a hysterectomy. This happened while I was living in Switzerland. My doctor at the time had the best bedside manner. She knew how to talk in layman terms. I asked her: "What would you do if you were me?"

She answered, "I would have the hysterectomy."

I trusted her judgment. Anyways, David and I finally agreed we weren't going to have children. I returned to the States to have the surgery.

It was December 10, 2010. I was ready to have it over and done with. I wasn't feeling well and I wanted to get my life back. I slept the night before like a baby. In the morning, David drove me to the hospital in New York from our home in Somerset, New Jersey. Interestingly enough, it was all women in that operating room—the anesthesiologist, surgeon, resident doctor, and nurse. We all laughed about that fact before they put me under.

"Wow, this is the first time I ever had surgery with an all-female surgical team. I know I'm in good hands," I joked. "You all will take good care of me."

In unison they replied, "We sure will."

And they did.

I came to the realization that I was indeed content. It was just me, my husband, and my Yorkie, Myles Davis. Just as David had been right there by my side, Myles had been a comforting companion for us both. We bought Myles in September 2001, shortly after 9/11. Here's my confession: in a small way, he was my response to not being able to conceive a baby. David knew it. We were watching the romantic comedy *As Good As it Gets,* starring Jack Nicholson, whose character is entrusted with caring for his neighbor's dog named Verdell. It was a Brussels griffon and I thought he was the cutest dog. I'm a huge Jack Nicholson fan and I loved the relationship he had with the dog in that movie. I hadn't had a dog since I was in junior high school. I looked at David and said, "I want a Verdell."

He replied, "No."

At that time, we had just moved into our house and everything was clean and brand new. "What are we going to do with a dog? I grew up with dogs all my life. I do not want any dogs," he grumbled.

But I wouldn't let go: "I really want this dog. Let's go look. Let's just go look."

David gave in: "Okay, let's just look."

We drove to the Shake A Paw Puppies pet store in Green Brook, New Jersey. I knew that I wanted a toy Yorkshire terrier, a dog small enough that I could carry him around and he could travel with me. We walked over to the cage where they had three Yorkie puppies that looked exactly the same, except two were boys and one was a girl. The owner of the store suggested, "Why don't you take them out and see which one you like?"

We brought the female puppy out first. She didn't really talk to us. She wasn't very friendly, as if she didn't want to be bothered with people. She just wanted to lie down in the cage and sleep, so I put her back. I took out the other puppy. We played with him a little. He was cute and spunky. He had a lot of personality. I laughed as he went under a little gap between the floor and the cage. Because he was so tiny, he fit underneath the space and then he stuck his little nose out. Nudging David, I said, "That's him."

He asked, "Are you sure?"

Without hesitating I answered, "Yeah. That's him."

As the pet store owner packed everything up—the puppy, a cage, wee-wee pads, dog food, etc.—he inquired, "So, what are you going to call him?"

I don't know, it just rolled off the tip of my tongue: "Myles."

He looked at me, eyebrows raised: "Myles?"

Again, without hesitation I quipped, "Yes. That's his name. Myles. Myles Davis."

Then David half laughed, "Sounds good to me."

I liked the name Myles and the puppy responded to it. We wanted to be somewhat respectful to the iconic jazz trumpeter Miles Davis, that's why we spell our Yorkie's name with a y.

We bought him home, stopping by my parents' house first. My father was cooking dinner; he turned, looked at the puppy side-eyed: "Where did you guys get that little puppy from?"

I proudly declared, "This is Myles Davis."

"Who?"

I was not missing a beat: "This is Myles."

Myles arrived to his new home and wouldn't sleep. He cried all night. He was the hardest dog to train. He would go to the bathroom wherever he pleased. For months, Myles and David fought tooth and nail. David was trying tactics his folks used to discipline dogs when he was a child. "With discipline, you don't let them get the upper hand," David told me. Well, Myles wasn't having any of that. It made him worse. David and Myles were two alpha males. You had this little two-pound puppy and David going at it every day. It was quite hilarious. Myles was barking and David was arguing. It was craziness for a few weeks.

One day, David got fed up. "Myles is going to pet adoption, today. Because he does not get it. I cannot take this anymore."

I told him, "You're not going to take my dog back. He's too cute to go back. We just need more patience."

That day, Myles decided to pee on the wee-wee pad and he's been trained ever since. It was like he'd turned a corner. I guess he knew David was taking him back. Well, at least that's what he said, and it seemed like Myles understood what he was talking about, as if he thought, *Oh, I guess I better behave, I better listen.*

He and David were inseparable. It's incredible how their relationship grew. David always spent more time with him, just given the nature of our situation with me working all time and David taking a backseat to my career when we moved to Switzerland. While I was at the office, it was David who fed Myles, walked him, took him to the vet to get shots, carried him to the groomers. When Myles was sick, he came to me because I was like the mommy. I would hug him and wrap him up in a little blanket—the whole bit. It's interesting, every time I had a surgical procedure or a lupus flare-up, Myles was so docile. Yorkies are energetic. Myles loved to bark, run around, and crawl under the bed. There were times when I was pretty much bedridden, and I would pick him up and put him on the bed and say, "Myles, I can't do anything. Just please lie down and go to sleep." And he understood that I wasn't feeling well. Myles would just lie next to me on the bed, not moving at all, and sleep.

Whenever David worked late, till one or two in the morning, Myles would be right there on the hardwood floor lying at David's feet. As soon as David rose, turning out the light, that's when Myles was ready to go to bed too. It was endearing to me to watch David interact with Myles in that nurturing, kind of fatherly manner. Fifteen years is unusual for a dog to remain so healthy. Last year, David and I took him to the vet for a checkup and an X-ray. Our heart sank when the veterinarian told us he found a mass in Myles's liver and that it was probably cancerous. He didn't believe Myles was going to live much longer.

"Oh my goodness," David said, as he and I stared at each other. Tears started streaming down our cheeks; this had been our child for sixteen years. He'd been our life. We hugged each other and then we looked at Myles. David muttered, "I'm going to take care of him for the rest of his days."

Champ that he was, Myles ran around like he was Superdog for another year. He passed away during the summer of 2017.

There is no be all and end all of your existence. You must paint your own picture about what you want your life to look like—with or without kids, with or without a partner. When you come home at night, if the loving face waiting for you is a short-haired domestic cat and you're totally happy, that's fine. Author, motivational speaker, and spiritual life coach Iyanla Vanzant offers up these powerful words: "You are enough."

The term *work/life balance* was basically coined to describe how women struggled by trying to do it all. But work/life balance for me is different than work/life balance for you, because we all have various priorities in our lives. As you climb up the rungs of that corporate ladder, you will have to learn how to find a harmonious balance between your personal and professional lives.

I like the perspective put forward in *Leading the Life You Want* by Stewart D. Friedman, a professor at the Wharton School and the former head of Ford Motor's Leadership Development Center. He profiles successful people who have achieved greatness, not by forsaking their work, families, communities, and private selves, but rather, by embracing these parts of their lives in what he calls "four-way wins." He surmises life can be better in all four domains, perhaps not all at once, but over the course of a lifetime.[110] Friedman expounds on his book in the *Harvard Business Review* article "Great Performers Make Their Personal Lives a Priority." He writes about how successful people have found creative ways to reduce conflict and replace it with a sense of harmony between work and the rest of life: "Having clarity of vision helps reduce conflict, stress, and strain."

At the core of an effective work/life balance are two key elements—daily achievement and enjoyment—declares WorkLifeBalance.com publisher Jim Bird.[111] "Achievement and enjoyment answer the big question: *Why? Why do you want a better income . . . a new house . . . the kids through college . . . to do a good job today . . . to come to work at all?*" Bird reasons that enjoyment does not just mean happiness. It means "pride, satisfaction, happiness, celebration, love, a sense of well-being . . . all the joys of living." Trying to live a one-sided life without enjoyment and achievement is why so many "successful people are not happy, or not nearly as happy as they should be."

The reality of life is that we have all made mistakes, exercised errors in judgment, experienced tragedy and loss, and learned to compromise. Both men and women can fully dedicate themselves to family and career at the same time. Women should not feel like they are to blame if they cannot manage to rise up the ladder as fast as men, plus have a significant other or an active family life.

---

110 Stewart D. Friedman, *Leading the Life You Want: Skills for Integrating Work and Life* (Harvard Business Review Press, 2014).

111 Jim Bird, "Work-Life Balance Defined," 2003, http://www.worklifebalance.com/work-life-balance-defined.html.

To hell with the boldface lie of having it all. Focus on having what matters most to you and on honoring who you are. *Own It: Oprah in Her Own Words* serves up Oprah Winfrey's most thought-provoking insights. Taken from an issue of *O, The Oprah Magazine*, in 2001, a passage on honoring yourself teaches us: "When you honor what you know your spirit is telling you to do, you are making the most conscientious decision, one for which you are willing to accept all the consequences."[112]

Accordingly, identify what matters most to you at work, home, and in the community. Act with authenticity. Do what you think is right for your sake and don't worry about if anyone judges your life choices. In short, DO YOU!

Key Steps

1. Don't overdo it. No one can do it all, all the time.
2. Prioritize what's most important to you—career, family, children, etc.
3. Always bear in mind: motherhood and womanhood are not synonymous.
4. Be honest and open with yourself about what you truly want to get out of your job and your career.
5. Don't allow your family, friends, or colleagues to pressure you or dictate what your life should look like.
6. Avoid beating up on yourself over the decisions or shifts you make in your career and your personal life.
7. Explore your options; there's no one way or a right way to accomplish something.

---

112 Anjali Becker and Jeanne Engelmann, *Own It: Oprah Winfrey in Her Own Words* (Agate B2, 2016).

8. Find a partner or spouse who has similar aspirations, dreams, desires, and goals.
9. Formulate a support circle of friends and family members you trust.
10. Seek out both achievement and enjoyment. Don't forsake one area of your life for another—strive for the four-way win.

IN THE FACE OF ADVERSITY—STOP, LOOK, LISTEN

Turn your wounds into wisdom.
—Oprah Winfrey

Our bodies speak to us in whispers, and if we don't listen to those murmurs, our bodies start to scream at us. Our bodies give us warning signs of waning health long before we get hit with the news that we have a potentially life-threatening illness. My body had been whispering to me for close to two years. I started getting signs that something was wrong long before I was diagnosed in 2006 with systemic lupus erythematosus, a chronic, inflammatory autoimmune disease. My doctors told me that I've probably had lupus most of my life, but the symptoms did not manifest into anything significant until my midthirties

In the summer of 2005, I was having bouts with fatigue, swelling, and stiffening around my elbows, wrists, fingers, knees, and ankles, and periodic muscle aches. The symptoms started happening once a month or so. Within a few months, the symptoms were becoming a lot more frequent. I was soon experiencing symptoms several times a month, and eventually daily. As time passed, I found it difficult to get out of bed. My joints were so stiff and swollen that I could barely move. By afternoon, the symptoms would taper off and I would start to feel like my normal self again, until the next morning when the vicious cycle would start all over again. I was also experiencing unusual hair loss and unexplained low-grade fevers. Every morning when I combed my hair, there would be clumps of hair left behind in the teeth of the comb. Over time, I eventually decided to wear extensions to mask the hair loss.

I wouldn't have all those symptoms at one time. One week I would have stiff joints and the next week I would have chronic fatigue. Flu-like symptoms came and went. So I ignored it for a while. I thought, *Well, I am getting older. These things happen.* On top of that, I was traveling quite a bit. I was always traveling to another city or country for my job. My rationalization was that when you travel a lot you get jetlag and your body reacts differently to foods you eat and water that you drink in foreign places. I just figured that once I slowed down a bit, everything would be just fine. I basically diagnosed myself. *Wrong!* A mistake too many professional women make.

It wasn't until I started getting severe headaches that I knew something truly wasn't right. I *never* get headaches. At least not like the ones that I was experiencing daily. These weren't migraines—although I don't even know what a migraine feels like. But it was a dull headache at the center of my forehead, almost like what you would experience when you have a sinus infection. It was pain in the frontal lobe and cheekbone. Even my teeth would ache for no apparent reason. I dealt with that sensation on and off for several months before I finally decided to see a doctor.

At age thirty-seven, I had become a statistic, a black female stereotype. The reality is that black women have high rates of many illnesses or health issues, such as hypertension, breast cancer at young ages, diabetes, strokes, and lupus. Black women are more likely to develop certain health problems than white women, according to the "Black Women's Health Study" out of the Boston University Stone Epidemiology Center, which since 1995 has recognized the need to understand the causes of these illnesses and determinants of good health. The BWHS has gathered information on many conditions that affect black women—breast cancer, lupus, premature birth, hypertension, colon cancer, diabetes, uterine fibroids—the list is long.

I can't say with certainty what caused my illness, but I do know that for years my body was talking to me and I ignored her. As women, we are guilty of self-neglect. Long before pop star Alicia Keys sang about being a "Superwoman"—as African American women we are all too familiar with this pattern of behavior. You know you're trying to be a superwoman if you feel pressured to be able to do it all; you feel overworked, overwhelmed, and overly committed; you feel exhausted, anxious, and stressed to the max. As outlined by the American Psychological Association, the "Superwoman syndrome" is used to explain the phenomenon of early onset of illness or disease among African American women in response to persistent chronic stress associated with meeting day-to-day demands and having multiple caregiver roles.

Life as a superwoman or a woman of power is no easy feat, but the same drive pushing you to reach the top of your profession may leave you battling a life-threatening illness or health issue sooner rather than later, reports *The Root*.[113] Masking up as superwomen is killing us—whether we meet with death as a result of suicide or the stress leads to heart disease and other serious conditions. While I was donning my cape and mask on the job, my body was battling lupus.

I may not have ever come to know I had this disease if

---

113 Lottie Joiner, "Black May Not Crack, But We're Aging Faster Inside," *The Root*, November 20, 2013, http://www.theroot.com/black-may-not-crack-but-we-re-aging-faster-inside-1790898981.

David and I hadn't decided to start a family. Even as donors, David and I still needed to get full health exams before we could go through the whole medical process of extracting my eggs and collecting his sperm.

It was the spring of 2005. I remember the doctor reviewing the results of my bloodwork and asking, "Does lupus or some sort of inflammatory illness run in your family?"

To which I quickly replied, "No, not that I am aware of."

Slightly puzzled, he said, "Okay, but I just find it strange that you have a positive ANA test, which is one of the symptoms of diagnosing lupus."

I totally discarded the comment. In my mind, there was no real evidence of any serious medical condition. Again, my body was yelling at me and I was essentially telling her: *Will you please shut up!*

In July 2006, I was undergoing my fourth surgical procedure to rid my body of the fibroid tumors that had plagued me for most of my adult life. It had been eight years since I'd first gone to the hospital to have fibroid tumors removed. Again, I never gave much thought to it because it is a fact that African American women are nearly three times more likely to develop uterine fibroids and suffer more severe symptoms. Not to mention that the hysterectomy rate among African American women is more than double that of any other ethnic group, with the majority performed to treat noncancerous fibroid tumors.[114] Looking back, I now know that as black women we can't shrug it off and accept fibroids as something as common as a cold.

114 Alicia Armeli, "African American Women & Uterine Fibroids: Why More Awareness Is Needed to Overcome This Health Disparity," Merit Medical, June 16, 2016, http://ask4ufe.com/african-american-women-uterine-fibroids-awareness-needed-overcome-health-disparity/.

Anyhow, on this occasion, my fibroid removal took place at Columbia Presbyterian Hospital in New York City. I was scheduled to have surgery at one p.m. and we were requested to arrive at the hospital at ten a.m. I was not very nervous at all since I had been on the operating table before. I sat calmly and quietly while I was being set up with IVs and other pre-operative procedures. As the anesthesiologist prepped me, he suggested, "After your surgery, you might want to talk to a doctor and have some additional blood work done because your SED rate levels are extremely high. You need to get that checked out."

A sedimentation rate, or SED, is a common blood test that is used to detect and monitor inflammation in the body. Here again, a medical professional was having a conversation with me about an inflammatory illness.

That was the final wakeup call. After the surgery, I went to see a rheumatologist. The first person I saw was very stoic and had a terrible bedside manner. During my first and only visit with him, he sat on a stool in front of me with limited eye contact. He did not break the news gently, he just casually stated, "We are sorry to inform you, but you do have lupus, or systemic lupus erythematosus, to be more specific. SLE is what it's called."

I looked at the doctor square in the eye and asked, "Okay, how do we treat this? What are my options?"

He rattled off a list of four or five medications that I should start taking immediately. I sat there deflated. I was rambling in my head: *How could I have been diagnosed with such a serious illness? I am a former athlete, exercise regularly, eat healthy, and maintain a relatively stress-free lifestyle . . . if there is such a thing. Why me?*

The only person I told at this point about my diagnosis

was my husband. I basically kept my diagnosis between the two of us. I then started to delve into all kinds of research about the disease on the Internet. Lupus isn't rare—around 1.5 million Americans, mostly women, are affected.[115] In lupus, something goes horribly wrong with your immune system, the part of the body that fights off viruses, bacteria, and germs ("foreign invaders" like the flu). Normally, our immune system produces proteins called antibodies that protect the body from foreign invaders. When you have lupus, your immune system cannot tell the difference between these foreign invaders and your body's healthy tissues, so autoantibodies are generated to damage and destroy healthy tissue. These autoantibodies cause inflammation and pain.

Shortly after my diagnosis, I was having those lupus flares on a regular basis, and it was starting to impact vital organs like my kidneys, my heart, and my lungs. One of my doctors told me: "You're not going to live to see fifty if you keep going down this road." I had to do something different.

Thank heavens that I had begun working with a wellness coach. It all started with those unexplained body aches. Sometimes the pain was so excruciating that I would end up in the ER, with a needle in my arm and a tube attached to an IV bag, getting a morphine drip to manage the pain. I would have to be given a narcotic because by this point, I was writhing in pain and crying out loud. It was *bad*. I didn't know it at the time, but this typically happens with lupus flares. I would have increasingly frequent bouts with swelling and pain, so I decided to get a wellness coach.

I was at the Chicago O'Hare Airport on my way to Switzerland. I had just attended a diversity conference and was looking forward to going home. I was in a bookstore and picked up

---

115 Lupus Fact Sheet, Lupus Research Alliance, New York, 2017.

a magazine; as I was flipping through it, I came across an article about Adrienne-Joi Johnson, more commonly credited as
AJ Johnson. She was an actress and a choreographer who had
made many guest appearances on sitcoms, television dramas,
and music videos. I knew of her from her supporting roles in
the films *House Party* and *Baby Boy*. She was Sharane, the best
friend of Sidney, played by Tisha Campbell in the Kid 'n Play
hip-hop *House Party* franchise, and she played Tyrese's mother
in John Singleton's coming-of-age film.

As I read the magazine article on the plane, I learned that
in addition to being an actress and dancer, AJ was a wellness
coach to celebrities, and the host of the VH1 reality fitness
competition series called *From Flab to Fab*. What's more, she
often held wellness retreats for her clients. Having lost her
mother to cancer at age seventeen, she was also the spokes-
person for the American Cancer Society and some weight-loss
products, not to mention she made various appearances for
Procter & Gamble, GSK Pharmaceuticals, and Walmart.

After arriving in Switzerland (where I was now living), I
called AJ's office the next day. By this point I was desperate.
Desperate to get my wellness back. I was willing to spend my
last dime to get healthy again. After literally harassing her
team for a few minutes to speak directly with AJ, she finally
got on the phone with me. We talked for close to one hour. I
recounted the exhausting story of my health journey up until that point. She offered to host a private wellness retreat
for me in Miami where we would have some real one-on-one
time to better understand my health situation and to put a
short- and long-term action plan in place. I was humbled by
the thought that a celebrity I didn't know would take the time
to help me reach my better self.

AJ and I met face-to-face for the very first time in Miami

on November 5, 2008, the day after Barack Obama was elected president of the United States. I was still reeling from the excitement of America having elected its first black president as I flew from Zurich to Newark International Airport. I had a connecting flight to Miami the very next day for the personal retreat that I was about to embark on with the woman who would ultimately save my life—and, most importantly, save me from myself.

That weekend featured fitness sessions like sunset yoga and strength training, meditation on the beach, and nutritional counseling. A vital discovery was that I was getting in my own way. AJ and I would work on this issue for several years. As an exclusive client of AJ's, I would have Skype calls with her that consisted of fitness and nutritional coaching, along with problem-solving exercises and homework.

My regimen with AJ was quite strict. I had gained thirty pounds from the steroid medication I had been prescribed by my physician to control the lupus flares and swelling. I was working out five days a week. With AJ, we were not simply focused on the physical health but mental health as well, utilizing many spiritual tools like books, music, meditation, and long lavender soaks in the tub. We addressed my eating habits. AJ advised me to reduce my sugar, salt, and intake of carbohydrates. We focused on increasing my protein intake. I reduced my consumption of red meat significantly and was eating a lot more fish and chicken. I reduced my caloric intake to 1,200 calories per day, which was quite effective in my losing the weight.

Another crucial lesson I learned from AJ was how to be my own health advocate when I went to the doctor, which was something I wasn't doing. She taught me all the things I needed to know to really be a real champion for myself when

I went to the doctor. I would just listen and take it all in. I wasn't writing anything down. I wasn't asking a lot of questions. I was basically sitting there and inquiring, "Okay, so how do we treat this?" Instead of asking, "So, is there a holistic method or some alternative method?"

I really was not as proactive as I could have been until one day AJ said, "Are you crazy? You're going in front of these doctors and you're not even asking questions? You're not even going in with as much as a pen and a piece of paper?"

Truth be told, I am not alone. Studies show black and Latino patients are less likely to ask doctors questions and to be as involved in the conversation as white patients. Poor communication is a cause of disparities in health among people of color and marginalized groups. According to research gathered by the US National Library of Medicine at the National Institute of Health, effective two-way conversations between patient and physician improve the overall quality of health care with respect to decision-making about subsequent interventions.

Under the old model, doctors told patients what to do and they did it—no questions asked. The new model is a mutually respectful partnership. So, never allow a doctor or other health care professional make you feel uncomfortable. "If you find it difficult to ask questions, ask a more assertive family member or friend to accompany you during visits," advises *Black Enterprise*, in the article "Become an Empowered Patient."[116] It's important for you to understand your illness, the article suggests. "Your doctor shouldn't feel threatened by your probing questions." I am now a lot more vigilant about going to the doctor for health checkups; getting my blood work done on a

116 Leslie E. Royal, "Become an Empowered Patient," March 11, 2001, http://www.blackenterprise.com/lifestyle/become-an-empowered-patient/.

regular basis. Even if the doctor doesn't suggest certain tests, I'll push: "Can we check this? Can we check that?"

I started to live differently with AJ's help. I made some real conscious changes to my lifestyle. I made subtle changes in my crazy travel schedule and day-to-day work environment. This meant getting more sleep at night; I was sleep deprived and I didn't even know it. I was operating on five or six hours of sleep at night. Who can do that long term? That's not sustainable for anyone's body. Instead of working twelve to fourteen hours a day, I started working eight to ten hours. Instead of working on the weekends, I took a break. Sunday became solely family time. I would spend the entire day at home or doing things with David and Myles Davis—even if it was just taking our beloved Yorkie for longer walks. We all just chilled out. Sunday was truly our day of rest.

Conversely, don't wait until you are diagnosed with a chronic illness before you take your health seriously and strive for a better work/life balance. Take a proactive approach and not a reactive one. Your health is affected by your workload and your surrounding environment. Let my situation serve as a lesson. Your health comes first—always!

Thank you to my sister-friend AJ Johnson for teaching me that lesson and saving my life.

Suffering in Silence

Another issue is the tendency for women to suffer in silence about whatever ails them. In my case, it would be another eight months after I got the initial diagnosis before I told my family I had lupus. The reason I didn't tell anyone, especially my parents, was because I just didn't want them to worry. It didn't take long before hiding my illness became a chore, and deep down inside I began to suspect my parents were on to me.

I went to visit with them one weekend as I normally do. We were in the kitchen and I announced that I had something important to tell them. "The doctor diagnosed me as having lupus," I blurted out. They were stunned, their eyes glassy. I described the nature of the illness, my long-term prognosis, and the course of treatment I was receiving.

I told my sisters at about the same time as I told my parents. They really didn't say much. It was more about, "Are you okay? How is it being treated?" Here's the thing: my twin didn't even disclose anything about herself at that time. Monique didn't say, *Oh, I have joint pain,* or, *Oh, I have swelling,* or, *I have headaches too,* or, *I have anemia.* We were suffering from similar symptoms but she didn't utter a word about her health issues over the years. It wasn't until she was diagnosed with lupus nearly two years after me that she mentioned any of this. Like me, she was partly in denial and unaware. Come to find out that her health issues were lupus-related.

They say lupus patients are like snowflakes: no two are the same, not even identical twins. Although Monique and I were only three minutes apart, my lupus looks very different than hers.

Now, take it from me: when you have a chronic illness, you need an ally at your place of work. Ask yourself if your chronic illness will require certain accommodations, like a different work schedule because of medications or the need for frequent breaks. If the answer is yes, then you need to be open with your manager or HR rep.

Little complications, as I would call them, of the illness were starting to present themselves to me on the job. I was having issues with my memory. My short-term memory loss was starting to become a lot more apparent, to me at least. I used to have a photographic memory, meaning I could look at a presentation, like a deck of thirty or forty slides, and I could memorize every single one. All I had to do was simply look at it one time. It was a gift that I possessed. My dad and my granddaddy also had this gift. I had always leaned on and relied on that gift. I used it throughout my career, and it was crucial to my way of operating as a leader every day. It was a skill I took a lot of pride in.

There was one situation during a leadership team meeting in Switzerland, where I was presenting some information, and my mind went completely blank in front of five hundred people. I lost my train of thought, I couldn't remember small words. It was probably only a minute or two where I was quiet, but it felt like days of silence in my mind. I was standing in front of these people—all eyes were on me—and nothing was coming out, my mouth was dry, my lips weren't moving. My heart sank. I was devastated. Afterward, everyone in that room remarked how I did a great job and that my presentation was *fabulous*. But when I arrived home that night and walked into the house, David looked at me and asked, "How did it go? How was your presentation?"

I collapsed into his arms, crying hysterically. I blabbered, "I'm losing my skill. I'm performing subpar and I'm not where I need to be. They're going to see right through me."

After that devastating scenario, I decided to tell my boss Thomas Ebeling, who was the CEO of the pharmaceutical division at Novartis. I walked into his office for one of our regular one-on-one conversations. I sat down in the chair directly in front of his desk. I didn't even go into my normal, *Here's an update in terms of what's happening work-related*. I told him: "Here's the situation: I have lupus."

I went on to explain to him what it was and it how was impacting me: "I'm not the same person I used to be. My memory comes and goes. I have swelling and inflammation occasionally. I have to be mindful about blood clotting and all of this other stuff. You might see some behavioral changes. I just wanted to tell you all of this, to let you know this information about my illness, because you're my manager and I trust you."

He looked at me solemnly and said, "I'm disappointed."

I didn't respond, but I looked at him like, *Disappointed?* Then he said, "I don't know why you didn't tell me this sooner. I'm disappointed in the fact that you felt you couldn't come to me with this before now."

Teary-eyed and all: "I don't want this to impact how you all perceive me as a leader in this company. I want to be treated like everybody else. I don't want to be identified as the sick one," I muttered. "You know, *Yeah, that's Michelle, the sick person.* I will do my best to continue to do great work, but I want to be treated like everybody else."

He was comforting, so compassionate, as he reassured me: "That's not an issue. Your secret is safe with me and I'm glad you told me."

He genuinely cared about me as an individual and not just because of what I was doing for him in the company. I was battling a chronic illness that could take my life and I hadn't even had the gumption or the courage to share it with him. He's a good friend to this day. I still reach out to him and he always asks, "Michelle, how's your health? How are things going? How are you doing?"

It wasn't only that I didn't open up to my boss. On top of that, I was working in the pharmaceutical industry. Can you imagine? Here I am, working alongside people who spend their days and nights trying to come up with a cure for cancer and other diseases. I was taking an antimalarial medication to help keep me well—which Novartis made—and I didn't even tell my coworkers I was on our own meds.

My illness was not a secret at work once I was at Harvard University in Cambridge receiving the Businesswoman of the Year Award by the Harvard Black Men's Forum. As part of my acceptance speech, I announced that I had lupus in front of approximately two hundred students, my colleagues, and my family. I received a standing ovation. That was a proud moment. A few students hugged me afterward and told me about their family members who also suffered from lupus. It felt like a weight had just been lifted from my shoulders. The secret was out. I can still see my mother's shocked expression; my family did not know that I was going to make this pronouncement to the world. She couldn't believe that I would openly share my health issues. I let her know: "If I can inform other young women and men about the symptoms of this illness and potentially save a life, I will continue to share my story."

I made up my mind that I was no longer going to hide my illness from anyone, not even future employers. When the executive headhunter representing Credit Suisse telephoned me saying that they had a chief diversity officer role available in Zurich, Switzerland, I didn't hold back. I went to speak with the recruiter and mentioned it during my initial meeting. I wanted to be transparent so that management at Credit Suisse knew exactly what they were potentially investing in by hiring me.

During the course of several months of over thirty interviews, I let everyone I spoke with know about my illness. I met with the CEO; I met with the chairman; I met with the CEO's direct reports and the members of the HR executive committee. Yes, it was a lot of different people. Everyone had a vote, a say about whether I got the job.

Those conversations went something like this: "Look, I'm not like everybody else. I have this autoimmune illness and it shows up in certain ways. Sometimes I have swellings. Sometimes I need to go to the ER to treat my flares. Sometimes I have joint pains, headaches, hair loss, and anemia." I went down the list.

They would look at me stoically and say something like: "Okay, thanks for sharing that, but you didn't have to."

I would declare, "Yes, I do, because I want you to understand that my symptoms can vary and change over time; my memory sometimes comes and goes. So, when it comes to you assessing me as a professional, keep that in mind. Don't just think at face value that because I look well that I *am* well."

To which the person interviewing me typically responded, "No problem."

This goes for anyone out there. You could have a person with MS who shows up to work every day. They're fine, then suddenly that person loses sight in one eye. Things happen. We all come to work with our stuff. I just let them know up front what mine was. They could have easily said, "Oh no." But they hired me despite my illness.

Legally, you don't have to disclose anything about your disease to your employer. And hey—if your illness never has and never will affect your job performance, then nobody needs to know your personal business. But if you think your health might impact your work down the road, you need to speak up. You should talk to the people you spend eight or more hours a day with, and help them better understand how they can help with your medical condition. A discussion with human resources is warranted. You can edit what you disclose to HR. Your objective is to make people aware and alleviate their fears about what to do if something happens to you on the job.

Getting a Handle on Stress and Work

In all honesty, I should have been up front with my bosses about my health long before my lupus diagnosis, because my workload was impacting my health. I believe that a lot of my health issues were related to the stress that I exposed myself to over the years. I suppressed a lot of stress between work and home. I'm not the type to wear my stress on my face or to lash out at people; everything is so inward with me. I had no family history of lupus; we don't know what causes lupus. It's not something I ate, an unhealthy diet. Nothing like that. Stress can cause chronic illness.

Don't just take my word for it. Countless research shows the correlation between stress and illness. Stress accelerates the aging of black female bodies, and "black women between the ages of 45 and 55 are biologically 7.5 years older than white women" of the same age, according to *The Root*.[117] According to the American Psychological Association, intense or prolonged chronic stress can be overwhelming on the body and a risk factor for several diseases—coronary vascular disease, obesity, diabetes, depression, cognitive impairment, and both inflammatory and autoimmune disorders.[118]

Unfortunately, this fact comes as no surprise: racial and ethnic minorities have medical issues far worse than the overall health of white Americans. Perceived discrimination has been found to be a key factor in chronic stress–related health disparities, such as hypertension and diabetes; and unhealthy behaviors such as cigarette smoking, alcohol use, substance

---

117   Joiner, "Black May Not Crack, but We're Aging Faster Inside."

118   Mary K. Alvord, Karina W. Davidson, Jennifer F. Kelly, Kevin M. McGuiness, and Steven Tovian, "Understanding Chronic Stress," American Psychological Association, http://www.apa.org/helpcenter/understanding-chronic-stress.aspx.

abuse, improper nutrition, and refusal to seek medical services.[119]

Catalyst research found evidence of an "emotional tax" that is levied on African American professionals "as they try to successfully navigate through their careers."[120] According to Catalyst, an "emotional tax is the heightened experience of being different from peers at work because of your gender, race, or ethnicity, and the associated detrimental effects on your health, well-being, and the ability to thrive" in the workplace when your unvalued work and unrealistic expectations are too much to bear.

It's not just our physical well-being but our mental health that is at risk when it comes to workplace stress, which can lead to feelings of helplessness or lack of control. Many of us know all too well that depression is a taboo in the black community. Some African Americans simply don't believe in depression even though many constantly face discrimination and negative stereotypes in and outside of the workplace. Even so, studies show that African Americans are 20 percent more likely to report serious psychological distress than whites.[121] We face a hard time expressing our emotions with family members and friends for various reasons, including the misperception that depression is not a "real issue" but rather something that you can just "get over."

My friend Terrie Williams explains her struggles and the stigmas attached to depression in her book *Black Pain: It Just Looks Like We're Not Hurting*. As founder of her own public

119 "Fact Sheet: Health Disparities and Stress," American Psychological Association, http://www.apa.org/topics/health-disparities/fact-sheet-stress.aspx.

120 Dnika J. Travis, Jennifer Thorpe-Moscon, and Courtney McCluney, "Emotional Tax: How Black Women and Men Pay More at Work and How Leaders Can Take Action," Catalyst, 2016, http://www.catalyst.org/knowledge/emotional-tax-how-black-women-and-men-pay-more-work-and-how-leaders-can-take-action.

121 "Mental Health and African Americans," US Department of Health and Human Services Office of Minority Mental Health, 2016.

relations agency, Williams represented the likes of Eddie Mur-
phy and Miles Davis. But in addition to handling a superstar
client list, Williams was also managing dysthymia, a form of
low-level but debilitating depression. For thirty years, she kept
on her game face of success, exhausting herself daily to satisfy
her clients' needs while neglecting her own. As she healed,
her mission became clear: break the silence of this crippling
taboo and help those who suffer. Williams sees *Black Pain* as
a guide to finding relief through faith, therapy, diet, and exercise, as well as through building a supportive network (and
eliminating toxic people). Williams encourages us to face the
truth about an issue that plunges our spirits into darkness, so
that we can step into the healing light.

I was never diagnosed with depression, but I've had many
down days dealing with my lupus. I've had my bouts with self-
pity and self-doubt. This illness, all these changes in my body
including my memory loss, yeah, I was shattered. Here it was,
I had been this great track athlete. Now I had this disease
starting to manifest itself in different ways and other people were
going to see I had a weakness. I felt like I couldn't run as fast as
my peers—I'm not that corporate athlete I used to be, I'm not as
smart as I used to be. I think we are all our own worst critics.

Don't get me wrong, there were people around me saying,
"Michelle, you still have it. I don't get it. You can give them
your C game and it's still an outstanding performance. You
didn't even have to give them your A game." I made it my
mission to surround myself with people who would reinforce
that I'm still talented, I'm still the same person, I still do a
great job, I still show up well. There were days when no matter
who was around me—that didn't work. I was self-conscious
and belittling myself.

It's hard for me even to this day, because life is full of

stressors. But I try to use my tools, the wellness trainings with AJ over the years, to help me cope. I take time out during the day to meditate. I do breathing exercises. I'm equipped to handle the stressors of life that occur every single day, whereas a little over ten years ago, I was left to my own devices to figure it out. I don't take my health for granted. None of us can afford to do so. I have gained a better understanding of work/life balance—what it could look like for me with AJ continuing as my wellness coach, helping to design it. My health had to fail me in order for me to make those lifestyle changes.

Dr. Janet Taylor, a psychiatrist based in Florida, reminds us that "the ability to maintain a healthy work and home life balance may seem impossible to women in high-profile positions, but developing healthy coping skills may help and may become easier with practice and positive reinforcement. Nothing is perfect. We all seek control, but life is full of challenges that we must learn from and continue to grow."[122] She thinks it's a good idea to acknowledge when congratulations are in order. "Women should congratulate themselves on their expectations and get real by prioritizing what's important as it relates to two things, passion and purpose," explains Taylor, who is a frequent contributor to CBS *This Morning, The Today Show,* and *Good Morning America* on the subjects of stress management, parenting, and work/life balance. "The goal is to identify those moments in a hectic day. Replace perfection by striving for purpose and passion every day," she advises.

My illness has brought about newfound passion and purpose in my life. This still ties back to my desire to help others

---

122 Brittany Dandy, "More Success More Problems: Power Women Prone to Higher Stress," *Black Enterprise*, April 17, 2015, http://www.blackenterprise.com/lifestyle/more-success-more-problems-power-women-prone-higher-stress/.

and to share my story. I've made it my mission to continue to educate myself and others about lupus. I now sit on the board of directors for the S.L.E. Lupus Foundation of New York. I talk openly about my illness because my feeling is that I could be saving a life, especially the life of a woman of color, because we are three times more likely to get lupus than our white female counterparts. Any time I talk about lupus, especially to a black audience, there's always three, four, five people who will walk up to me and say, "I have lupus," or, "My mother had lupus," or, "My aunt has lupus." I'm educating people about a chronic disease that is more prevalent than MS (multiple sclerosis) or some of the other autoimmune diseases.

I remember when celebrated *Good Morning America* anchor Robin Roberts beat breast cancer in 2007. Five years later she was on national television revealing to the world that she had myelodysplastic syndrome (MDS)—a type of bone marrow disease with around twelve thousand new cases diagnosed each year, according to the American Cancer Society. Robin has described herself as a "walking miracle," because doctors told her that she had two years to live without a transplant. She began speaking more candidly than ever before, opening up about the challenges she faced after her life-altering diagnosis, and all of the people who loved her through it, including her longtime girlfriend, Amber Laign.[123] When the news broke in 2012, it was the first time that Robin had acknowledged publicly that she was in a relationship with another woman. One of the comments that Robin made during a TV segment in talking about being a breast cancer survivor was that she was going to "make a message out of her mess." I told myself, *Maybe that's why I was chosen*

---

123 Sharon Cotliar, "Robin Roberts Feels Like She's a 'Walking Miracle,'" *People*, April 16, 2014, http://people.com/celebrity/robin-roberts-feels-like-shes-a-walking-miracle/.

to have this illness: to shed light on lupus. Perhaps I was supposed to talk to other patients who have this illness.

Consequently, I began to talk to lupus patients in support groups and visit with them in the hospital. I see women in wheelchairs. Women who look like us—black women—who are stroke victims, who are amputees, who are dealing with stem cell transplantation or implantation. I also began to befriend other individuals with lupus like Zenay Arnold. Veteran singer and actress Tichina Arnold is best known as the quick-witted Pamela James from the classic sitcom *Martin* and the family matriarch on the sitcom *Everybody Hates Chris*. She is also a lupus advocate and cofounder along with her sister Zenay of the We Win Foundation. It was formed to help individuals, as well as the families and caregivers who support those suffering with lupus and other related autoimmune diseases.

I met Tichina in February 2013 at a fitness event in LA that was hosted by *Essence* magazine and Nike, the day prior to the *Essence* Black Women in Hollywood luncheon. I had read about Tichina's We Win Foundation and the fact that her sister was a lupus patient. As Tichina entered the room, I walked straight up to her and introduced myself. I told her about my having lupus and my working with AJ. I offered to assist her with the great work that her foundation was doing to support lupus patients and caregivers. We exchanged contact information and I reached out two days later. Tichina was gracious with her time. She provided me with her sister's contact information as well.

Zenay was thirty-two when she woke up one morning and her body refused to move. She had to be rushed to the hospital. The test results showed several autoimmune diseases had taken her body hostage. One of the more aggressive diseases was lupus.

Ten years later she is thriving, and winning, with lupus

and six other autoimmune disorders. Zenay is one of the kindest women I have ever met. She is so knowledgeable about the illness and suggests holistic methods for treatment when I need them. We talk about our illness and we share our stories; we share our remedies.

Tichina and Zenay honored me at the very first We Win Foundation Awards event held in Phoenix a few years back. The Arnold sisters have been such a blessing in my life. We have established a very close bond and keep in touch regularly. Whenever I am in LA or they are on the East Coast, we make it a point to try to see each other. They are my sister-friends and I love them dearly. AJ and the Arnold sisters helped me realize that sucess should not be measured by status and wealth alone, but also by our health and wellness.

As African American women, if we are working twice as hard and suffering twice as much from certain illnesses than other groups, then we need to pay heed to the correlation. Something in our immune systems suffer if we are constantly battling adversity in this unrelenting determination to succeed. Yes, at times we all must make sacrifices. In striving to rise higher in your career, one of those sacrifices cannot be neglecting your physical and mental health. Trust me, meditation, acupuncture, and regular spa days will do the mind and body good. Seek mental health counseling or life coaching—which is not a sign that you're weak or crazy—when stress starts to affect your mood, activity, sleep, eating habits, or weight. I know that for me, if I don't do these things, I won't be here. And believe me, I want to be here. And so should you.

Key Steps

1. Listen to your body. Pay attention to warning signs of waning health.

2. Don't neglect yourself. Get plenty of sleep (eight hours a night is ideal). Maintain a healthy diet—eat breakfast, lunch, and dinner, and drink plenty of water.

3. We're not meant to be superwomen. Take off that mask and cape. You don't need to do everything, be everywhere, and aide everybody.

4. Learn how to manage stress, improve focus, and increase resilience.

5. Schedule annual health and wellness checkups with your doctor. Be your own advocate—ask plenty of questions.

6. Use your vacation time—you've earned it. Try not to work while on vacation. It's okay to check in once in a while. Appoint a deputy or another colleague to look after your work while you are out of the office.

7. Set aside time for yourself to replenish weekly—warm bath soaks, meditation, or reading good books.

8. Try not to schedule more than four meetings in your workday. Be sure to incorporate some desk time.

9. Don't suffer in silence. Get support from other people who can help you cope with whatever ails you.

10. Yes, we all need to earn a living. But to lead a happier and more fulfilling life, our mind, body, and spirit must take priority.

9

FINDING MY FEARLESS SELF

I learned that courage was not the absence of fear,
but the triumph over it.
—Nelson Mandela

In February 2017, Tampa Bay Buccaneers quarterback Jameis Winston addressed a group of fifth graders at a school in St. Petersburg, Florida. Here's what the youngsters were told, as reported by the *Tampa Bay Times*:

> "All my young boys, stand up. The ladies, sit down," Winston said. "But all my boys, stand up. We strong, right? We strong! We strong, right? All my boys, tell me one time: I can do anything I put my mind to. Now a lot of boys aren't supposed to be soft-spoken. You know what I'm saying? One day y'all are going to have a very deep voice like this (in deep voice). One day, you'll have a very, very deep voice. But the ladies, they're supposed to be silent, polite, gentle. My men, my men supposed to be strong. I want y'all to tell me what the third rule of life is: I can do anything I put my mind to. Scream it!"[124]

Later, Winston tried to recant, explaining he used "poor

---

124   Tome Jones, "Jameis Winston's Pep Talk to Kids Sends Wrong Message," the *Tampa Bay Times*, February 22, 2017, http://www.tampabay.com/sports/jones-jameis-winstons-pep-talk-to-kids-sends-wrong-message-wvideo/2314204.

word choice." Instead of empowering all the students in that auditorium, he chose to tell a group of fifth graders that girls need to be silent and boys need to be strong. Women deserve to have a voice. Little girls have the right to speak up. We can't continue to teach our girls that there is only one way they should act. If they come across as strong, then they're behaving like boys. Nor can we continue to raise our boys to play rough and tough all the time.

Gender roles, and how we express those roles, are imposed upon us from the day we are born. Blue is for baby boys and pink is for baby girls. Toy trucks and Legos are for little boys while dolls and playhouses are for little girls. Boys must play rough otherwise they're labeled a *sissy*. Girls must be passive in their play or they'll get labeled a *tomboy*.

I was never one to accept restrictive gender roles. It was okay with me for little girls to love their G.I. Joe with the Kung Fu Grip as much as they loved their Barbie doll. Little boys could jump double-dutch and still race toy cars on a track. Girls and boys alike can love sports as much as they love dance. Men and women alike can be adept at plating a five-course meal, donning a chef's coat, or building a two-story home wearing a hardhat. Couples—gay or straight—can shed tears during a romantic comedy and then fist bump watching a bone-cracking martial arts flick. Need I say more?

As a little girl, I learned to speak up for myself and to stand up for others. Growing up in North Edison, where there weren't many children who looked like me, you had to fight for your place in the world—or at least in my neighborhood. You had to do things to make yourself known and to differentiate yourself. If not, it was almost like—as a little brown-skinned girl—I'd be diluted some kind of way in a pool of white children. When it came to fighting for or standing up for others, I've always been the type of individual who just had to help whenever I saw another kid getting a beat-down. I did it with my twin sister. If anybody was teasing or messing with Monique, I would make it a point to holler, "Hey, leave my sister alone!"

Though I'd stand up for anyone, being in an area where there weren't many other brown boys and girls instilled in me early on the need to stand up for those who were silenced, marginalized, and made invisible because of race, gender, or sexual orientation.

When Monique and I were fourteen, there was racial tension in our junior high school among some of the white and black girls. I can't recall what started it all but I was arguing with one of the white girls at school when her mother and a few of the other white women in the neighborhood pulled up in their cars. This mother jumped out and screamed at me: "Why are you attacking my daughter?"

We weren't really attacking her. There was no physical altercation between her daughter and me. But this woman started to throw blows. She grabbed me, pushed me up against the car, and pulled my left arm behind my back. It was quite a scene. Here it is, I was out in the street fighting with someone's mother. I was basically defending myself and my friends— really, every other minority who was there at that school.

This tiny altercation was now a big ordeal. It swelled into a mini race riot. The police were called, but no one was arrested. The girl's mother wanted to press charges. Within a few days, there was a meeting called at the municipal building near the police headquarters. All the kids who were involved in the incident and their parents were in attendance. A well-respected businesswoman and neighbor, Bertha Griffin, also was in the room that day. Bertha, who is African American, was an influential figurehead in our community. She was respected by whites and blacks alike. She made it her business to attend the meeting to ensure that everyone was treated fairly and justly. There was a great deal of tension as both sides had an opportunity to air their grievances. Since no one was hurt, no property was damaged, and we were all basically good kids with no previous incidents of trouble, we were simply instructed to apologize to one another.

This incident, and others, shaped who I am. It laid the foundation, paved the way for a fulfilling career in human capital and diversity. I would need to be fearless if I wanted to be successful in a field where I would be standing and speaking up for myself and others.

I'm a fighter. Innately, that's my personality. Undeniably, I have a slight Napoleon complex—which is typically defined as people of short stature with overly aggressive personalities. I'm five foot two and a half. So I always felt the need to make my presence known, whether it was slamming doors as a girl or walking into a room and being the first one to talk. I've always had a knack for drawing attention to myself and others.

When I started working at Novartis, its African American employee resource group was in its infancy. African American professionals at the company decided to convene an employee network to discuss issues that were unique and germane to them in the workplace. They wanted the group to come up with solutions to make it a better environment.

In general, employee resource groups (ERGs) and affinity groups are voluntary, employee-led groups made up of individuals who band together based on a shared set of common interests, experiences, perspectives, backgrounds, or demographic factors. ERGs serve as a resource for members and organizations by fostering a diverse, inclusive workplace aligned

with the organizational mission, values, goals, business practices, and objectives. Other benefits include the development
of future leaders.

I was representing HR and the diversity function as a representative of senior management as the executive director
of diversity at Novartis. I was also a member of the African
American ERG (called the African American Network—
AAN). At first, other members of the AAN at Novartis exercised caution about what they said around me, not knowing
if I would share that information with senior management. I
gained their trust once I told them: "I know how to straddle
the line between you all trusting me, and me giving high-level
themes of what's happening with us as a community at this
company. I know how to do both, and I would hope that you
would trust me enough."

The AAN comprised about twenty-five active members
who led committees and programming, and everyone else who
would show their support simply by attending the events. That
was fine by us. We just wanted to see some representation of
ourselves at the signature events where senior leadership was
invited. There was a nice cross-divisional representation of
AAN members who frequently showed their support. There
were more women than men—mainly because most of the
male members were in senior roles and felt that they did not
have a lot of time for planning and execution. In my experience, it's usually the female employees who will roll up their
sleeves and dive right into the work no matter what level they
represent on the food chain. The AAN made it a point to collaborate with the other ERGs. It was important to do so since
most of them had more critical mass, especially the women's
network, and had been established a little longer.

I spoke of the employee engagement survey in Chapter 4,

and how the results revealed that African American employees were unhappier than any other demographic employed at Novartis during that time. This links back to when Sallie invited me to sit at the table during that boardroom meeting and I dared to speak up about the dissatisfaction among and departure of African American employees. No one really knew why we were unhappy, nor did anyone care or dare to ask us why. At least until I seized the opportunity to present the problems and propose solutions to aid the African American employees.

Another black female colleague and I put together a slide presentation outlining the current state of affairs. We discovered that the African American employees were not getting promoted as readily as other populations. There was no pipeline development opportunity for them. Instead of talking about the problem with HR and helping to solve it, the African American employees were resigning and leaving the company. HR was not looking at the exit interview data to figure out why they were quitting.

What's more, the AAN was held back by the fear factor. It was this sense of being misjudged by their bosses who might think, *There they are, starting trouble.* As black people, we can get so caught up in the optics of what it looks like to others if they see us coming together versus the things that we can do collectively to make the workplace better. Three or more black people sitting together in the cafeteria, talking in a meeting room, or gathering in the hallway—*why, they must be up to no good, right?* That is what we presume is the perception on both sides. Whereas the white women would sit together, the Asian employees would sit together, or white guys would sit together, and no one said a word about it—nor did any of them look like they were fearful of anything or anybody.

Hence, many of the African American employees were more concerned about not making trouble than making a positive difference at Novartis.

My colleague and I presented our findings to the executive committee and the CEO. She was there to present the information and I was there in full support of what was being discussed, straddling the fence between being an African American employee and a diversity practitioner. On more than one occasion we both heard: "Well, nobody cares about us. I don't know why you're wasting time creating this slideshow. It's not like they're going to do anything." In any case, we felt compelled to do it—to present our findings to executive leadership.

The presentation took place after lunch in the executive boardroom. The audience was thirteen men and three women. My colleague and I were the only people of color in the room. We were a little nervous about the discussion as we weren't sure how the information would be received. All that we knew was that we had a problem and wanted to be an integral part of the solution. Senior management accepted our recommendations. Next thing I knew, the chief operating officer volunteered to be the executive sponsor of the African American employees, to better understand what our issues were and to help us by providing support and strategic guidance so that we were aligned with, and supportive of, the company's business objectives. That would not have happened had we not shown that presentation and had a conversation with senior management.

To that end, Novartis' Diversity & Inclusion Council consisted of senior leaders and members of the employee resource groups. In addition to supporting recruitment, retention, and career development strategies and initiatives, the ERGs brought about greater multicultural awareness and respect among all employees at Novartis. There were a few other fledgling ERGs with similar missions and visions. We all tried to work collaboratively.

The AAN would meet once per month. We would talk about the opportunities to mitigate and remedy our circumstances. Our goal was in part to not be perceived by management as a threat or as a group of employees who were complaining about what was wrong with the company; we wanted to be perceived as appreciative workers coming to the table with some meaningful solutions to help make the company a place for us to have fulfilling long-term careers. So we created all kinds of career development programs. We would bring in guest speakers during Black History Month. We shared the best diversity practices from other companies.

We were a tight-knit group. Some of the African American employees at Novartis remained skeptical and never attended any of the AAN meetings. Those of us who showed up were convinced that we were doing good work at the company. We cared enough to create a better work environment and contribute to the company culture, which would help us all be successful. We all saw the bigger picture.

Benefits of Joining Employee Resource Groups

It wasn't just our network at Novartis that was struggling to gain its footing in a large organization. As a matter of fact, the African American ERGs in *every* company I've worked for seemed to struggle, which included efforts to secure financial backing. In general, budgets for ERGs will vary depending upon the size and scope, as well as their relevance to the business. While black ERGs struggled, the women's ERGs could plan these wonderful forums and get the necessary funding.

Maybe it's because there was a more critical mass of women working at these companies. Or perhaps it was because African American employees remained paralyzed by the fear factor, or they simply did not see or demonstrate the value in ERGs. And yet, such networks were initially established on our behalf.

ERGs were started as race-based employee groups in response to racial tensions in the 1960s. Xerox Corporation was cited for its groundbreaking approach toward discrimination and achieving equality in the workforce. Taking action after violent race riots in Rochester, New York, in 1964, black employees at Xerox established the company's first regional caucus in 1965. The Bay Area Black Employees (BABE) group at Xerox Corporation formed in 1969 to support the hiring, development, and promotion of qualified minority applicants—a move that followed race riots tearing apart inner cities across America in 1968 after the assassination of Dr. Martin Luther King Jr. Xerox founder Joseph Wilson wrote a letter to his managers calling for increased hiring of African Americans.[125] In 1970, Xerox founded the National Black Employees Association (NBEA), a national caucus group of African American Xerox employees. In 1986, Xerox furthered its efforts when sixteen female employees started the Black Women's Leadership Council.

Nearly fifty years later, ERGs have evolved from networking groups that promote diversity and inclusion of African Americans and women to key contributors in business strategy and operations. Almost 90 percent of Fortune 500 companies report having ERGs, per research from Catalyst.[126] Because of

125 "Diversity at Xerox," News from Xerox, 2008, https://www.xerox.com/downloads/usa/en/n/nr_Xerox_Diversity_Timeline_2008.pdf.

126 "Employee Resource Roundtable: How Effective Is Your ERG?" Catalyst, 2014.

the rising popularity, many companies have adopted practices and have begun financially supporting ERGs. Beyond advocating for equal pay and equal opportunity, ERGs allow an opportunity for voices of employees to be heard and to gain greater visibility with, and access to, senior executives. Catalyst understands that a powerful ERG enables organizations to increase employee engagement, connect to communities in which business is conducted, and enhance the bottom line. Accordingly, the Catalyst Employee Resource Leadership Initiative engages and connects ERG leaders across companies, industries, functions, and regions to share ideas and practices.

There are issues beyond the control of even the best companies that have philosophical practices and principles around diversity and inclusion. Having such groups not only indicates an investment and commitment to challenges facing women and ethnic minorities in the workforce, but it also demonstrates a bottom-line impact.

What if you believe your ERG at work is ineffective? Then get in there and make it count, much like the way my colleague and I created that presentation. You should even consider becoming an ERG leader, because in doing so, you will get to rub elbows with members of senior management. Your direct report will likely be a director or above, typically a vice president. Likewise, leading an ERG—managing a team of coworkers and a budget—provides a window of opportunity for you to build a relationship with a potential sponsor.

Belonging to an ERG can be incredibly beneficial if you're a double minority. Take General Motors employee Sabin D. Blake, who graced the July 2011 cover of *Black Enterprise* magazine. In the GLADD Media Award–winning article "Black and Gay in Corporate America," Blake shared how he navigated professional obstacles throughout his career. Currently serving as community outreach manager at GM, Blake began his career as a seventeen-year-old freshman co-op student in the Buick Motor Division. For years, he kept his sexual orientation hidden for several reasons, "including fear for his personal safety. Once keeping the secret became too disheartening, Blake made the decision to gradually reveal his sexual orientation to fellow GM employees." He attributed his level of comfort to GM's workplace: "I know that GM has strong language in their antidiscrimination policies and very strong support of their employee network groups," Blake told *Black Enterprise*.[127]

GM is headquarted in Detroit. Michigan is one of the states where workers can be fired for being LGBT with little to no legal recourse.

> Since its inception in 1993, the 200-member GM *Plus* LGBT ERG has actively campaigned for equal treatment and safe, acceptable working conditions for all employees at the multinational corporation. GM *Plus* has made sure that the company is on the right side of workplace policies. Sexual orientation was added to GM's nondiscrimination policy in 1999 and GM, Ford, Chrysler, and the United Auto Workers (UAW) jointly announced the auto industry's first same-sex domestic partner health care benefits a year later. The automaker added policy protection for employees based on gender identity and gender expression in 2006."[128]

GM—which is on the Human Rights Campaign's "Best

---

127 Carolyn M. Brown, "Black and Gay In Corporate America," *Black Enterprise*, July 2011, http://www.blackenterprise.com/mag/black-and-gay-in-corporate-america/.

128 *Ibid.*

Places to Work" list—"joined a coalition sponsored by HRC to support the Employment Non-Discrimination Act," a bill sitting in Congress since 1994, to provide national protections against workplace discrimination based on sexual orientation or gender identity.

In "Black and Gay in Corporate America," GM Plus chair Adam Bernard noted that such "internal and external efforts of corporations such as GM have provided open, inclusive, and supportive environments that have made it less daunting for LGBT workers and managers to be 'out at work.'" General Motors Corporation has twelve ERGs, whose members represent GM's diverse workforce, including the African American Network, the Hispanic Initiative Team, the Chinese Affinity Group, and GM Women.

Being black, female, and a lesbian makes you a triple minority in the workplace, shares Rosalyn Taylor O'Neale. Since the start of her career, O'Neale has always been clear about what it means to be an African American, a woman, and a lesbian in corporate America, but it never stopped her from successfully pursuing her goals. In *Black Enterprise*'s "The 'Coming Out' Challenge," O'Neale recounts that in 2000, she "was conducting a cultural assessment of the employees of an outside company to develop their training and diversity initiative. The CEO was not aware of her sexual orientation. 'I told him some of your lesbian and gay employees are concerned that it is not comfortable for them to come out,'" she recalls in *Black Enterprise*.[129] "'He said, *It's not, and I'm going to ask HR for those names because I'm going to fire them*. I knew as a lesbian that I couldn't work under those circumstances.' O'Neale willingly walked away from the contract." O'Neale

129   Brittany Huston, "The 'Coming Out' Challenge," *Black Enterprise*, November 1, 2009, http://www.blackenterprise.com/small-business/thecoming-outchallenge/.

also thinks she was fired in the early eighties because she was a masculine-looking lesbian. "'When I first entered corporate America, I was in my *boy days*, meaning I had short hair and wore pantsuits with ties,'" she told the magazine.

O'Neale (Roz to me), sixty-five, has over thirty years of experience leading diversity and inclusion efforts. Most notably from 2008 to 2012, she served as vice president and chief diversity and inclusion officer for Campbell Soup Co., where she was responsible for helping her organization create a diverse and inclusive culture around the globe, focusing not only on attracting diverse candidates, but on issues around retention, development, and engagement. Today, Campbell is recognized as a leader around employee resource groups, which the company calls "business resource affinity networks." As Campbell's diversity and inclusion initiative developed, six other groups were granted official network status, including the OPEN LGBT network.

O'Neale's experience resonates with African American corporate executives who identify themselves as LGBT. For those who choose to pass as "straight," they expend a great deal of time and energy covering up their personal lives or avoiding certain colleagues and company events. O'Neale, a fellow member of the Alpha Kappa Alpha sorority, has been with her partner for twenty-plus years—one of the 18,000 legally married couples in the state of California. She acknowledges that in the black community there is a history of excluding and marginalizing LGBT individuals. At the same time, LGBT African Americans can feel invisible within the general LGBT community. For these reasons, African American LGBT workers often struggle with fitting in with either ERG.

Having Our Say in the Face of Danger

Regardless of sexual orientation or gender identity, black women grapple more with speaking up at the workplace. We can be so afraid of retaliation that we would rather sit in silence sometimes, and just let certain incidents happen. Yes, it depends on the company culture. But in my view, you need to find a way to have these tough conversations around race and gender, where you're not going to throw yourself under a bus. You make your point so that people understand what it is that you're saying and it's not viewed as overly offensive or aggressive. They're called peek-a-boo moments.

We know that workplace harassment and hostility is all too real. We have heard accounts about displays of racially offensive symbols such as a swastika, Confederate flag, a noose, KKK letters, a racist cartoon or drawing at the workplace, which create a hostile environment. Antidiscrimination and harassment laws prohibit speech or acts that create a hostile or abusive work environment. No matter, complaints of harassment are on the rise across all industries, increasing from 25 percent to more than 30 percent of all the charges received by the Equal Employment Opportunity Commission.[130] When it comes to preventing harassment in all its forms, it boils down to how executive leadership handles these incidents when they occur.

There was one incident in 2005 that rattled me a bit. I had recently been promoted to vice president of diversity for the US at Novartis. I had been with the company for nearly two years and was now the successor to a white woman who was very popular in the organization and who was assuming an-

---

130 Chai R. Feldblum and Victoria A. Lipnic, "Select Task Force on the Study of Harassment in the Workplace," US Equal Employment Opportunity Commission, June 2016.

other leadership role. I left work and went home on a Friday like I normally do. I closed my office door during the course of the evening, and when I reported back to work on Monday morning, I opened the door and looked on the floor. Someone had slipped a note under my door. *Nigger* was written many times in a small font across a white sheet of paper. Red fingerprints—they looked a bit like blood to me—were left on the paper as a scare tactic.

Someone else may have trembled—not me, I was rock solid. My thought was, *You are likely to be a target if you're being effective and impactful.* I was being effective and impactful. I was stunned though. I was shocked, because there wasn't any provocation leading up to the note. In that moment, it all seemed bizarre to me. It meant that sometime over the weekend or shortly after sunrise on Monday, someone had left that note for me to see. The cleaning crew, who were Hispanic, had always been very friendly with me. I would speak to them often. I didn't believe any one of them wrote that racist note.

Immediately, I picked up the phone and contacted security. I called HR and my boss to let them know what had happened. The CEO of pharma for the Americas rang me on the office phone, his voice resolute: "Michelle, this is terrible. This is unacceptable. I can't believe this happened to you. We're going to take care of it. We're are going to do everything that we can to ensure that you are safe and protected."

I was still pretty calm. It wasn't until security showed up and began talking about what they were planning to do that I became rattled. Two representatives from Novartis security came to my office. For them, this was a serious matter: "Michelle, you know, we'll take great care of you."

When they started using that kind of language, I got a bit

alarmed. Suddenly it hit me like a ton of bricks—somebody at work had actually threatened me.

Security escorted me to my car. They asked if I wanted to be escorted in and out of the building every day and I said no. It was summertime so it was still daylight out when I'd leave at six or seven o'clock. I felt safe because usually at night I would walk out with another colleague who worked in HR. I would call her when I was leaving and say, "Hey, you ready to go home?"

She'd say, "Yeah. Let's go."

We would walk out together unless I was working on a project or a presentation that kept me there late at night.

That evening, I went straight home and immediately told David what had transpired. He was as stunned as I was. I also called my parents to let them know of the incident. They were clearly shaken and requested that I be aware of my surroundings at all times and follow the instructions of the security team. Leadership took the incident very seriously. The CEO reacted promptly, letting it be known that this type of behavior would not be tolerated in the organization. Management was aggressive in trying to right the wrong. Since no one wanted to alarm the entire organization, there was no mass e-mail that went out to all employees, but there was a town hall where the CEO talked about the importance of diversity, how he was serious about it, how he was committed to it. He spoke about intolerance. Since I was not harmed physically, my advice to him was to not make a big deal of it and accidentally encourage copycats.

Sometimes when a situation like this happens to you, it makes you want to do even more. I told myself, *You know what? I'm going to continue to do this work because I'm clearly getting to somebody. I must be doing a good job because I'm pissing somebody off.* I was making a name for myself in the diversity space at that point. There is some pushback whenever you introduce change in an organization. One of the reasons Novartis hired me in the first place was because of my reputation as a change agent.

Once I knew the CEO and his executive team were on board with diversity initiatives and workplace harassment wouldn't be tolerated, I went in guns blazing. I was more visible. I showed up in more meetings, did more presentations around the business case for diversity at town halls, talked about the significance of diversity, intolerance, and unconscious bias. I made it my mission to educate more people and to talk about these issues; not just in the context of people of color and the things that are quite visible to us, but other dynamics as well. I let them know it's about all of us.

While I was not afraid to speak up, that is not the case for many other women. Research shows that regardless of industry, a much smaller proportion of women share their opinions or raise their voices at work when compared to men. In the *Forbes* article "Speaking Up As a Woman of Color at Work," Ruchika Tulshyan writes about *speaking while female* in reference to a *New York Times* article by Facebook's Sheryl Sandberg and Wharton School Professor Adam Grant, who talk about how when a woman speaks in a professional setting, she walks a tightrope.[131] "Either she's barely heard or she's judged as too aggressive. When a man says virtually the same thing, heads nod in appreciation for his fine idea. As a result, women often decide that saying less is more," they write.

"Male executives who spoke more often than their peers

---

131 Ruchika Tulshyan, "Speaking Up As a Woman of Color at Work," *Forbes*, February 10, 2015, https://www.forbes.com/sites/ruchikatulshyan/2015/02/10/speaking-up-as-a-woman-of-color-at-work/#2f9cd96f2ea3.

were rewarded with 10 percent higher ratings of competence,"[132] whereas female executives who spoke out more than their peers were punished by them with 14 percent lower ratings, according to a study that was cited.

Backing up these comments, Ruchika says that speaking up at work may be a challenge for women of all backgrounds, but recognizes that there is a difference between speaking up as a white woman versus other women: "Add in the complication of speaking as a woman of color, when prevailing stereotypes rear their ugly heads."

One commenter on Sandberg and Grant's article aptly described challenges in corporate jobs that Ruchika personally faced as a woman of Indian heritage. Swati B, who self-identified as an Indian woman, wrote: "I face huge biases not just due to my gender, but also due to my race, which is commonly associated with people that are good at *doing* work, and not so much at *selling* themselves." She found that she was only considered good if she kept her ideas to herself. "When I spoke up, and asked for promotion, and pointed out that the work given to me was of subpar quality, I faced much resistance from my colleagues and *name calling* . . . I was made to feel unwelcome at work."[133]

I was in a position where I dealt with a number of circumstances around gender discrimination or sexual harassment. But it's hard to prove allegations like, *I was discriminated against because of my gender, my race, etc.* As you know, there are always two sides to every story. When you have all parties in the room, there's always some misunderstanding about what someone said. The HR business partners typically would take

132 Sheryl Sandberg and Adam Grant, "Speaking While Female," the *New York Times*, January 12, 2015, https://www.nytimes.com/2015/01/11/opinion/sunday/speaking-while-female.html.

133 Ruchika Tulshyan, "Speaking Up As a Woman of Color at Work."

on those issues and situations. Occasionally, I was brought in if the HR business partner felt that it was of benefit for me to be in the room during those meetings, to add value to the conversation.

Correspondingly, there were women who would come talk to me about the lack of opportunity, who would ask, "I'm not getting promoted quick enough—how do I do that?" I would help them figure it out. I would conduct a constructive or meaningful coaching session, where we would discuss what she could do to get noticed, how she could present herself to get the stretch assignments, what type of conversations she should be having with her manager.

If you believe that you are being harassed or bullied in the workplace, the best thing to do is to speak to your HR business partner about it. If your company has an anonymous help line that investigates internal employee relations issues, call the number and leave a message. That's the first step.

Boldly Embracing My Natural Hair in Corporate America

Where I come from, *good hair* is fine and straight—no exceptions. Once a month, my mother would use a hot comb to straighten my sisters' and my hair. She would place the iron comb on the stove just above the pilot. When it got hot enough, she would take the comb and gently rake it through the hair several times, stopping only when she was satisfied with the new smooth texture—and at the expense of physical harm. I have been singed many times in the name of vanity. By sixteen, I was chemically straightening my hair every six months to get that smooth, silky look. I shared this personal story "On Embracing My Natural Hair in Corporate America—and How It Changed Everything" in *Marie Clare*.[134]

134 Michelle Gadsden-Williams, "On Embracing My Natural Hair in Corporate America—

Cut to many years later as the chief diversity officer for a Fortune 500 company. Like many executives, I needed to adhere to the corporate uniform: suits, conservative dresses, and flat-ironed hair. Much like when I was a little girl, this process with my hair would take up to twenty minutes each morning—if I didn't wash it first. But it was worth it. As a woman of color, I had to be mindful of the way I navigated corporate America. We all know there are unwritten rules. No one is going to come out and tell you that your hairstyle is a problem. You will likely figure it out over time, when you're continuously passed over for a job, a promotion, or a particular assignment.

"The 'Good Hair' Study: Explicit and Implicit Attitudes Toward Black Women's Hair" reveals how natural hair hurts black women in the workplace.[135] "Women of color in the workplace, particularly those with natural hairstyles, are penalized because they often do not conform to traditional notions of beauty. No one has ever empirically measured the various biases people have about different types of hair and whether or not certain styles are *professional*,"[136] until a new study examined "how women of color face major barriers to success . . . Its authors asked the question: *Is society biased against black women based on their hair? The answer is, Yes.*"

The "'Good Hair' Study," using the first Hair Implicit Association Test (IAT), which Perception Institute created, and an extensive online survey, offers unprecedented evidence on

and How It Changed Everything," *Marie Claire*, May 3, 2016, http://www.marieclaire.com/beauty/features/a20285/straightening-hair/.

135 Alexis McGill Johnson, Rachel D. Godsil, Jessica MacFarlane, and Linda R. Tropp, "The 'Good Hair' Study: Explicit and Implicit Attitudes Toward Black Women's Hair," Perception Institute, February 2017.

136 Carolyn M. Brown, "Natural Hair Hurts Black Women in the Workplace," *Black Enterprise*, February 1, 2017, http://www.blackenterprise.com/news/hot-topics/natural-hair-hurts-black-women-workplace/.

implicit and explicit biases against natural and textured hair. "This study confirms what most black women have known and experienced: wearing natural hairstyles has deep political and social implications," explains Alexis McGill Johnson, "cofounder and executive director of Perception Institute, a consortium of researchers, advocates, and strategists who translate cutting-edge mind science research on race, gender, ethnic, and other identities into solutions that reduce bias and discrimination."

"From the classroom to the workplace, bias against natural hair can undermine the ability of black women to be their full selves and affect their professional trajectory, social life, and self-esteem," Johnson writes.[137]

You must be bold and brave to be a self-identified *naturalista* woman. Truthfully, I wasn't so daring until I had a health issue that compromised my flat-iron hair routine. During the summer of 2013, my annual mammogram revealed that I had a suspicious mass in my right breast. The mass turned out not to be cancerous, but the procedure left me with a two-inch incision and stitches that were extremely painful. I was out of the office recuperating for two weeks. As I was healing, I had difficulty lifting my right arm to comb my hair. The pain from trying was excruciating—I felt a stinging sensation that traveled from my bicep to my armpit. I paused. *What would happen if I simply washed my hair and let it air dry?* By the time of my surgery, I had been chemically processing my hair my entire life. I was worried: had I ruined my natural wave and curl pattern with the years of hot comb and chemicals?

For the first time in more than thirty years, I washed my tresses and let them air dry—and I watched my curly ringlets come to life. The more my hair dried, the happier I became. I

---

137 *Ibid.*

tried this method for a few days, experimenting with a number of shampoos and conditioners specific to curly hair. After a few attempts, I enjoyed the bouncy, curly results. As I planned to return to the office, I started to research natural hair maintenance. Would I be able to keep this up? After a consultation and styling, I decided that I wanted to live a healthier lifestyle from the inside out—which included nutrition, exercise, and an end to chemical processing altogether. I decided to stop chemically treating my hair for good.

I woke up two hours early on my first day back. I felt anxious about revealing my new hair to the world. What would my colleagues think? Could I pull off the new me? Would they think I was attempting to make some kind of political statement? I was seized by another, more pressing question: would this new style be acceptable in the boardroom? On that same day, we had a global leadership team meeting, which meant that all of my colleagues from around the world would see me. I decided to wear my best dress, coif my hair in a soft, curly style with a side part, put on my makeup, and go to work.

As I suspected, my hair was a topic of conversation for many at the meeting. One female colleague pulled me to the side and said, "Why on earth did you do that?" *Could I pull off the new me?*

And then a black female colleague stated, "In my opinion, some hairstyles are just not appropriate for the workplace."

I was deflated. Ironically, my superiors were extremely complimentary. The CEO and his chief of staff told me how much they liked my new look. Several female peers praised me for having the courage to show a more authentic side of myself. A few of the more junior women even told me they had considered letting their hair go naturally curly and that I'd helped pave the way. I'll admit that I was afraid: first, of the conversations it would spark with my peers and superiors, both black and white; and second, of the deeply ingrained racial issues regarding what constitutes *polished*—I just wasn't prepared to address them at the time.

It's been four years since I stopped straightening my hair. I am a lot less preoccupied with what others think about it. Understandably, as a woman of color, if you have aspirations to reach the next level of leadership, you have to play ball— something I did for years.

A groundbreaking new study commissioned by Essence, *in partnership with Added Value Cheskin, found that black women are significantly more likely than non-Hispanic white women to downplay certain aspects of their personality in the workplace.* The reason? An overwhelming fear of reinforcing negative stereotypes, such as the Angry Black Woman. *Eighty percent of black women surveyed felt they must make adjustments to their personalities to succeed [in the office, while] just 62 percent of non-Hispanic white women felt the same. Additionally, 57 percent of black women also feel that they must physically appear a certain way (straightened hair, a certain style of dress) in order to receive a promotion. Only 39 percent of non-Hispanic white women share that sentiment. As a result, 50 percent of black female millennials, 42 percent of Gen Xers, and 30 percent of baby boomers strive to be seen as the Accul-turated Girl Next Door, a professional who is unthreatening and willing to conform.*[138]

138 Taylor Lewis, "Hiding Your Authentic Self at Work Can Damage Your Career," *Essence*, April 2, 2015, http://www.essence.com/2015/04/02/essence-study-hiding-authentic-personality-work-damaging.

The *Essence* study found that black women in the C-Suite, however, have varying views on how they want to be perceived in the workplace. Thirty-nine percent of black women executives want to be known as "inspiring stars," women who take risks, open up, and share traits that make them different from others.[139]

The *Essence* study about "black women's experiences in white-dominated workplaces shows that altering key aspects of our identities in order to blend in is not only psychologically damaging, but it could also be keeping us from scoring the promotions we deserve."[140]

"Scores of us are so worried about being perceived negatively that we hide our authentic selves in the workplace, choosing instead to tone down our appearance, soften our demeanor, and hold back in our conversations . . . Switching between *work me* and *personal me* is exhausting and doing us more harm than good. When you hide your true self behind a mask at work, it's like walking around with your hands tied," Kym Harris, EdD, president of Your SweetSpot Coaching and Consulting in Atlanta, told *Essence* magazine.[141] "When you use so much energy being something you're not, you don't have enough left to be the best you can be."

"Black women in the upper echelons of corporate America (CEOs, CFOs, CDOs, and so on)" should strive to be their authentic selves if they want to make real change. We must be cheerleaders and campaigners on behalf of others. When

---

139 Rhonesha Byng, "*Essence* Magazine Takes a Closer Looks at the Challenges for Black Women at Work," *Her Agenda*, April 8, 2015, http://heragenda.com/essence-magazine-takes-a-closer-look-at-the-challenges-for-black-women-at-work/.

140 Tamara E. Holmes, "Black Women at Work: How We Shape Our Identities on the Job," *Essence*, April 2, 2015, http://www.essence.com/2015/04/02/black-women-work-how-we-shape-our-identities-job.

141 *Ibid.*

I was promoted to the executive ranks and I knew that I had a seat and a voice at the table, I understood that came with responsibility. You know the expression: *To whom much is given much is required.* I couldn't just sit back and let things happen and then pretend as if I wasn't even there in the room, and in a position of power and influence—never mind how limited that power might be. As far as I'm concerned, what's the point of being a leader if you're not going to act like one? You're just going to wear the badge, have a nice title, work in a nice office in the corner, but you're not going to advocate for people who look like you or anybody else who's underrepresented in the company? I recognized I was representing those of us who weren't anywhere near that corner office, anywhere near the boardroom.

As people of color, when we progress into these managerial roles, especially at the most senior levels, we must take that responsibility seriously—I sure did. Some of the things I would say to top leadership were not popular at all, but I knew they had to be said. It's all about what you say and how you say it too. No, I'm not Angela Davis with my fist pumped up in the air in the boardroom. It's all in the approach, and it's all about being tactful. Yes, you've got to adhere to or at least acknowledge that politics exist. But how you show up and speak up—or not—in the workplace says a mouthful about you.

Key Steps

1. Speak up for yourself. As women, we must advocate for ourselves and one another. Yes, it is important for all young people to be well-mannered, but we must also teach young girls to be strong and to have a voice.
2. Join employee resource groups. You should belong

to appropriate ERGs (African American, Hispanic, Asian, Women, LGBT, employees with disabilities, etc.) at your organization if you haven't done so already. If you are member, assume an active role—a position of leadership. This will put you in the room with senior management. Managing a team of coworkers and a budget can work to your benefit in gaining sponsors and moving a few rungs up the ladder.

3. Bond with your coworkers. Identify and cultivate allies (multifaceted and multicultural) in the workplace. This requires being open, sharing yourself, and connecting with others on issues that you are passionate about.

4. Find your fearless self. Meaning, have the courage to be free, to be yourself. Yes, you may have to look the part according to your organization's culture, but don't suppress who you are and hide behind a false identity.

5. Report incidents of gender or racial discrimination. Document ongoing infractions. If your manager blows off your complaint, take it up with HR. If senior leadership does not rally behind you, you need to decide at that point if this is the right work environment for you.

6. Take risks. Find the confidence to take risks in the workplace and to move outside of your comfort zone. Be willing to disrupt gender and racial stereotypes.

7. Act like a leader. If you are in a leadership role, advocate for people who look like you or anybody else who's underrepresented in the company.

10

REACHING BACK, PULLING OTHERS ALONG

*Our ambitions must be broad enough to include the aspirations and
needs of others, for their sakes and for our own.*
—César Chávez

On January 20, 2017, the day of Donald Trump's inauguration, I hopped into my Porsche 911 convertible to drive from New York City to Washington, DC. I wasn't on my way to see the swearing in of the forty-fifth president of the United States of America. On the contrary, I was heading to the Women's March along with womenfolk across the world, who were coming out in droves to protest and advocate for policies and legislation regarding myriad issues, including women's rights, immigration reform, LGBTQ rights, racial equality, and worker's rights.

Granted, it took awhile to settle on theme and the intent. The organizers eventually adopted the title "Women's March on Washington," invoking the civil rights movement's 1963 March On Washington for Jobs and Freedom.[142] The mission of the Women's March was not to simply protest, but to empower women to move forward and to send a bold message to the new administration on Trump's first day in office—and to the world—that women's rights are human rights.

---

142 Nina Agrawal, "How the Women's March Came into Being," the *Los Angeles Times*, January 21, 2017, http://www.latimes.com/nation/la-na-pol-womens-march-live-how-the-women-s-march-came-into-1484865755-htmlstory.html.

This was my first time ever participating in a march of any kind. I was totally elated all the way around that day. Since I was to be en route to DC on Inauguration Day, I was worrying a little about, *So, what's traffic going to be like? Am I going to be stuck bumper-to-bumper with oodles of vehicles for five hours or more on the turnpike?* In my mind, I thought that because of the presidential inauguration, all the hotels would be sold out in DC and I would run into all sorts of crazy road traffic.

As I was driving down the New Jersey Turnpike, I noticed other women in vehicles. Some of them had pink flags. Many of them were waving. Others were mouthing, *Are you going to the march?* And if you mouthed back yes, they would give you the thumbs-up. There was a lot of affirmation and support along the way. It really was like a mass caravan, if you will, where several cars just followed each other down the highway on the way to DC. It was great. To my surprise, it took me no time. I departed around twelve noon and arrived at four p.m. It was smooth sailing the whole way.

Honestly, I was totally looking forward to the march. As a matter of fact, I was a member of the planning committee. Although most of the planning team had already been assembled, I came onboard at the back end. The team put in a lot of hours and effort. There were round-the-clock phone calls and e-mails. A very good friend of mine, Tamika Mallory, one of the four women masterminds behind the march, asked me if I wanted to participate in some way. I was honored to have been invited to get involved.

How the Women's March came into being was best outlined in the *Los Angeles Times*. It was November 8, 2016, and Donald Trump had just won the presidency, when Teresa Shook woke up sad and dumfounded. "With some help from friends online, the retired attorney and grandmother living in Hawaii created a Facebook event page calling for a march on Washington after Trump's inauguration," reported the *Los Angeles Times*.[143] "She went to bed that night with about forty responses" and woke up to over ten thousand.

Meanwhile, fashion designer, CEO, and founder of Manufacture New York Bob Bland proposed a march, posting to Facebook on November 10: "I think we should build a coalition of ALL marginalized allies + do this." She went on to state, "We will need folks from every state + city to organize their communities locally, who wants to join me?!?"

According to the *Los Angeles Times*, "Bland consolidated various protest pages, including Shook's, that had cropped up on Facebook and recruited three longtime, New York-based activists to be cochairs of the national march."

These other organizers were Linda Sarsour, a Brooklyn born Palestinian-American Muslim civil rights activist, executive director of the Arab American Association of New York, and cofounder of Muslims for Ferguson; Carmen Perez, executive director of Gathering for Justice, a nonprofit founded by Harry Belafonte, as well as cofounder of Justice League NYC and founder of Justice League CA, two state-based task forces for advancing the juvenile and criminal justice reform agenda; and my sister-friend Tamika Mallory, a longtime social justice leader who worked closely with the Obama administration as an advocate for gun control, among other issues, and served as a national organizer for the fiftieth anniversary of the March on Washington.

I first met Tamika through a mutual friend about six years ago. I was still living in Switzerland at the time and she was the outgoing civil rights activist serving as the youngest executive director of Reverend Al Sharpton's National Action

---

143 *Ibid.*

Network at the time. Tamika and I were introduced over dinner with Angela Rye, a political commentator on CNN and an NPR political analyst. Angela is also the CEO of IMPACT Strategies, a political advocacy firm in Washington, DC.

Tamika and I would typically catch up every couple of months. We were due for one of those phone calls, so I sent her a text saying, "Hey, we've gotta catch up."

She replied, "Yes, we do. But I want to get you involved in something, let's catch up soon."

We spoke a couple of days later. She told me about the Women's March—what the organizers' objectives were, and what they were aiming to do. She asked, "Do want to play a role?"

And I exclaimed, "Absolutely. I would love to!"

She wanted to know: "How do you want to be involved?"

I said, "How do you want me to be?"

She probed, "Would you be open to lending your name to cochairing a women of color breakfast on the morning of the march, along with a few other high-profile women: New York congresswoman Yvette Clarke and Valeisha Butterfield Jones, Google's head of black community engagement?"

It goes without saying that I leaped at the chance.

I spent the night before the march—and that entire weekend—at the home of my younger sister Alicia, who lives on the Maryland side of the DC border. I went to see Tamika when I arrived on Friday afternoon to lend a helping hand. The team was still having a lot of prep and some final planning meetings. Model and political organizer Janaye Ingram was responsible for the logistics. A lot of people didn't know this, and she didn't receive a lot of attention for her critical role. But she played an integral part in getting all the permits and taking care of things on the ground. Janaye was there that evening, along with a host of other people. I saw Michael Skolnik, a civil rights activist and political director at Russell Simmons's GlobalGrind.com, and many others. Everyone who was anyone in the advocacy space was there in that room. It was fantastic.

I got up early Saturday morning, around five a.m. I wore my ski jacket, a pair of black Timberland hiking boots, comfortable dark-blue jeans, and a matching top. I anticipated cold weather, but it turned out to be a pleasant day; I had my coat open the entire time. I took an Uber into the city, avoiding the headache of trying to find parking, to the headquarters of the National Council for Negro Women. That was the location of the kickoff breakfast. As I entered the building, I saw a portrait on the wall of the illustrious Dorothy Height. What a marvelous feeling to be at the pulse of an organization formed more than eighty years ago by Mary McLeod Bethune. NCNW's mission remains as relevant today as it was in 1935—offering a unified voice to address the economic, social cultural, and spiritual needs of black women, their families, and their communities, according to the homepage on their website.

The breakfast was by invitation only for black women leaders. It was for VIPs and luminaries. Meaning, you had Congressional Black Caucus members and executive members of a number of women's organizations in attendance. The theme of the breakfast was "Formation," a play on the Beyoncé song from her *Lemonade* album, which some have characterized as her Black Power anthem. Before a roomful of women, mostly sisters of color, the other cochairs of the kickoff breakfast and I gave opening remarks about how important the day was, and the need for all of us to galvanize our collective wisdom and represent ourselves well, to march in the spirit of gender equality.

Afterward, we all loaded on a bus which shuttled us to the drop-off point where the stage program would begin, followed by the official march. A wide range of speakers and performers cutting across generational lines rallied near the Capitol building before marchers made their way toward the White House. The kickoff rally is what most people witnessed on television. The main stage program turned into a star-studded event, with celebrities such as Madonna, Janelle Monáe, Scarlett Johansson, America Ferrera, and Ashley Judd making appearances. The mothers of the slain gun-violence victims like Trayvon Martin and Sandra Bland, also spoke. Hillary Clinton did not attend the march but tweeted her gratitude: "Thanks for standing, speaking & marching for our values @womensmarch. Important as ever. I truly believe we're always stronger together." The actual march did not occur until later that afternoon.

Some women were chanting while others were waving signs. You locked arms with whomever was next to you. It didn't matter who it was, we were all there walking in solidarity. I took many different photos of a diverse throng of women—Muslim, white, black, Latina, and Asian. There was the LGBT constituency; women from different organizations and the sororities all had a terrific showing. Everyone was represented. It was nice to see such diversity among the women together. Just a lot of terrific energy that day—emotionally moving. I didn't stay for the very end. Some of the ladies and I went to a restaurant for dinner and drinks to celebrate how momentous a day it had been. We reflected on the experience in its entirety.

As many as half a million people participated in the Women's March on Washington that Saturday, per news accounts.[144] The Washington demonstration was amplified by

144   . Jason Silverstein, Larry McShane, Cameron Joseph, and Adam Edelman, "Half

gatherings around the world, with march organizers listing more than 670 events occurring in cities from London to Los Angeles, Melbourne to Miami, Paris to Philadelphia, Berlin to Boston, Tel Aviv to Tucson.[145] Worldwide participation was estimated at five million overall. The Washington march had been so well executed that there was not one incident of violence reported. I don't think any us really expected it to be as successful as it was. We knew it was going to be something special, but we could not have predicted that around the world there would be this kind of rallying cry for women's rights.

This is not to say that we were all in agreement. Long before the first buses rolled out to DC and sister demonstrations jumped off in other cities worldwide, contentious conversations about race erupted among marchers, which left some women exhilarated while alienating others. The Women's March came under scrutiny due to perceived division amongst coordinators and participants around issues of race and privilege. This was made very clear to me as a member of the planning committee, as I witnessed how some of the women reacted to the four primary female organizers. Some women wanted to throw everybody into the same basket and say, "Okay, all women's issues are the same, and we're talking about all of us." Many women of color had a different opinion. There needed to be an acknowledgment that we are not the same, and that we don't all share the same experiences.

The *New York Times* article "Women's March on Washing-

a Million People Show Up for Women's March on Washington as Others Flock to Sister Marches Across Globe," *New York Daily News*, January 21, 2017, http://www.nydailynews.com/news/politics/women-march-washington-attendance-dwarfs-inauguration-crowd-article-1.2952170.

145 Karla Adam, "More than 670 Sister Events Staged Worldwide in Support of Women's March on Washington," the *Washington Post*, January 21, 2017, https://www.adn.com/nation-world/2017/01/21/people-worldwide-rally-in-support-of-womens-march-on-washington/.

ton Opens Contentious Dialogues About Race" highlighted how a fifty-year-old white woman from South Carolina took offense with a post written by a black activist from Brooklyn who advised "white allies" to listen more and talk less. The post also chided those who, it said, were only now waking up to racism because of the election, asking them to check their white privilege.

During a news interview, the white woman from South Carolina remarked, "This is a women's march. We're supposed to be allies in equal pay, marriage, adoption. Why is it now about, *White women don't understand black women?*"[146]

The national organizers of the Women's March made a deliberate decision to highlight the plight of minority and undocumented immigrant women, to provoke uncomfortable but necessary discussions about race. The march's Facebook page posted a quote from bell hooks, author, social activist, and black feminist, about forging a stronger sisterhood by "confronting the ways women—through sex, class, and race—dominated and exploited other women."[147] A debate then ensued about whether white women were just now experiencing what minority women experience daily, or were having a hard time yielding control. Gloria Steinem, honorary cochairwoman of the march along with Harry Belafonte, lauded the organizers' approach. In an e-mail Steinem wrote: "Sexism is always made worse by racism—and vice versa."[148]

The White Lies Around Sisterhood

We witnessed how race, gender, nationalism, and societal

---

146   Farah Stockman, "Women's March on Washington Opens Contentious Dialogues About Race," the *New York Times*, January 9, 2017, https://www.nytimes.com/2017/01/09/us/womens-march-on-washington-opens-contentious-dialogues-about-race.html.

147   *Ibid.*

148   *Ibid.*

privileges played out in our political arena during the 2016 presidential election. Many political analysts predicted that the Democratic candidate and former secretary of state Hillary Rodham Clinton would become America's first female president. But Republican candidate Donald Trump beat the first female major-party candidate to run for the US presidency. (While she didn't succeed, Shirley Chisolm became the first African American to seek nomination for the presidency with a major political party in 1972.) CNN contributor Van Jones claimed the election and Trump's unexpected rise ultimately came down to *whitelash*—backlash from white Americans against other races.[149]

White women were accused of selling out the sisterhood by voting for Trump. Women did vote overwhelmingly to elect Clinton, except for white women, reported the Edison national election poll. "Overall, 54 percent of women voted for Clinton," higher than the percentage of women who voted for Trump. Just 51 percent of college-educated women voted for Clinton compared to 45 percent for Trump. "His most enthusiastic supporters were white men across the board," but 64 percent of non–college educated white women voted for him, "while 35 percent backed Clinton. This figure is far higher than non–college educated black women, of which 3 percent voted for Trump, and [among] non–college educated Hispanic women, of which 25 percent voted for Trump."[150]

During his run to become America's forty-fifth president, "Trump tried to pit straight white men against everyone else—

149 Josiah Ryan, "'This Was a Whitelash': Van Jones's Take on the Election Results," CNN, November 9, 2016, http://www.cnn.com/2016/11/09/politics/van-jones-results-disappointment-cnntv/index.html.

150 Aamna Mohdin, "American Women Voted Overwhelmingly for Clinton, Except the White Ones," *Quartz*, November 9, 2016, https://qz.com/833003/election-2016-all-women-voted-overwhelmingly-for-clinton-except-the-white-ones/.

women, people of color, people in the LGBTQ community, immigrants—and white women decided [that] they wanted to vote on the side" of white men, said *Slate* associate editor L.V. Anderson, in a column written following the election. She noted: "Most white women still identify more with white men than they do with black women, Latina women, Muslim women, transwomen, and every other woman."[151]

In the *Huffington Post* column "Dear Fellow White Women: We F**ked This Up," Sarah Ruiz-Grossman wrote that white women failed to show up to the polls to elect the first woman president—a white lady, no less—and instead chose white privilege: "After all the supposed progress we've made, pains-takingly trying to change a white feminist movement into an intersectional one (and for that we have only the hard work of women of color to thank), white women didn't show up to fight back against a man whose rhetoric and policies directly attack women of color, immigrant women, Muslim women, LGBTQ women, and more."[152]

She went on to say, "Tell me we came through for our sisters of color, I begged, at least this one time. We didn't. So, I am ashamed. I am ashamed of my country. I am ashamed of white people. But more than anyone else, I am ashamed of white women. Is this who we really are? Clearly—and it is who we have always been."[153]

The truth of the matter is that the results of the 2016 election were indeed consistent with voting patterns from

151 L.V. Anderson, "White Women Sold Out the Sisterhood and the World by Voting for Trump," *Slate*, November 9, 2016, http://www.slate.com/blogs/xx_factor/2016/11/09/white_women_sold_out_the_sisterhood_and_the_world_by_voting_for_trump.html.

152 Sarah Ruiz-Grossman, "Dear Fellow White Women: We F**ked This Up," *Huffington Post*, November 9, 2016, http://www.huffingtonpost.com/entry/dear-white-women-we-messed-this-up-election-2016_us_582341c9e4b0aac62488970e.

153 *Ibid.*

previous elections and implied that America's political party affiliation is greatly mediated by one's race and class. "In 2004, George W. Bush got 55 percent of the white female vote" and John McCain got 53 percent to Barack Obama's 46 percent in 2008, while Mitt Romney got 56 percent to Obama's 42 percent in 2012.[154]

In part, what continues to be problematic are the constraints endemic to identity politics. For example, since the beginning, the women's movement has treated all women, black and white, as having similar goals and suffering similar inequities. As authors Melinda Marshall and Tai Wingfield explore in their book *Ambition in Black and White: The Feminist Narrative Revised*, neither the women's movement nor the civil rights movement "recognizes the particular challenges [African American women face] in the workplace, nor their singularly fraught path toward equality."[155] They further argue, "At the intersections of race and gender, both then and now, black women have labored unseen, even to those lobbying for their advancement."[156]

"The intersection of race and gender appears to be a far more lethal combination for black women than for other persons of color," notes a former senior vice president for global philanthropy at JPMorgan Chase.[157]

In the article "Women's March on Washington Opens Contentious Dialogues About Race," the *Times* recognized this

---

154 John Cassidy, "What's Up with White Women? They Voted for Romney, Too," the *New Yorker*, November 8, 2012, http://www.newyorker.com/news/john-cassidy/whats-up-with-white-women-they-voted-for-romney-too.

155 Melinda Marshall and Tai Wingfield, "Getting More Black Women into the C-Suite," *Harvard Business Review*, July 1, 2016, https://hbr.org/2016/07/getting-more-black-women-into-the-c-suite.

156 *Ibid.*

157 Carolyn M. Brown, "White Lies," *Pink*, May 20, 2013, http://www.littlepinkbook.com/white-lies/.

brand of feminism—frequently referred to as "intersectionality"—which asks white women to acknowledge that they have had it easier. "It speaks candidly about the history of racism, even within the feminist movement itself. The organizers of the 1913 suffrage march on Washington asked black women to march at the back of the parade,"[158] noted the *Times*.

In a *Washington Post* column, Kimberlé Crenshaw wrote about how it's been nearly three decades since she first put a name to the concept of intersectionality.[159] Crenshaw serves as the executive director of the African American Policy Forum and is a professor of law at Columbia University and UCLA. She cited the 1976 discrimination lawsuit against General Motors filed by Emma DeGraffenreid and several other black women, "arguing that the automaker segregated its workforce by race and gender . . . According to the plaintiffs' experiences, women were welcome to apply for some jobs, while only men were suitable for others. This was of course a problem in and of itself, but for black women, the consequences were compounded. You see, the black jobs were men's jobs, and the women's jobs were only for whites," wrote Crenshaw. "Unfortunately, for DeGraffenreid and millions of other black women, the court dismissed their claims."

Crenshaw construed that the reason for this was "because the court believed black women should not be permitted to combine their race and gender claims into one." Consequently, "the discrimination that happened to these black [female workers at GM] fell through the cracks . . . As a young law professor, [Crenshaw] wanted to define this profound in-

---

158 Farah Stockman, "Women's March on Washington Opens Contentious Dialogues About Race."

159 Kimberlé Crenshaw, "Why Intersectionality Can't Wait," the *Washington Post*, September 24, 2015, https://www.washingtonpost.com/news/in-theory/wp/2015/09/24/why-intersectionality-cant-wait/?utm_term=.6e17ca1bfd66.

visibility in relation to the law." Intersectionality was her "attempt to make feminism, antiracist activism, and antidiscrimination law do what [she] thought they should—highlight the multiple avenues through which racial and gender oppression were experienced so that the problems would be easier to discuss and understand."

Intersectional erasures are not exclusive to black women; Crenshaw went on to say: "People of color within LGBTQ movements; girls of color in the fight against the school-to-prison pipeline; women within immigration movements; trans women within feminist movements; and people with disabilities fighting police abuse—all face vulnerabilities that reflect the intersections of racism, sexism, class oppression, transphobia, able-ism and more."[160] She further recognized that "intersectionality has given many advocates a way to frame their circumstances and to fight for their visibility and inclusion."

Looking at intersectionality in corporate America, the problem still lies in the fact that white women, just as much as white men, are often in denial of race as a significant factor at work. The harsh reality is that many high-ranking women of color believe that "white women are afforded many of the same privileges as white males by being part of the majority class in the corporate arena." And what's more, "many white women are shirking their responsibility as sisters in the gender movement."[161]

"White women need to remember to honor the covenant between all women," explains Sandra Finley, president and CEO of the League of Black Women, in *Pink* magazine's 2008 article "White Lies." She continues, "They need to stop

---

160 *Ibid.*

161 Carolyn M. Brown, "White Lies," *Pink*, May 20, 2013, http://www.littlepinkbook.com/white-lies/.

saying, *That could happen to anybody*. The reality is that what happens to black women is different. Our experiences are unique."

I completely agree with Finley; we experience the workplace differently than our white counterparts, our white sisters. Yes, there needs to be some acknowledgment that we walk through life differently. White women and women of color need to coexist better. Not to say that we don't, but we need to do a better job of trusting each other, relying on each other, and understanding our unique qualities.

In that same "White Lies" article, Michelle Johnson, then director of supplier diversity for Home Depot, makes a bold statement, noting: "White women don't have parity with white men, but they're a rung above women of color on the ladder. White men in corporate America look at white women and see their wives, mothers, grandmothers, sisters, aunts, daughters, nieces, granddaughters." In contrast, she explains, "Many of the same men still see women of color as clerks. And even some white women secretly view black women as their support—*the hired help*—not equal partners striving for common ground with the men."[162]

In "White Lies," Finley also recounts that "she was mistaken for a parking attendant or assumed to be a guest at the professional club where she's a member. She [said] more of such embarrassments happen to African American women due to racial bias than to gender bias, a fact that white women need to know. 'It's the two-punch double whammy,'" she said.

I know from personal experience that this still rings true today—brown and black women are often perceived as the hired help. I can recall one time when I was standing in the driveway of my home in Somerset County, New Jersey. My

---

162 *Ibid.*

neighbor, walking with her newborn baby in her arms, came over to talk to me. She asked if I would like to hold the baby. I extended my arms to her to hold the child. Not long into our conversation, a FedEx van pulled up into the driveway to deliver a package. As the driver approached the house, I could tell that he automatically assumed the house was hers and not mine. He walked up to my neighbor and addressed her as the lady of the house—Mrs. Williams. She was white, I was black. Besides, here I was, holding a white baby, so he must've thought to himself that I was the nanny—even though I was standing in front of my own home. I have learned that you have to meet people where they are regarding these types of situations.

Our Separate Ways: Black and White Women and the Struggle for Professional Identity is the first book that I am aware of that dared to compare and contrast the backgrounds and career paths of successful black and white women in corporate America, exploring the roles that race, wealth, education, and family background play in shaping women's lives.[163] Based on a groundbreaking multiyear study into the life journeys of female managers and executives, authors Ella L.J. Bell and Stella Nkomo attempted to illustrate the complexities between black and white women as they climbed the corporate ladder. The authors proficiently delineated "the prejudices that create special problems for black women in the executive suite, without losing sight of the experiences they share with white women." They concluded that there is an "enduring power of gender discrimination in the workplace, the extent to which managerial careers are steeped in patriarchal ideology."[164]

163 Ella L.J. Edmondson Bell and Stella Nkomo, *Our Separate Ways: Black and White Women and the Struggle for Professional Identity* (Harvard Business Reviews Press, 2003).

164 "Review: *Our Separate Ways*," *Publishers Weekly*, https://www.publishersweekly.

Essentially, the big take-away for me from the book is that we know that while there are similarities among all women in the workplace, there are also differences that create an un-level playing field for minority women. The epilogue in *Our Separate Ways* offers suggestions on how to begin sometimes difficult dialogue between black and white women executives. It was in this regard that I found the book to be instrumental when I was at Novartis, as we were just embarking on those types of conversations between white women and women of color at the senior levels.

I remember one of my Novartis colleagues basically con-fessing: "I feel like a cleaning woman in a suit when I come to work every day." The white women at the company really didn't understand what she meant by that. We welcomed these cou-rageous conversations that demonstrated our commitment to appreciating the differences that we all experience in life and ultimately bring to the workplace.

Are You Your Sister's Keeper?

All women in the workplace need to take a personal assess-ment of how they honor the sisterhood. What does it mean to be our sister's keeper? It requires that we guard, protect, and attend to her. We can't be our sister's keeper if we harbor resentment, envy, and scorn toward her. Also, when it comes to looking out for someone else, this isn't about those whom we call our friends, but includes everyone around us.

I grew up in industries where it was mostly male dominated. Subsequently, I didn't encounter any real female rivalry. Most of the women around me—black and white—were incredibly helpful and genuinely invested in my advancement. It might be that in my role as a diversity officer, they saw me as the

com/978-1-57851-277-5.

quasi–civil rights leader of the company and wanted to see me succeed. After all, it didn't benefit them to undermine my efforts; quite the contrary. However, I do know plenty of colleagues and other women who have horror stories about female saboteurs. Unfortunately, these happenings are not that uncommon. "One of the biggest barriers to female career advancement that could have been largely overlooked until now [are] other women."[165]

"Women take competition with other women at work too seriously, and it could be damaging their own career prospects," new research from UCL School of Management reveals.[166] Professor Sun Young Lee found that competition with female coworkers can tax women's work relationships and cause women to struggle to interact with female coworkers, becoming overly cutthroat and mean, which can restrict their career progression. "On the other hand, hierarchical ranking and competition is natural in male peer culture, so men's work relationships do not suffer from competing with other male colleagues."

Lee's research on the relational perspective on same-gender competition forms the basis for a paper that was published by Selin Kesebir and Madan M. Pillutla (both from the London Business School) in the *Journal of Personality and Social Psychology*. After four separate studies involving close to eight hundred participants, the paper—labeled as the "sisterhood ceiling" study by the *Telegraph*—"concludes that women are more likely to fall out with female colleagues whom they sus-

---

165 John Bingham, "The Sisterhood Ceiling: How the Final Barrier to Women Reaching the Top Is . . . Other Women," the *Telegraph*, April 13, 2016, http://www.telegraph.co.uk/news/2016/04/13/the-sisterhood-ceiling-how-the-final-barrier-to-women-reaching-t/.

166 Sun Young Lee, "Competitive Workplaces Hold Women Back," UCL School of Management, April 13, 2016, https://www.mgmt.ucl.ac.uk/news/competitive-workplaces-hold-women-back.

pect of trying to elbow them aside on the career ladder than they would with men."[167]

"As a woman who has worked across the world, I've long observed that women take competition with other women much more personally than men take competition with other men—my research provides support to such an observation," states Lee.[168]

Further analyses showed that "female participants perceived competition with their same-gender coworkers as less desirable"[169] than competition with their opposite-gender coworkers. In contrast, notes Lee, "male participants perceived competition with their opposite-gender coworkers as less acceptable than competition with their same-gender coworkers."[170] She goes on to "explain that women's responses showed that they expected much more 'relational damage' with female colleagues because of workplace competition."[171]

But the paper's authors emphasize that their findings do not confirm caricatures about women having workplace "catfights." As a matter of fact, "the evidence suggests the contrary," they write. "Women reported higher relational damage only under competition, and not under cooperation."

Lee believes that "bosses need to be aware that competitive career structures that are effective to men may be detrimental to women. At the same time, women should be aware that taking competition too seriously could be holding them back from leadership positions."[172]

167 John Bingham, "The Sisterhood Ceiling: How the Final Barrier to Women Reaching the Top Is… Other Women."

168 Sun Young Lee, "Competitive Workplaces Hold Women Back."

169 John Bingham, "The Sisterhood Ceiling: How the Final Barrier to Women Reaching the Top Is . . . Other Women."

170 *Ibid.*

171 *Ibid.*

172 *Ibid.*

We expect women to help support each other's advancement, but the reality is that insecurities, along with the competitive nature of the workplace, set the stage for female rivalry. This dynamic is spelled out in the *Forbes* article "The Dark Side of Female Rivalry in the Workplace and What to Do About It" by Bonnie Marcus.[173] "Another contributing factor to female rivalry is the workplace itself," asserts Marcus, who is also the author of *The Politics of Promotion: How High Achieving Women Get Ahead and Stay Ahead.* "The male-dominated workplace sets women up to compete due to increased scrutiny and a scarcity of top leadership positions for women. The psychosocial factors along with the workplace culture together create female rivalry at its nastiest!" explains Marcus.

She points to research around "the extent to which individuals believe they can control events affecting them," which confirms that women are more likely to believe their decisions and life are out of their control and influenced by outside factors of fate, whereas men tend to believe that they are the captains of their fate. Our personalities "can dictate how sensitive we are to outside factors influencing our achievements." Thus, "if we lack the confidence in our innate talent to help us reach our goals, we are more competitive, and anyone is a potential threat, especially other women in a workplace that fails to offer sufficient advancement opportunity," Marcus surmises.

Furthermore, Marcus cites Katherine Crowley and Kathi Elster, coauthors of *Mean Girls at Work: How to Stay Professional when Things Get Personal,* who states, "Women are complicated. While most of us want to be kind and nurturing, we

---

173 Bonnie Marcus, "The Dark Side of Female Rivalry and What to Do About It," *Forbes,* January 13, 2016, https://www.forbes.com/sites/bonniemarcus/2016/01/13/the-dark-side-of-female-rivalry-in-the-workplace-and-what-to-do-about-it/#20f766915255.

struggle with our darker side—feelings of jealousy, envy, and competition. While men tend to compete in an overt manner—jockeying for position and fight to be crowned *winners*—women often compete more covertly and behind the scenes. This covert competition and indirect aggression is at the heart of mean behavior among women at work."[174]

Susan Shapiro Barash, author of thirteen books about women's issues, agrees: "A lot of it is covert. It's our dirty little secret that we're really jealous and competitive with other women. And in *Tripping the Prom Queen*, I parse out the differences. I found that competition can be healthy. It certainly is for men. *I'll fight you for what I want.* There's envy. *I want what you have.* And then there's *jealousy. I want what you have and I want you dead.* And the darkness of it is really frightening."[175]

We expect women to collaborate with and mentor each other to be successful; but that's not necessarily what happens. According to Marcus: "The dark toxic side is triggered by the increased scrutiny that women experience. The female rivalry is fueled by a workplace culture that does not provide a level playing field for women, equal pay, and/or equal opportunity for women to reach leadership positions."[176] She concludes that women are set up to compete with each other in the workplace because only so many women are tapped for the C-Suite.

Here's a wakeup call: women need to get a reality check and to finally admit there's a problem. Are you constantly festering over the unfairness of a situation at work? Are feelings that you are not in control of your life and your career consuming too much of your energy? Well, focus on what you can

174 *Ibid.*

175 *Ibid.*

176 *Ibid.*

control in a positive and productive manner. Build a powerful network to protect your reputation from those who may seek to hinder your success. Who are the influencers? Key stakeholders? You want key stakeholders to understand your value in case a manager or boss offers negative comments about you.

"If you fear that someone is out to damage your reputation and slander you in the presence of powerful executives, make sure that you include these people in your network," Barash advises. Once again, this circles back to why you need to create relationships with powerful mentors and sponsors: they can protect you and give you advice on how to navigate around toxic people, and how to deal with them on a day-to-day basis.

In addition to female rivalry, among African American women there is a perception that we don't like to help other black women. This impression has permeated the business culture and has left many women believing that their own race and gender are hindering them from achieving success and moving up the corporate ladder. Fact or fiction? The harsh truth is that some sisters are fearful of helping other sisters. This may often be the case when you're the *only one* in a position of power and you might not want to have to deal with the potential backlash from reaching out   trying to help another woman along in the workplace. I've heard these types of comments around advocating for other minorities. African American managers, in speaking about promoting African American employees, sometimes express being accused of favoritism or told, *Well, you're just doing this because it's another black person.* And yet, white people do it all the time—in terms of hiring recruits and promoting other employees into senior management positions. Their actions within the corporate leadership structure are not perceived as, *Well, you're hooking somebody up.* Yet with African American managers, they always must be mindful of how they are being perceived.

It is my view that it is our responsibility to make sure another woman succeeds, and to a certain extent it is our responsibility to make sure that a new female hire at our organization succeeds. This requires that you check up on her to see how she's doing. We know from research that women of color don't get a lot of constructive feedback from their managers. As a woman of color, if you're messing up or you're not doing your job well, you're not likely not get any feedback from the majority population. Your colleagues and even your boss might just sit there and watch you spiral downward or go off the rails. This is why it is so important for us to reach out to other women—especially women of color. You don't leave another woman to her own devices to figure out how she is going to make it in the organization. That's how you end up failing, especially if you're a seasoned employee coming into the organization from someplace else. When you enter a new business culture at a very senior level, you don't know the unwritten rules, you don't know the rules of engagement. You don't always know the key players, you don't know where the bodies are buried. The next thing you know, you're about to get fired because you're not delivering based on something you simply weren't aware of, or there's a landmine that you just stepped on.

As women, we must be better stewards and better advocates for each other instead of seeing each other as the competition.

There was one African American woman whom I worked with at Novartis—I remember having a conversation with her in the company parking lot. We were talking about the African American Employee Network and she told me: "Michelle, if you continue pushing the African American Employee Network, none of this is going to work." In other words, *You're do-ing yourself a disservice and you're going to end up getting yourself into trouble by being this pro-black advocate. It won't be in your best interest or anyone else's.*

I was very disappointed with that response. Because she didn't want to get on board with our employee resource group, I felt that reflected her fears and insecurities, not mine. I re-sponded to her: "I'm here to help people, and if you choose not to go down that path, that's on you." I was mad at her for three days, because she was one of the highest-ranking Afri-can American women at the company. Here she was, basically letting me know, *I'm not helping anybody, not at my stride.* Any-how, I pressed on, pushing the agenda of the African Ameri-can employees at Novartis during my tenure at the company.

I do hear from a lot of African American women that there is a "Queen bee syndrome" in the workplace, which is this idea that there is only going to be one person on top. Hence, a "Queen bee" is a successful woman who, instead of using her power to help other women advance, undermines her female colleagues or is unwilling to support another woman. The "crabs in the barrel syndrome" is still very much alive and prevalent in some cases. It is the cultural belief that as a group, African Americans will pull each other down, a way of thinking that goes, *If I can't have it, neither can you.*

I remember having a conversation with another African American female colleague who held a very senior position. Actually, she was more senior in the organization than I was at the time. We were talking about how we pay it forward and help other minorities, particularly African American folk. *How do we help them advance within the firm? What are some of the things we need to focus on in order to prepare them for that next level of leadership?* She said to me: "Look, I'm not going spend a whole lot of my time on that, because I didn't have anybody helping me along the way, and I had to fend for myself, so they're going have to work it out on their own." In other words, *I had to get mine so now you get yours on your own.* I was so stunned. I just didn't expect that comment to come from her because this was a person who supposedly supported diversity and talked a lot about inclusion. In front of our colleagues, especially leadership, she was putting forth an image of herself as an advocate for propeling minority employees through the pipeline. You know, *Look, this is what I'm doing, because I'm a senior leader and all eyes are on me. So I'll talk a good game externally, but behind closed doors, the reality is I'm not helping anybody. Because nobody helped me.*

I'm not going to generalize and say all African American women are like that, but some are. Women must be here to help each other; to support each other; not hurt each other. Not just some of us; this applies to all of us. Marianne Cooper writes in the *Atlantic*: "The basic idea is that since all women experience sexism, they should be more attuned to the gendered barriers that other women face. In turn, this heightened awareness should lead women to foster alliances and actively support one another."[177]

If your attitude is that you're not going to help another woman because nobody helped you, or for whatever reason, then shame on you. Especially if you are a leader, because as a person in charge—be it a small staff or an entire division— you are supposed to help others realize their own ambitions. No matter how you got to where you are, and even if you had harder experiences and traveled tougher roads than oth-

---

177 Marianne Cooper, "Why Women Sometimes Don't Help Other Women," the *Atlantic*, June 23, 2016. https://www.theatlantic.com/business/archive/2016/06/queen-bee/488144/.

ers, you are still a pioneer. People still look up and see you as someone they aspire to be at some point in time. You have to set the example and clear the path—instead of pulling up the drawbridge after you've crossed.

Throughout this book I have communicated what it was like growing up, not only as a woman, but a person of color, climbing up the ranks in corporate American, trying to find my place in the world. My own experiences, good and bad, have served me well. I have had a thriving career and a wonderful existence thus far. I have learned some powerful life lessons. But one thing is clear: I have not forgotten who I am in the process. All that I've ever wanted to do was to leave a company in better shape than when I entered. I can honestly say that I have moved the needle ever so slightly in each of the corporate environments where I worked. I am proud of my achievements within those organizations, but even more so, I am proud of the impact I have had on the people around me.

Some people like to call me a feminist. I gladly take ownership of that label and wear it as a badge of honor. But truth be told, I advocate for *all* individuals. My ultimate aim with *Climb* has been to compare and contrast the experiences of women—both majority and minority—utilizing myself as the protagonist. My intent is not only to touch on the many differences that we each bring to the table but to illustrate how you leverage those differences. We all have work to do—both men and women—to ensure that there is equity and parity in the workplace.

Our upbringing can certainly help or hinder our success. In my case, it certainly did assist me. When I look back over my career, I realize how blessed I have been in many ways. I had parents who set the bar high for themselves, and for all three daughters, to effectively use our God-given gifts and

talents; who encouraged us to take risks and assume total responsibility for our failures; who taught us to be relentless in
the pursuit of our passions and to be courageous enough to be
vulnerable and different.

Similarly, Facebook's Sheryl Sandberg points out in her
book *Lean In*: "We all want the same thing—to feel comfortable with our choices and to feel validated by those around us.
So, let's start validating each other."

As women, we have each had a different career journey.
We are not one and the same when it comes to our experiences in the workplace. We need to acknowledge that some
of us must work a little harder to rise above the fray and to
be counted. My hope is that true equality is drawing near and
that it will soon be realized for everyone across the board.

I have made it my mission to continue to break the cycle—
whether it be as an executive working for a Fortune 500
company or as an entrepreneur. Scaling the corporate ladder
involves a series of steps that you must go through; sometimes you might even have to move down a peg and then up
over again, just to gain more power in a company and rise to
the top, from an office cubicle to the C-Suite. Do away with a
narrow-minded view that there is a linear way to get to the top.

Trust me, I get it. I understand that for many women,
getting to the C-Suite may not be the final goal. Yet doing
a great job and executing on your purpose should always be
the endgame. You should strive to be successful, always think
more broadly about the role that you play at work. Constantly
do self-assessments with regard to where you are adding value
to an organization. It is my sincere hope that every person
reading this book accomplishes every life ambition and career
aspiration. Interlock your true passion and purpose—that is
how you *CLIMB!*

Key Steps

1. Commit to the idea that you are your sister's keeper by helping other woman advance in their careers.
2. Don't stop reaching back once you cross over into a management or leadership position.
3. Look for the alternatives in every situation. There should be a Plan A, B, and C.
4. Don't allow feelings that you are not in control of your life or your career take ahold of you. Focus on what you can control in a positive and productive manner.
5. Stay in touch with your network so you can tap into it when needed. These are individuals who are invested in your success.
6. Leverage your differences and experiences in life to help you thrive in the workplace and rise higher in your organization.
7. Make sure your voice gets heard, whether that involves attending a civil rights, LGBT rights, or women's rights march, participating in an employee network, speaking on a conference panel, or simply opening up at office meetings.
8. Never lose sight of who you truly are in the process, the journey.
9. Strive to leave a company in better shape than when you arrived.
10. As you climb, remember to take every step of your life's journey with courage, hold fast to your convictions, and take calculated risks to achieve success and a thriving career.

Acknowledgments

Now I understand what authors mean when they say this is the hardest part of the book to write. When it's time to acknowledge every single individual who played an integral part in your life and success over the years, it is no easy feat. Any omissions are inadvertent.

First and foremost, I would like to thank my husband, David Jamal Williams, for being my biggest supporter and advocate. Thank you for allowing me to dream big and work hard at bringing those dreams to fruition. You've been on this journey with me from the beginning. You are the most patient and loving person I know. Thank you for choosing me to be your best friend and your wife. I love you to the moon and back!

To my parents, Herbert Gadsden, Jr. and Anna L. Gadsden; my sisters and brothers-in-law, Dr. Monique Witherspoon, Esq., Dr. Craig Witherspoon, Alicia R. Martin, and Agypon Martin; and cousins, Jaheed A. Grant, Raheem I. Grant, and Sakinah Grant—thank you for your unwavering love and patience throughout this process as I forced you to read every chapter and verify all of my facts. Everything I do . . . I do it for you!

To my nephews, Cameron G. Gardner and Aiden X. Martin, I am excited by your mere presence and look forward to watching you grow into the great men that you are destined to be.

To my extended family, Essie C. Williams, Jennette L. Williams, Theresa G. Brown, Al Winston, Jerri E. Harrell, Jasmine Francis, Mike Francis, Keenan D. Harrell, Cedric Harrell, Randall L. Brown, Dr. Bianca Brown, Randolph E.

Brown, and Rodney Brown—thank you for welcoming me into your family more than twenty years ago. I love you all!

To my godmother, Dr. Emily (Cissy) Houston, you are the strongest woman I know. Thank you for being the epitome of what the strength of a woman looks like.

To my mentors and sponsors, Ernie Bell, Ted Childs, Thomas Ebeling, Alex Gorsky, Paulo Costa, Ann Fudge, and Sallie Cunningham, there are no words sufficient to express my deepest gratitude for taking the time to identify and nurture my talents. I am where I am because of your strategic guidance and friendship.

To my publishers, Akashic/Open Lens—Marva Allen, Marie Brown, Regina Brooks, Johnny Temple, Shantel Whitaker, Ibrahim Ahmad, Johanna Ingalls, Susannah Lawrence, Aaron Petrovich, and Alice Wertheimer—writing this book was a challenge. You see your vulnerable self on every page. I paused on a number of occasions out of fear that I was exposing too much of myself. Each day became easier and easier, until I finally accepted the fact that my example and truth can save a career or even a life. Your constant coaching from the sidelines made me feel like my average story was not only good but in a lot of ways extraordinary. Genius has been defined as working toward excellence, ceaselessly, with every element of your being. I put everything that I have into this book. It was certainly a team effort. Thank you for investing in me and my genius!

To Carolyn M. Brown, my collaborator—it has been the greatest gift to have you on this journey with me. Thank you for believing in me and this project, and for pushing me beyond the boundaries to share the best version of myself. Your genuine curiosity forced me to dig deeper to unveil the real me. The end result was my personal masterpiece: this book.

To the wonderful companies, and their leaders, where I have had the honor and pleasure of working—Macy's, Phillips–Van Heusen, Wakefern Food Corporation, Merck & Co., Inc, Novartis Pharma AG, Credit Suisse, and Accenture.

To my sister-friend Loren Nicole Artis and her husband Brad Artis, you've raised five awesome young men who are all my godchildren. I could not be more proud to be their godmother, and I'm even prouder to call you my sister and brother.

To my sister-friend AJ Johnson—when we met the day after Barack Obama was elected president, that weekend changed my life forever! Thank you for pushing me to wellness and to my fullest potential. Love you, AJ!

To my sister-friend Dena Craig—there are no words that can sufficiently express my unwavering gratitude to you. You are the most selfless person I know. Thank you for cheering me as I wrestled my way through the process of writing this book.

To all my sorors of Alpha Kappa Alpha Incorporated, your love and support over the years mean so much! Love you all!

I am eternally grateful to all of my family and friends for the support I have received to bring this book to life. This book is for you.